T0278350

BE
FUNNY
OR DIE

BE FUNNY OR DIE

HOW COMEDY WORKS AND WHY IT MATTERS

Joel Morris

First published in 2024

Unbound
c/o TC Group, 6th Floor King's House, 9–10 Haymarket, London SW1Y 4BP
www.unbound.com

Typeset by Jouve (UK), Milton Keynes

A CIP record for this book is available from the British Library

ISBN 978-1-80018-310-0 (hardback)
ISBN 978-1-80018-311-7 (ebook)

Printed in Great Britain by Clays Ltd, Elcograf S.p.A.

1 3 5 7 9 8 6 4 2

MIX
Paper | Supporting
responsible forestry
FSC® C018072

With thanks to the patrons of this book:

Charlie Brooker
Goo Flah
Adam Tandy FRSA
Alistair Wallace

To Julia

CONTENTS

... AND THE PUNCHLINE

I have read plays by people who had never written anything before and enjoyed them and the same goes for novels, but I have never laughed at a good comedy script by someone who has never written one before ... There is a skill in making people laugh.

Marty Feldman

Disclaimer

Comedy seems to be hardwired into us. It changes the way we see the world and helps us to navigate our lives. And, maybe because of this, it belongs to us in a way that no other art form does, with the possible exception of music. Like music, the comedy that grabs you as a teenager is often the stuff you can't shake off. Our comedy and music tastes, our favourites, are equally deep, instinctive and inexplicable.

Comedy climbs into our hearts at vulnerable times. It can be a comforting fixed point during turbulence and change (teenage, see?). It can help declare our values when we want to say who we are, or feel our identity is under threat. It can neutralise danger with absurdity. It can provide relief when we need cheering up. It can help us bond with friends. What makes us laugh is as much part of our identity as what makes us dance, or cry.

We like what we like. We don't like what we don't like. And that tells us what *we're* like. So, the first disclaimer is that I'll draw examples from the comedy I love. This is affected by what I grew up with, and my own tastes, and I might leave out some of your favourites, so sorry in advance. I'll try and make sure stuff I refer to is popular enough to be assumed as comedy currency, but I will tend to grab things that I can easily reach for, and those will necessarily be revealing of my own comic preferences.

The other, trickier, disclaimer is that times change, and people (especially comedy people) can be peculiar, and occasionally do and say things that are less than admirable. Because of that, please assume that a reference to someone's work is meant to be just that. It's not an endorsement of that creator as a person, or their views or behaviour. This book has some pretty abstract ideas in it between the jokes, and to help us not get lost, I'm going to use some major landmarks on our shared comedy maps, so we can find one another.

This book is set here, in my own comedy landscape, because it's the one I know. And I'd like, if I may, to reserve the right to enjoy some of the beautiful buildings, even if I might not want to have dinner with the architects. Because some of them, I'm sad to say, are capable of being complete arseholes.

I hope you feel able to do the same.

Comedy is Important

Humor can be dissected, as a frog can, but the thing dies in the process and the innards are discouraging to any but the purely scientific mind.

E. B. White

I promise by the end of this book to reveal the secret of comedy. Really. I promise.

I'm not going to pretend this is the first book to promise that, but this time I'm going to do it. Because comedy is really important.

Comedy is sometimes looked down upon because it's foolish and messy, nonsensical and unexpected, unruly and disrespectful. But that's like nobody taking music seriously because it's 'so soundy'. Comedy's wayward, disobedient, surprising, silly features aren't a problem – they're part of its definition. Comedy uses expectation and surprise to push us off-balance, then while we're a bit wobbly, keeps us happy playing quick, absorbing games of guess-what's-next.

Because it relies on surprise, comedy breaks the rules of expectation, so it sometimes seems to be wilfully badly behaved. In comedy, you're meant to think you know what's coming, but never be sure whether you'll be satisfyingly right or outrageously wrong. And that means that comedy's well-judged leaps into the absurd sometimes appear very, very silly indeed.

But the purpose of comedy is completely serious. Humans spend an awful lot of time making each other laugh. It's a big drain of brainpower and time. So, joking must be vital to our survival or we'd have stopped doing it. And we *do* all do it.

Think about the things that have made you laugh the most. Something your mate did, or your mum did, or a comedian did on a show you like. Maybe it's something clever someone said. Perhaps it's some perfect choice of words that always cracks you up. A precise skewering of human existence. A barbed piece of satire. Or a joyful little burble of nonsense. Maybe it's just something that somebody wore on their head, or fell into. It all seems fairly silly. And it made you laugh.

Surely stuff like that can't be serious?

Comedy is an art form whose peaks of expression for me personally would include a 1950s greaser in a transport café singing 'Mr Boombastic' on a Kirby wire, a drag Viking miming extremely tight raspberries, and an American newsreader playing jazz flute to strangers under the door of a toilet stall. It's the art form in which the magic words 'for you, Lord Delfont...' can act as a bonding signal to old friends, and where the happiest moment of your childhood might be you and a sibling crying with laughter as you pass each other a spoof advert featuring a smiling man furiously pedalling a bicycle wheel that goes up his arse. Its craft is contained in the book title *Doctor Who and the Shreddies of Nabisco*, the name of the American football star 'Quiznatodd Bidness' and the little village of Wabznasm. It's a man in a bowler hat eating wax fruit, a huge Gaulish warrior eating most of a cake, and a schoolgirl eating a colossal Wagon Wheel so marshmallow goes all over her face. It's a cat chasing a mouse that is suddenly two more enormous mice who turn out to be circus elephants in disguise. It's a man who starts to tell you a story but can't because he farts continuously for three minutes straight. It's hiding a cow creamer from a fascist lingerie entrepreneur in ridiculous shorts.*

That all seems pretty stupid.

But comedy's job is to keep us alive.

Jokes and comic ideas train us to stay alert, to be sharp and clever. Social laughter helps us feel stable and secure. Funny stuff keeps our various tribes bonded together, for safety and strength. Comedy declares who we are, and who we are not. It defines us, and defends our values and standards. It's about pretty much everything that makes humans human, and everything that got us here alive.

Gathering together in groups and giggling to ourselves is as much a part of our humanity as flying and emitting pellets is a part of an owl's essential *owliness*.

Comedy is who we are.

And thanks to an explosion of new outlets, from streaming to social media to podcasts, there is more comedy around us than ever before. You might not be a professional comic, but you're very likely joining in comic exchanges every day on your social media feed, or joking over email and messaging apps, or being encouraged to add some jokes to spice up a presentation at work, or using humour to break the ice at meetings both virtual and face-to-face. It used to be possible to avoid having to be funny with anyone but your closest friends until you were forced to give a speech at a wedding, but now we're almost expected to make one another laugh all the time.

Comedy is a vital part of who we are, and the social advantages of being funny are huge. And the social

---

* These are, off the top of my head, references to some of the times I have laughed most in my life. I could have gone on forever. If you're playing spot the reference, I've put these all at the end in an appendix.

hazards of *not* being funny when you thought you were being funny are equally big.

That's high risk.

Maybe it's time to have a look at how comedy works, in case we get custard pie in our faces.

IT'S FROG-KILLING TIME

So, how can we analyse comedy? And what's the point, when everyone always says it's impossible?

One problem facing anybody looking for an abstract analysis of comedy is that the people who are most often asked how comedy works are comedy performers, because they're the most famous. But I suspect performers are precisely the people most likely to say they simply don't know.

Some don't want to jinx it. Some think it's pointless on principle. The unpredictability of audiences, the terror of trying out new material in hostile spaces, where good jokes can die and hack material can fly on golden wings, all mitigates against overanalysis of the comedy itself. Sit in a room with stand-ups exchanging war stories, and you'll find the major areas of analysis are audience response, performance technique, and moaning about how hard it is to get car insurance. How jokes work is often reduced to a glossary of half-dismissive professional shorthand (reversal, pull out and reveal, Langdons, call-backs, act-outs, squeakers and so on).* Nobody is making many friends backstage by dissecting the magical frogs on which all comics rely to make a living.

---

* Anyone wanting a terrific and evolving resource of (mainly UK) comedians' and comedy writers' private terminology should visit *Veep* and *The Thick of It* writer Andy Riley's wonderful blog *How To Talk Comedy Writer,* misterandyriley.com/2016/10/31/how-to-talk-comedy-writer-updated/

But I'm not a performer. So I don't give a crap. I'm quite happy to leave a great swathe of chopped frogs in my wake, like a cross between Genghis Khan and Miss Piggy.

The job of the for-hire room writer, the script fixer or the hands-on comedy producer involves absolutely *shitloads* of forensic frog-killing. It's usually done using other people's precious material. That's a rare advantage, because it's a brave person who can be technically dispassionate about their own stuff. (Everything I've ever written myself, for instance, is of course Mysterious and Chaotic, and mustn't be analysed. Which is why I shall not be accepting notes. Thanks.)

If your working day is about fixes and punch-ups and brainstorms, sometimes on other people's precious projects, you get to see a different side of comedy, where pulling jokes apart isn't a heresy, it's the job. It is a unique luxury to be invited to look at a piece of comedy from a sufficient remove to be able to see its underlying shape, and then also to be encouraged to make changes to it to make it work better. The frustrated internet critic who is convinced they can see exactly where some piece of comedy crashed and burned doesn't get to see if their amazing suggestions for repairs would work. But the backroom script editors and producers and writers-for-hire do.

This inevitably means that people in this blue-overalls backroom corner of showbiz think comedy probably isn't as mysterious and impossible as all that. In fact, you realise quite quickly that it might be handy, when plying your trade as an emergency comedy plumber, if you know where the stopcocks are, and don't airily insist they are 'in the hearts of all mankind' or 'about saying the unsayable' or 'an expression of human frailty'.

The answer you want to have to hand is 'under this sink'.

STAND BACK, CITIZENS: THESE FROGS
WILL RUE THE DAY

I'm a comedy writer, and have earned money from jokes since I was at school. I've been doing this stupid job for a long time, and I think I've worked out a few things. And then, because I wanted to write this book, I have also talked to a lot of clever people – writers, comedians, producers, editors, scientists, journalists, various experts in their fields. I've picked through groaning shelves of books, old and new, about how comedy works. And I've even stared out of the window and had biscuits. I've given myself a headache. I've bored a lot of people in pubs and cafés when we were meant to be talking about stuff other than comedy theory.

And this is the result. This is how comedy works.

I reckon.

And from my position I'd say my reckon's as good as the next guy's. I mean, we keep Freud's books on comedy in print, and his focus on the comedy of sexual repression is so narrow and obsessive it only really explains the later *Carry On* films. We must be able to do better than that.

Come! It is time to kill some frogs. Because only by killing these frogs can we work out how we're going to keep ourselves alive. It's us or them.

Forward! Let the war on the frogs begin.

PART ONE

COMEDY IS HUMAN

The Funniest Joke in the World

OK. Now what?

Richard Wiseman, 2002
(Punchline to the winning entry in a scientific
survey to find the 'funniest joke in the world'*)

This idea for this book came from an assertion which I thought was self-evident, and which I'd made many times. It's this:

The funniest joke in the world is any joke shared between siblings at a funeral.

But one day, someone challenged me to say why. And I found I couldn't quite stand it up. So I disappeared down a thinking hole for a year or so, and ended up writing this enormous book, and now here we all are. It's a valuable lesson: even if something seems self-evident to you, do try and know why, in case someone asks.

---

* Here is the full joke, if you want it:

Two hunters are out in the woods when one of them collapses. He doesn't seem to be breathing and his eyes are glazed. The other guy whips out his phone and calls the emergency services. He gasps, 'My friend is dead! What can I do?' The operator says, 'Calm down. I can help. First, let's make sure he's dead.' There is a silence, then a shot is heard. Back on the phone, the guy says, 'OK, now what?'

The funniest joke in the world is any joke shared between siblings at a funeral.

I think it's solid. Most of us can confirm that the laughter produced by this category of joke is of a deep and irresistible type that is hard to find anywhere else. The joke itself need not even be very good. It can be a dumb observation you've made a million times before, or a reference to something silly from childhood. But this weapons-grade variation of a normal gag, delivered in perfect conditions, is a clue to how comedy works, and why humans joke at all.

It's the same joke we whisper in the back row of a stern teacher's class, or the funny comment we mumble to a friend in the rear seats of a taxi while an intimidating work colleague rides up front. It's the sort of joke that might get us in trouble, but the act of sharing the joke is more important than any potential danger. It creates a tiny temporary conspiracy, a tribe within our tribe, cementing a giggly kinship through exchanging a private comic token.

This is probably because the important part of sharing a joke isn't the joke, it's the sharing.

The ideal sibling-funeral gag will use common references and rely on a mutual sense of humour. It will be unexpected, possibly even shocking. It usually threatens to cross a socially agreed line without actually doing so. Telling it at all will seem like a mad thing to have done. Has the teller taken leave of their senses? Who even are you? You know the rules!

The one-person audience takes a moment to realise that this joke is purely for them, not the wider congregation. There will be a gasp-beat of confusion, and then a moment of relief that nobody heard. Nobody is in danger. Every atom of the siblings' bodies will want to laugh out loud, spreading the joke across the room, but they know they mustn't. The capping of this potential big-yucks-volcano will build up pressure, making the laugh impulse stronger and stronger.

I've exchanged a few of these. None of them bear repeating. They were like site-specific works of art. But the feeling of bottled hysteria – the recognition of common values, the hint of transgression, the moment of relief, the warmth of ownership and intimacy, the sharing – is the pure essence of comedy.

So, to make the funniest joke in the world, you will need:

Ingredients
2 or more siblings (to taste)
1 funeral

Method
1. *Light joke touchpaper, quietly.*
2. *Stand back.*

What could be simpler?

Human Laughter

Man is The Animal that Laughs. But so does the monkey.

Mark Twain

Mark Twain's careful use of comic capitalisation (above) is a wry warning that humans shouldn't think we are Something Special because we can get the giggles. Scientists have observed plenty of animals laughing, or at least employing what are called 'play vocalisations'. These are sounds that indicate that rough-and-tumble activity is non-threatening. It's the wildlife equivalent of advancing on a toddler, wiggling your fingers and saying 'heeeeere I come' in a silly voice before tickling them.

Because an actual attack might trigger actual distress, we need a noise to say 'don't worry, it's just a tickle'. We need an all-clear as much as we need an alert klaxon, and so laughing is one of the first sounds we learn to make as infants.

It's the 'nothing to worry about' cousin of the cry, the other wordless noise we learn to make very early. A cry requests help. A laugh says that we're fine. Those are the two basic noises a baby needs to make to interact with the world. A robot baby, if you can imagine such a thing, might have a red light and a green light. Laughing is the green one: no danger.

But though animals share laughter as a play signal, humans seem to be the only animal that makes jokes. There is, as far as we know, no comedy in the animal kingdom.

Scientific literature on humour often makes reference to a gorilla called Koko who seemed to make comedy to amuse herself and her human friends. Before Koko's death in 2018, she learned a thousand signs, and was even filmed swapping comic riffs with an hysterical Robin Williams, which is one of the most adorable ideas in science. Her research team claimed she would pretend to be other animals, using simple props, and to mistake objects for other objects for comic effect, like a small child might, or an improv comedian. Robin Williams had probably gigged with worse.

But Koko's experiment has never been successfully repeated, and many neuroscientists dismiss the conclusions as confirmation bias: the researchers merely found the ape comedian they wanted to find. Observations of Koko's style of 'primate comedy' in the wild are non-existent, and impressions of ape behaviour in captivity are confounded by the animals' exposure to humans. Significantly, Koko never laughed at jokes made by the researchers, and the laughter of humans in response to her antics could easily reinforce patterns of behaviour. Koko may simply have learned to repeat any action that went down well with the human audience, and then laughed sociably because the rest of the room was laughing. The experiments may have demonstrated a normal loop of group primate laughter, not the animal's glee at her own comic invention. Or perhaps gorillas are just too classy to laugh at their own jokes.

PICKING LICE OFF THE AUDIENCE

Most of the things humans do to make each other laugh seem to have evolved from primate grooming: the social stroking, cleaning and preening that apes perform to solidify bonds and reassure one another. Grooming also facilitates co-operation, signals non-threat, manipulates status within the group, de-escalates conflict, indicates shared attitudes and can help attract a mate. You can probably see parallels with why humans tell jokes in a lot of those motives. It's a vitally important act for all of us. When apes laugh and smile, it's mostly due to this sort of physical contact. We simulate that action using jokes.

Charles Darwin in *The Expression of the Emotions in Man and Animals* called humour the 'tickling of the mind'. Language processing allows us to tickle one another with words and ideas. Notice the way that the amount of physical tickling we do to our children tends to decrease as they master language, and we can make them giggle with the one about what's orange and sounds like a parrot* instead. It's all about breaking the patterns we think we know, for a laugh.

We don't have to sit in each other's hairy laps and phys-ically stroke each other, or play-fight, or tickle, to feel soothed because we, uniquely amongst the apes, have evolved to use language for this job. This evolutionary shift from touching to talking was triggered by the enlarge-ment of social groups, as we moved from small packs to villages, towns and cities. It's not clear which way round this happened – language allowing us to groom in larger groups, or larger groups speeding the evolution of language – but we seem to have developed linguistic

---

* A carrot.

grooming around the time it became impractical for us to sit and pick the nits off everybody in prehistoric Antwerp.

LANGUAGE AND LAUGHTER

Our human language processor is the system we hijack to make jokes, because understanding language requires us to guess what's coming next. We understand words by running slightly ahead of ourselves, like the predictive text feature on your phone. The brain takes in information, and then uses what we have received so far, and our expectations of what is likely to follow, to have a stab at what's up next. We process language at great speed by staying a half-step ahead.

According to some theories of human consciousness, our whole method of perceiving reality works in a similar way. To sort the incoming data from our various senses, the human perceptual system takes repeated guesses, and, if we get it wrong, we go back and check, adjusting our expectations so we don't get caught out next time. We collect old patterns and perfect new ones to understand what the hell is going on.

This is vital for our survival. The humans who were good at turning experience into fresh templates that helped them guess what might come next could survive unexpected threats, and leave plenty of offspring. The ones who were bad at guessing, who didn't pay attention, or failed to apply what they had learned might not get the chance. We are, statistically, the products of the imaginative, careful people.

Comedy is a game of incongruity – puns, twists, moments of slapstick surprise, things we didn't see coming. If we are to enjoy being tricked, we first need to have expectations. Even though this is a habit sharpened by our language processor, and its half-step-ahead method, this model doesn't just apply to verbal comedy. A pun plays on this facility just the same as the unexpected but wordless arrival of a stepladder in a clown's face. The world is a strip cartoon, rolling past our senses, one block of information at a time, and we love a surprising final frame, even if it's got no speech bubbles in it, as long as it's playing a satisfying game with what we thought might happen.

3

Human Comedy

You can't underestimate how fired up people can get over Comedy – which might seem, to the outside world, the very definition of trivial.

Brent Forrester
(writer, *The Simpsons*)

To borrow the rhetorical technique of the desperate best-man's speech, let's reach for the dictionary. The first two definitions under 'comedy' I find in the free online version of the *OED* that I don't have to sign up and pay for (because I don't have that sort of money because I'm a comedy writer) are:

1. *Professional entertainment consisting of jokes and sketches, intended to make an audience laugh.*
2. *A film, play, or broadcast programme intended to make an audience laugh.*

And I'd argue that the difference between *laughter*, as experienced by other animals, and *comedy*, as practised by humans, is that idea of *intent*.

Mel Brooks famously said:

Tragedy is when I cut my finger. Comedy is when you fall into an open sewer and die.

I'd argue that falling into a big stinky hole isn't necessarily a decent definition of comedy, even if it's really funny and happening to someone else. But Mel Brooks' *quote* is comedy, because there is an evident intent to delight and amuse. And you can tell that because, well, look at it. The joke is beautifully assembled and does its job like a dream.

And think about your response. If someone actually fell down a manhole, you might run to help. But you don't feel any distress response at hearing this joke. You know exactly how you're meant to react, even if you don't laugh. You can tell it's a joke. There is clear intent. So it's comedy.

So how about this?

> *Comedy is the intentional desire to amuse by encouraging someone to process comic input and react.*

The worst thing someone can say after you tell them a joke is, 'Was that meant to be funny?' The answer is usually 'yes', but the failure to communicate intent is what will distress the joke teller. 'Of course it was meant to be funny! Or I wouldn't have said it!' Comedy is a conspiracy. We agree that we understand the rules: we know someone was trying to make us laugh and we agree to play this game with them.

The aim of comedy is that a fellow human will follow your thread of ideas, and that this will produce a reaction that acknowledges your intent to amuse. Once the receiver has finished chewing over your input, they will laugh, smile, or at some minimal level acknowledge you were trying to amuse them. I'd also argue that the results don't matter. If the comedy maker fails to get that reaction – the receiver might be angry, might say it's not funny – it's still comedy. Just as art is anything that the artist intends to be art, comedy is anything the comedian intends to be comedy.

This means that while laughter and smiling may be a reaction or a mood indicator, just as it is in apes and other animals, comedy – the remote transmission of that basic feeling of primate grooming, with all its purposes and signifiers – is a form of communication. It might succeed or it might fail, but it is an attempt to transmit a 'grooming' state of mind.

Humour's social-grooming function is pretty universally agreed on by comedy boffins, as Professor G. Neil Martin notes in his *Psychology of Comedy*:

> *[Humour] may have evolved for all sorts of reasons, including the promotion of social bonding (Dunbar, 1996), the facilitation of co-operation (Jung, 2003), the prevention of pursuing counterproductive paths (Chafe, 1997), the signalling of non-threat (Hayworth, 2002), a desire to signal the initiation or maintenance of social co-operation (Li et al., 2009), the manipulation of status (Alexander, 1986), the resolution of errors in a pleasant way (Hurley et al., 2011), to attract and select a mate (Miller, 1997) or signalling an awareness that we share attitudes and preferences with others (Flamson & Barrett, 2005).*

Comedy is like a yawn, a ticklish feeling that spreads from person to person within a social group, to make the members of that group feel playful and reassured. Even the most aggressive, toxic, edgy material has that aim: to declare that we are all together in a place of safety.

Even transgressive, dark or shocking comedy is still meant to reassure, by testing the boundaries of our group values. Shock comedy can be a way of 'othering' non-members of the group whom we wish to test or drive away, but every offensive joke that horrifies an outsider solidifies the in-group by contrast. The terms of membership of the joke teller's tribe can be as basic as 'enjoying the sort of horrible joke that goes against my declared values', but even that is a bonding activity. (Just not for everyone.) I'll deal more with ideas of offence, taboo and shock in the third part of the book, when I look at comedy's tribal function.

SOCIAL COMEDY

Humans are social animals, and comedy is used within human social groups both as a lubricant and as a glue. Usually, something that is sometimes a lubricant but also sometimes a glue is less than useful; for example, when you're anxiously staring at the bottle before pouring it into your car engine or using it to fix tiles to a wall. (Maybe that is the secret of comedy after all: surprise.)

When I spoke to cognitive neuroscientist Professor Sophie Scott about her love of the spoof adventure series *Ripping Yarns* for my *Comfort Blanket* podcast, she stressed the social nature of comedy and the importance of sharing:

> *There's something special about comedy in the fact that laughter is magnified by social contact. Watch a programme on your own, you won't laugh. Watch it with someone else, you will ... It's not just your aesthetic appreciation of something that you find engaging. It's something that you share with people. In that, it has something in common with music ... A lot of what we mean by friendship is the people we can find a better mood together with by finding things to laugh at. It's always sharing laughter that matters.*

Of course we can enjoy comedy on our own – I love nothing more than sitting and reading a funny book or comic to myself – but we laugh more readily and more often when we are in company, because laughter is intended to be a social act, a signal of mutual safety and reassurance. In fact, I've caught myself happily reading a comic novel to myself, and then stopping to take a picture of the cover, or clipping out a particular passage, to share on social media, or running off to find someone to read a bit out loud to, as if to say, 'Enjoying myself on my own, here! Who wants to join in?' Even at its most deliberately solitary, comedy can pull naturally towards the sociable.

FOLDING OUR ARMS TO MAKE SOME SORT OF POINT

Our love-hate relationship with laughter tracks on television comedy programmes is a good demonstration of comedy's social function. Although we are conditioned as primates to respond warmly to group laughter, fake-sounding laughter makes us bristle. 'Who are these arseholes and why do they find this crap funny?' And we reject the invitation to join this group.

In a live environment, it is hard not to laugh when a room is laughing, but if you do decide that the comedy isn't to your taste, you will most likely become angry and distressed, no matter how hard you try to hide it. I can't remember a time where I have sat in a room full of people laughing at something that I didn't find funny and felt relaxed and sure of myself, even if I was totally confident in finding it unfunny. Feeling alone in a laughing crowd is horrible.

If you follow comedy fans on social media, you may have witnessed this first hand: 'I must take to the internet and explain why this particular comedy wasn't in fact funny.' It's a fruitless exercise when the sound of laughter indicates that people *are* enjoying themselves. Something is funny if people find it funny. Funniness is a subjective judgement, not an objective fact. That you personally didn't laugh is a valid observation, and may be part of an important statement of your identity, but it's not an empirical measure of the quality of the comedy.

The unusual level of anger generated around comedy that is seen to have 'failed' compared to other forms of art is probably down to humour's hyper-social origins. Being the only person laughing, or not laughing, in a room can trigger an elementary distress response; being cast out of the tribe is a panicky feeling. Remember *The Good Life*'s Margo Leadbetter (in the beautiful 'Windbreak War' episode) breaking into drunken tears as her fellow Surbiton neighbours shake with laughter? Her voice wheedling like a wounded child:

But... why is it? Why is it funny?

The distress in Penelope Keith's face at this moment is perfect, and incredibly human. It's never comfortable being the one person in the social group not being preened, cleaned and soothed by the act of collective comedy.* It's a moment that isn't just a lovely comic character moment, but a clue as to the function that comedy performs for us as a species.

---

* *The Good Life* creators John Esmonde and Bob Larbey loved writing characters who didn't get the joke. The first scene of *Ever Decreasing Circles* where Martin Bryce meets new neighbour Paul Ryman in his and Ann Bryce's suburban kitchen is a masterclass in how miniature tribes break out based on senses of humour. Uptight Martin offers a series of thin, socially acceptable pre-prepared gags, which fall flat, while Paul jokes easily and naturally, reacting and offering genuine warmth. Martin's frustrated bafflement and Ann's increasingly conspiratorial amusement are a microcosm of the show's themes, and a mirror held up to us as social creatures. There are many similar scenes dissecting the human exchange of social humour in *The Office*, a show whose co-creator Ricky Gervais is a vocal fan of *Ever Decreasing Circles*.

4

Freud Never Played Glasgow Empire

Freud's theory was that when a joke opens a window, and all those bats and bogeymen fly out, you get a marvellous feeling of relief and elation. The trouble with Freud is that he never had to play the old Glasgow Empire on a Saturday night after Rangers and Celtic had both lost.

Ken Dodd

Anyone who works in comedy professionally will recognise the knee-jerk prejudice that serious people sometimes have about funny stuff. Because the primary aim of comedy is to make people laugh, not think (though that is often a by-product), there's an assumption that comedy itself is a silly thing to do. 'What are you playing at in there? Seems to be an awful lot of laughter. . .'

Michael Palin has said that BBC management regarded him and his *Monty Python's Flying Circus* colleagues as naughty boys. The Pythons had done their job exactly as required to a world-class standard, but were categorised as disobedient, chaotic, disruptive. It was as if the creation of The Ministry of Silly Walks was something to be stoically borne by the powers-that-be, not warmly approved of in the way they would have unquestioningly applauded a hard-hitting documentary, or a drama about a sad policeman.

I've heard from some academics that the same mistrust of the 'silly people' can sometimes extend to scientists researching laughter. This unease would never be expressed around someone analysing the human response to, say, music. Certainly, if you look for mainstream books about the science of humour on the shelves of your local bookshop, you'll find that titles on the science of music outnumber them by a ludicrous factor, even though explaining the often verbal process of comedy on the page is much easier than trying to nail down the abstract shapes of music.

But there is a palpable fear that comedy itself – an art form that works by disrupting order – is too anarchic for study, that the sound of laughter might do structural damage to an otherwise august institution.

RIDEO ERGO SUM

All humans joke, but different cultures value laughter differently (and it must be said that the centrality of humour to British and Anglophone culture is remarkable), but accusing someone of having no sense of humour is almost universally perceived as hurtful. Academics Sharon Lockyer and Michael Pickering introduced *Beyond a Joke* (their collection of serious essays on humour and offence) by making a bold claim for the centrality of humour to our sense of self.

> *To claim that we lack a sense of humour is to launch an assault on our self-esteem, on an attribute of ourselves that helps to define us as an integrated person, worthy of being known. It is tantamount to declaring us deficient as personalities, as being 'literally an incomplete person'.*

We all know that comedy and jokes are important. In a 2007 survey published by R. Lippa in the *Archives of*

Sexual Behavior, 200,000 people across fifty-three countries, men and women, gay and straight, were asked to
name their most desirable features in a mate, and sense of
humour was always in the top three.* It might express our
hope that a possible mate will be able to join us in laughing
at life's ups and downs, or it might be simple evolutionary
preference: humour can be a demonstration of our ability
to think in unusual and flexible ways, and that's a valuable
characteristic which is attractive to potential partners.

Humour is a game we play using our internal pattern-
detection processor: predicting, responding to surprise,
and demonstrating our mental adaptability to new
information. Showing off that your processor is working at top capacity by making little displays of comic
invention is like doing chin-ups, but for the brain. And
just as doing a headstand or a cartwheel demonstrates
to a potential partner that you're physically fit and
would be able to run away from a tiger if required,
making jokes shows your brain is able to sift data, react
quickly and play with information. That's a skill that
might be useful for working out where tigers are hiding,
like they do, the deceitful stripy buggers. Maybe you'll
avoid ever having to run (or cartwheel) out of the way
of tigers altogether. This is probably why the stereotyped comedy writer isn't that sporty: because we're
convinced we don't need to be.

HOW TICKLED WE ARE

Legendary Liverpool comic Ken Dodd was a sharp thinker
about the nature of jokes, and it's difficult to find fault

---

* There is a notable statistical bias towards prioritising humour as a desirable
trait in a potential partner by women, which may explain why some men seek-
ing to attract females feel being funny is a competitive act.

with his fundamental definition of comedy (given in an interview on BBC Radio 3's *Night Waves* in June 2012):

> *[Comedy is] the performance of humour to obtain laughter.*

But up at the top of this chapter you'll see he is quoted, in the *Guardian* in April 1991, with his trademark warning on the perils of analysing comedy. Here it is again, because it's a long walk back to the start:

> *Freud's theory was that when a joke opens a window, and all those bats and bogeymen fly out, you get a marvellous feeling of relief and elation. The trouble with Freud is that he never had to play the old Glasgow Empire on a Saturday night after Rangers and Celtic had both lost.*

It's a great observation, and made it into the *Oxford Book of Quotations*. But I prefer the concision of an earlier version of the same gag, quoted by critic Michael Billington in a 1973 review of Dodd at the Liverpool Playhouse:

> *[Dodd] quotes Freud's opinions that a laugh is a conservation of psychic energy; but, as he says, the trouble with Freud is that he never played Glasgow second house on a Friday night.*

In both versions, Dodd is denying that comedy can usefully succumb to analysis. But I'd argue that we can learn something about how to analyse comedy by analysing Ken Dodd's joke about how we mustn't ever analyse comedy. (Yes. I'm unbearable.)

Dodd has tinkered with his joke between 1973 and 1991 to make sure it can't fail. The comic has put himself in the position of a potential audience member, calculating where any confusion (the enemy of comedy) might occur, then cut it out or clarified it. He may have done this mechanically (as craft), or instinctively (by feel), or experimentally (by dying repeatedly on his arse with the gag, until one night it took the roof off) – most probably a mixture of the three.

Each of the concepts in the original 1973 joke (Freud and Glasgow) has had information stapled to it over the years, so by 1991 we are given a colourful illustration of the idea of psychic energy ('bats and bogeymen'), and a context in which we might judge the mood of an audience we've possibly never experienced ('after Rangers and Celtic have both lost'). Dodd has sacrificed some pace and rhythm, and swapped it for comprehensibility. Now the gag plays to a bigger room.

I suspect that my preference for the earlier version is not just because it's faster, tripping me over more unexpectedly, but because it's a tradesman's joke designed to be shared with other comics. The first one belongs to me and my comedy mates; the later version is for auditorium use. In terms of 'grooming', I feel less special as part of the second version's tribe.

Look at the 1973 version again:

> [Dodd] quotes Freud's opinions that a laugh is a conservation of psychic energy; but, as he says, the trouble with Freud is that he never played Glasgow second house on a Friday night.

I'm familiar with both the ideas of Freud about comedy, and the reputation of a Glasgow comedy crowd. So, I got the references, and that felt nice. This is a welcoming bit of tribal social grooming for the comedy monkeys, if you're lucky enough to feel included (as a theatre critic such as Michael Billington might). I'll confess I don't really know what the 'second house' is like at a 1970s comedy gig, but I can work it out from the context. It feels like being given a little glimpse into Ken Dodd's secret professional world, which is flattering.

So, in 1973 Dodd has an express version of the joke that plays with his peers (and pricks the ear of a critic who feels included enough to quote it in print). But he also needs a clearer gag that 'grooms' a bigger social group. So he develops version 2.0 with all the information packed inside and nothing assumed. This is the one that can cut across the rowdy stalls.

It might even work in the mythically tough second house at the old Glasgow Empire on a rough night. I hear that can get a bit lively.

BACK OFF, MAN, I'M A SCIENTIST

The process of making comedy is worth analysing, even if you're making a joke about how it isn't. Underneath the nonsense, it's perversely logical. Comedy is about manipulating human beings to induce a seemingly involuntary reaction of laughter, warmth and fellowship. To do so, the comedian needs to understand human beings, and how human brains absorb information. And that means comedy creators are relying, whether they want to admit it openly or not, on a combination of neuroscience, anthropology and craft.

Scientists may have a suspicion of comedy, but comedians often have an equal suspicion of the science behind what they do. Hence the old *dissecting a frog* warning, and Ken Dodd's caution that science is no use out in the field when the football's gone to shit. One side considers forensic analysis of the funny to be beneath them. The other side reckons looking too closely at jokes is not only being a bit up yourself, but of no practical use.

Comedy seems to be unique as an art form that both

serious and frivolous people consider equally out of bounds for examination. Yet musicians are happy to break their craft down to some serious levels of scientific nerdery without objection. Any decent muso will know a natural A note above middle C registers at 440 Hz, and won't consider that knowledge as wrecking their ability to play or compose. And professors of music will happily discuss the melodic influence of simple folk tunes and nursery rhymes without thinking it's silly. But with comedy, there is an unspoken rule about never breaking the comic machine open and showing the simple levers and pulleys inside. It's a perfect situation for preserving mystery, where both sides, academic and craft, have agreed it's not really worth talking about.

Anyway, sod that. Let's talk about the science of comedy.

5

What Clever People Have Reckoned

HUGH: Are you a doctor, then?
HANCOCK: No. I never really bothered.

Hancock's Half Hour, 'The Blood Donor'
(written by Ray Galton and Alan Simpson)

Although taking comedy seriously remains a niche academic pursuit, that doesn't mean plenty of excellent brains haven't had a swing at it, presumably while doing some serious chin-stroking about proper things. In Jimmy Carr and Lucy Greeves' energetic popular study of joke science, *The Naked Jape* (a great example of co-operation between an academic and a working comic to try to fathom the mysteries of comedy), the authors exhaustedly report that they have uncovered over a hundred different theories on how humour works.

Reading most of these theories, however, I'm always struck more by what they leave out than what they manage to include. Regardless, I'll offer a few insultingly simplistic pocket summaries of the major ideas that have arisen from philosophy and science about how funny works, so we can blow raspberries at them one at a time (as comedy requires).

Plato (fifth to fourth century BCE)

Plato talked about humour, but dismissed it as a malicious interruption of serious thought, and his suspicion of giggling has found sympathetic ears amongst puritan and academic communities throughout history. I think of him as a bit Mr Spock, a bit Lady Whiteadder, a bit Margo Leadbetter. But not as funny as any of them.

Aristotle (fourth century BCE)

Aristotle was one of the first thinkers to properly tackle the mystery of humour and astutely hinted in his *Rhetoric* at what would eventually be called 'incongruity theory': he insisted that comedy relied on setting up expectation and then providing 'a twist'. This is a solid observation with which no current theorist would disagree. He even went down to a technical level – 'The effect is produced even by jokes depending upon changes of the letters of a word; this too is a surprise' – an explanation from 2,300 years ago of the innocent fun of those '#BeatlesCurry'* hashtag games. But then he ruined it by going in to bat like a maniac for 'superiority theory' instead. Superiority theory is the idea that we mainly laugh at the ugly and the unfortunate. This restrictive and mean-spirited definition of what's funny was cited and proposed again and again by learned experts over the next millennium and a half – René Descartes, for example, regarded all comedy as an exercise in *Schadenfreude* – and makes you wonder whether science used to have an admissions policy that might be described as 'arseholes only'.

---

* Paperback Raita – that's your usual starter. Sgt Poppadom. Your Mutter Should Know. I'll stop now.

Thomas Hobbes (seventeenth century)

Hobbes, building on Aristotle's ideas, said that we laugh at a moment of 'sudden glory', when we realise our superiority over the butt of the joke. 'They got the pie in the face; I didn't.' This vision of comedy fits neatly with Hobbes' generally competitive, aggressive view of humanity, and may be related to the dominance play of primates (which, we shall see later, may not strictly be anything to do with humour at all). The problem, which you can probably point out as easily as Immanuel Kant eventually did, is that 'sudden glory' doesn't tell us why we enjoy victimless wordplay, whimsy or nonsense, and has no place for the affirmative recognition laugh we get from shared observational comedy or the chuckling warmth we feel towards favourite sitcom characters. I'm not saying this was Hobbes' intention, but while 'sudden glory' is a great technique if you're ever asked to perform a tight ten for Adolf Hitler, it's not going to help if you're punching up sketch material for *Sesame Street*.

Immanuel Kant & Søren Kierkegaard (eighteenth to nineteenth century)

Incorporating ideas proposed by the poet James Beattie and the philosopher Francis Hutcheson, Kant and Kierkegaard (and others) refined what is known as 'incongruity theory'. This was the first big challenge to the idea that all comedy is about ugly strangers falling down wells. Laughter, according to this theory, is a response to the resolution of a perceived incongruity. We see something that doesn't make sense, try with all our might to measure it against expectations, and when we realise someone is just being silly, we laugh. What we saw wasn't *meant* to make sense, so we can stop fretting and chuck it in the box marked 'funny'. The action of filing-under-funny makes us happy, because at least we're not confused any more. The poor dog had no nose, but it was just a joke and we don't have to call the RSPCA. Kant famously described this as 'the sudden transform-ation of a strained expectation into nothing' and called the usual human humorous response to apparent absurd-ities a 'play with thoughts'. This moved humour theory away from a simplistic cruelty to others, towards an acknowledgement of the common human enjoyment of mental games and the usefulness of play. Incongruity theory at least makes an effort to explain all the comedy that can be defined as 'not someone being injured'. Because it stresses the idea of patterns and the breaking of patterns, for me this is a major breakthrough.

Herbert Spencer (mid-nineteenth century)

Herbert Spencer borrowed a typically Victorian allegory for human feelings from the hissing tanks and pistons of the Industrial Revolution. Our emotions, he thought, were like a hydraulic system, with energy being built up and let go. And our emotional engine vented laughter just like steam. Spencer blended this image with contemporary ideas of 'psychic energy' and theorised that the human condition was to be trapped between the build-up of this energy, through expectation and tension, and its release through physical action, in this case laughter. It's a more elaborate version of the 'heeeeere I come' tickling game with a toddler; the more the subject builds anticipation, the longer they hold that energy in, the bigger the laugh. Spencer was helped here by an increased contemporary understanding of the nervous system, and his theory incorporates elements of the now familiar fight-or-flight idea, where the body gets ready to react by winding itself up like a coiled spring. The difference with comedy, Spen-cer observed, was that this reaction to stimulus wasn't *useful*, like running or fighting, but a release in itself; laughter was the product, because where else would that energy go? This is called 'relief theory'. We build up tension, but when it turns out that we are not threatened, the stored energy needs to be vented. This is one of the key factors in the efficacy of my favourite siblings-at-a-funeral joke, and Spencer's repress-and-explode idea was to be a big influence on Freud.

Sigmund Freud
(late nineteenth to early twentieth century)

Freud was, as you'd expect, obsessed with how comedy exposed the forbidden or suppressed parts of our inner selves. Anyone who's read Freud's theories, and the jokes he uses to illustrate them, will suspect he was slightly more interested in the repression part than the joke part. Like Hobbes, Freud restricted his definition of comedy to make it fit his worldview, except that where Hobbes reckoned we were all competitive savages, Freud thought we were the cast of a *Carry On* film: randy, miserable wretches with one thing on our mind and steam coming out of our collars. A lot of comedy does enjoy saying the 'unsayable', and Freud's insistence that every gag was a secret sex joke or an outburst from the darkest corners of the brain works fine when explaining double entendre, embarrassment humour and shock comedy, but leaves out almost everything else. Speaking personally, I find the problem with Freud is that, in trying to find an explanation, he promises you a big one that will really satisfy, and then ignores all the mothers. Others.

THE BIG THREE

So, in the history of human enquiry into comedy, there have been three main schools of thought. For ease of universal comprehension, I propose to define them using the following well-loved cartoon characters, performing their signature moves.

Superiority Theory:
Nelson Muntz the bully from *The Simpsons* pointing at a floundering victim and going 'ha ha'.

Relief Theory:
Shaggy from *Scooby-Doo* giggling nervously because it was just an old sheet all along, Scoob.

Incongruity Theory:
Rick and Morty from *Rick and Morty* doing absolutely anything at all.

Of the three, the last one strikes me as the most inclusive and useful. It is certainly the one most widely accepted by twenty-first-century scientists studying the subject. Sure, it's funny watching someone fall down a manhole (superiority). And it's funny watching someone not fall down a manhole and thinking 'phew' (relief). But what both of these potentially comic situations have in common is surprise. The action of suddenly falling, or suddenly not falling, when something else was anticipated is incongruous. With a bit of thought, you can see that the label of 'incongruity' also applies to all the basic old faithfuls of comedy.

Incongruity covers puns, juxtapositions, parodies, misunderstandings, exaggerations, bathos, weird facial expressions, strange dances, silly walks, slapstick routines, underreacting, overreacting, one-song-to-the-tune-of-another, adults behaving like children, humans behaving like animals, women dressed as cows, men dressed as hot dogs. It includes inability to see the obvious, blindness to our own shortcomings, excessive self-belief and inappropriate cowardice. Incongruity is what's funny about throwing custard pies in a posh restaurant, presenting the news in a field, things being too big, things being too small, piss, spunk and vomit all up in the wrong places, unexpected public nudity, being caught in embarrassing clothes, and disgracing yourself generally around priests, bosses, monarchs or parents. Incongruity is the engine that drives over-complex excuses and under-cunning plans, goofy anachronisms, characters breaking 'the fourth wall' by talking to the audience, mismatched couples, flatmates from hell, unexpected frankness, needless euphem-ism, butlers who appear out of nowhere like a shimmering miracle, henchmen who go *clongggg* like an iron water tank when you boot them in the knackers, and unseen spouses described as filigreed monsters. It's absurdity, surrealism, unlikely coincidence, bursts of excessive cartoon violence, declarations of drunken love, grannies doing a rap, punks having tea and cucumber sandwiches, being exactly the wrong guy for the job, kissing the wrong person by mistake, saying you'll never catch me doing that and then doing exactly that, cheeking a policeman and saying 'he's standing right behind me, isn't he?' It's an idiotic lack of boundaries, clumsy misjudgement, overextension, rudeness and dis-gust. It's lists that become comically much longer than they need to be, but find a strange rhythm pulsing within them, and then over time evolve into rhyme, and pretty damn soon develop a tune, and seem to be jokes in themselves.

It's all that.

Incongruity is expecting one thing and getting another.

And that's how comedy works.

6

Surprise!

Whatsoever it be that moveth laughter, it must be new and unexpected.

Thomas Hobbes

Ignoring the clever people for a moment, if you've ever tried to make comedy yourself, and are somehow able to observe what you're doing (which is as hazardous as thinking about walking while walking), you might find yourself able to agree with the following statement:*

Comedy is a game that humans play which challenges other humans to guess what is coming next.

All storytelling of any sort does this: treating a series of events as a puzzle that the audience is invited to solve. We agree to play a game, to follow clues, to learn patterns of character behaviour and story shape, and try to guess what happens next.

Comedy (unlike drama, of which more later) plays this guess-and-reveal game over very short distances, often as fast as a one-liner. And the key element is surprise. A pattern is set, then broken. It's basic primate rough-and-tumble

---

* With the caveat that this is true of lots of other things as well, but, hey, we have to start somewhere.

play, like teasing-out-the-wait-and-then-tickling, but with physical intimacy replaced by mental games. No matter how sophisticated the structure, a regular swing between anticipation and surprise is the common factor in all comedy.

Human cognition is a lot about guesswork. As information pours in, our brain (or more specifically, the frontal lobe) behaves like a goalkeeper in a penalty shootout, scuttling to the side of the net where we think the next ball is going. (Patients with damage to their prefrontal cortex have huge difficulty planning, predicting or sorting their ideas.) The idea of our processing engine being thrown into disarray is scary. The fear and distress we might associate with 'madness' (in its literary rather than clinical sense) may be down to us knowing how vital it is for humans to be able to predict patterns.

Because of this, our brains look out for the unexpected. Unusual input goes straight to the front of the processing queue because an urgent response is required. What if the surprise means we're in danger? And sometimes this very serious game of ensuring our survival by processing and resolving incongruity becomes really good fun. And that's comedy.

SETTING OFF THE FIRE ALARM FOR A LAUGH

Obviously not all surprises are funny. If we're waiting for a latte and the barista pops a scorpion on the counter (even if it's been put in a cup with our name on it), we might scream and run away. Humans are vulnerable animals with plenty of predators, and incongruity, if not immediately resolved, can trigger our fight-or-flight response.

Scientists have used fMRI brain imaging technology to look for specific areas of the human brain involved in recognising, resolving and elaborating the sort of incongruity that we find routinely in life, and also in comedy and humour. It's a highly complex system, and there is no single part of the brain that is dedicated to this one job. We don't have a 'comedy cortex' you could poke with a scalpel and get a laugh (though that would make open-mic nights easier), and different sorts of joke, such as puns, seem to light up different parts of your brain, which is a fascinating idea.

The process seems to be co-ordinated by the prefrontal lobe, which matches input against memory to analyse expected threat and reward, and attempts to resolve conflicts when it detects inconsistencies between expectation and reality. Way below that is the limbic system, the brain's primitive paleomammalian engine room, long regarded as the home of our lower emotions, such as fear and aggression (though, as always, the human brain turns out to be more integrated and complex than that). Down here, our quick-reaction trigger, the amygdala, also appears to respond to funny stimuli, which may point to a connection between the sort of incongruity we enjoy in jokes and the broken patterns that we need to look out for to survive.

Perhaps it's the link between our incongruity-twitchy amygdala and our laugh response that causes nervous laughter. (There'll be more on that later.)

All this stuff is serious kit. The incongruity alert systems are the bits we evolved as our tiger klaxon. When this network of monitors, analytics and responders is triggered, our brain readies us to think faster, react more quickly, become hyper-alert and responsive to threat. If this system is doing its job, it calls up our learned patterns of expectation, detects that something doesn't fit – *TIGER!* – and sends us into red-alert mode, to stand and fight, or run like hell.

When we consume horror and thriller fiction, our desire

to trigger this system, to deliberately put ourselves through all that stress and tension, may be nothing more than a handy fire drill to check the machinery is working. Deliberately setting off the alarm while we know we're safe could be seen as a version of Aristotle's ideas of mimesis and catharsis in Classical drama: that we can purge emotions by enjoying a simulation of them. This fits with Herbert Spencer's machinery analogy; we're testing the capacity of our panic engine by filling it with pressure and then releasing it. As with most fiction and a lot of art, we may be sharpening our mental and physical toolkits in a safe space, by running our survival procedures while we are not in any real danger.

HORROR VS COMEDY

It's worth noticing here how many skilled comedy writers, directors and performers do excellent work in the horror genre. Off the top of my head, I'd name John Landis, Alice Lowe, Jordan Peele, Sam Raimi, the various *League of Gentlemen* creators, Charlie Brooker, Matt Holness, Ben Wheatley, Gareth Tunley, Roald Dahl, Joe Dante and Joe Cornish.

Edwardian comic writer E. F. Benson created the witty *Mapp and Lucia* books alongside the most terrifying ghost stories of his era. Screenwriter Craig Mazin went from the goofy *Hangover* film franchise to Cold War tech-horror *Chernobyl* and zombie apocalypse dystopia *The Last of Us*. Dalek creator Terry Nation started out writing for Tony Hancock. The BBC's tradition of chilling Christmas TV ghost stories was kicked off by *Beyond the Fringe* comedy star Jonathan Miller. Barely anyone now remembers that the writer of *The Exorcist*, William Peter Blatty, honed his craft in comedy, writing the screenplay for the second *Pink Panther* film *A Shot in the Dark* (as well as several comic novels). 'The sad truth,' Blatty said, 'is that nobody wants me to write comedy. *The Exorcist* not only ended that career, it expunged all memory of its existence.'*

Switching between these two seemingly opposite genres is possible because the same game of setting up expect-ation, following patterns, then breaking them, works for both comedy and horror. Checking that our incongruity alarm is functioning properly seems to give us pleasure, regardless of whether it makes us happy or stressed.

The difference between horror and comedy is the audi-ence's reaction to the surprise. When we enjoy well-made horror or engaging thrillers, we don't laugh when the bomb goes off, or a vengeful ghost appears in the shadows. That's because we laugh with relief, and horror denies us that relief, keeping the tension going. Herbert Spencer's Victorian pressure-engine works whether you keep the steam topped up, for a big release, or let it go in little spurts. I'll go into this further later, but it's a good demon-stration of how comedy differs from other pattern-spotting games, through its speed of release.

Comedy keeps returning us to safety, defusing the ten-sion. A joke with the mounting, seemingly unresolvable extended unease we find in thrillers would either not work, or at best be termed 'a Shaggy Dog Story'. Our enjoyment of extended jokes (where the expected rules of quick release are deliberately broken) is very different from how we respond to a burst of slapstick or a snappy verbal gag. Again, more on that later.

THE GHOST WAS OLD MAN JENKINS ALL ALONG!

In a horror film, when the source of the unexplained noise in the fruit cellar turns out to be nothing but a clumsy cat,

---

* Having found this out, I am now obsessed by Clouseau/Satanic possession movie crossover potential. *'Your minkey sucks cocks in hell...'*

we may laugh (especially if we are part of a cinema or theatre audience). These laughs within an extended horror or thriller narrative are a natural part of a release of tension, because, for a moment, everything makes sense again. There is an ordinary normal everyday cat in the cellar. Not a monster. If the surprise of the cat jumping out were not followed by a moment of relief, and maybe a laugh, we would be indicating to ourselves and others that we were somehow worried by an unexplained noise that has now been explained. But of course in horror, this incongruity is not totally resolved. Tension sustains.

We know that the actual answer to 'what is down in the cellar?' will never just be 'the cat'. This is the game we have agreed to play. It's a horror story. Our laugh was a mistake. We relaxed too early. The monster is still out there.

Because the use of incongruity and the pattern of reveals and surprises is so similar in comedy and horror, I would argue that it's the moment of relief that defines comedy, by making something unexpected into something funny. In comedy, instead of incongruity ramping up our anxiety, we immediately see an alternative model by which the nonsense makes sense. Sure, what just happened was mad, but this character does mad things. The pun made no sense until we heard the word the other way. The puzzle is swiftly resolved, and we feel relief. It's OK. Green light. And so we laugh, rather than hold our breath to choke the scream.

7

What's Brown and Sticky?

How do you tell the difference between a bugler and a burglar?
One of them has a bugle. And the other one is really upset that his bugle's been stolen.

John-Luke Roberts

In 1972, psychologist Thomas Shultz studied children to see how they attempted to make sense of surprise elements in cartoons, and came up with his 'incongruity resolution theory'. This idea was confirmed by later researchers, who observed that whenever the brain trips up, it retraces its steps until it makes some sort of sense out of the apparent nonsense. This mental skip-back-and-forth is the moment we experience pleasure from comic stimuli. When the process works and returns a 'that makes sense' result, the conflict is resolved. We relax, we feel safe, and therefore we laugh.

One of my favourite 'proper joke' jokes I've heard in recent years was shared by the music writer Pete Paphides, which means I think of it as *his* joke. He didn't make it up, just passed it on, but we value the sharing of humour so much as a species that a joke may 'stick to' the teller and engender affection, even if the gag wasn't their own creation.*

---

* When the prolific comedy writer Barry Cryer died, I noticed that almost none of the jokes we told and enjoyed in his name were actually *written* by Barry

Anyway, here's Pete's joke (that isn't his):

A man goes to the doctor and says, 'I'm having trouble
with my hearing.'
The doctor says, 'Can you describe the symptoms?'
And the man replies, 'Well, there's Marge. She has blue hair.'

The first time you hear it, it seems to stop too quickly.
Then you retrace your steps and work out where the misunderstanding has happened. What's lovely about this one
is that the point where the incoming data splits into two
parallel streams is slightly earlier than you expect. You
would commonly anticipate a joke on the last word: maybe
a pun that depended entirely on the word 'symptoms', or a
gag about the nature of the medical problem; something
about ears, perhaps, or hearing. Instead, the split in meaning happens earlier, on the word 'describe' (or, it might be
argued, on the phrase 'Can you . . .'). In the patient's reality,
the doctor is suddenly asking a general-knowledge quiz
question about a TV show. The divergence of the question
into two senses (medical, quiz) is neatly explained by the
hearing problem in the set-up, but the pleasure comes from
the audience not quite spotting exactly where one sense
forked into two and having to go back to check.

I call this part of any good pun 'the hinge', and the earlier it comes in the phrase, the happier I am, because it
means the misdirection was cleverer than I was expecting.
My brain keeps wanting to go back and play with it, like
a satisfying 1980s executive desk toy. I want to set the
thing off again and again, watching the little silver balls of
meaning whizz off in two directions at once.

---

himself, though he may have expertly polished their telling. He'd merely acted
as a benevolent conduit for some great gags, and it was clear that the world
loved him for it. The good feeling, the sense of generosity and sharing, had
rubbed off on him.

When it turns out that the misunderstanding wasn't a problem, just a reasonable mistake based on having reached for the wrong pattern, you can laugh and, importantly, learn.

Humans reward ourselves with a little jolt of pleasure after learning because it's good for us, and jokes are enjoyable because they aren't just play, they're practice.

STICK STICK STICK STICK, STICKY STICKY STICK STICK

To demonstrate how we process this sort of comic incongruity, imagine that a kid has brought this vintage howler back from the playground:

KID: What's brown and sticky?

Now imagine you have never heard this joke before. It's far-fetched, but imagine you are like some sort of sinless and untainted foundling, raised by wolves in a medieval wildwood, discovered on the steps of a monastery by the brethren who are prompted by your presence to ponder whether a soul raised without knowledge of scripture can possess knowledge of the divine within it, or if the very idea of divinity is transmitted through the word of God alone. Imagine it's like that, but with the brown and sticky joke, rather than fundamental questions of medieval theology. Is this helping?

Anyway. Imagine a kid tells you this joke and you've never heard it before:

KID: What's brown and sticky?
ADULT (THINKS): Brown? And sticky? That's probably a poo. Isn't it? I know where this is going. And it's straight down the lavatory. Typical.

KID: A stick! Ha ha ha.
ADULT (THINKS): A stick? Whaaaaat! My mind is
blown. Where did that come from? Brown, sure, but
are all sticks covered in honey? Are all sticks poos?
Weren't we doing poo? This is insane. Everything I
believed in is in ruins! Aaaargh! Oh, hang on. Yeah.
Brown and sticky. I get it. Great.
KID: Do you get it?
ADULT: Ha ha ha.

All the distress of an ambush, but it wasn't a monster, it was a trick. Or rather a stick. How silly that we tried to make the information fit our preconceptions! Looking back, it all makes sense. We just made an understandable mistake. But don't worry: 'brown and sticky' still also means what we thought it did too. Phew. Our well-practised pattern-detecting software was working after all. Just a false positive.

We pop the bit we didn't see coming happily away in a mental box marked 'funny', and laugh to signal that we know we are safe, and maybe to let others nearby know that nothing bad is happening. In this context it even seems credible that Victorian hydraulics buff Herbert Spencer was on the right track, and that the stored nervous energy of the initial panic response vents itself safely like steam from a pressurised tank, creating a pleasurable smile or laugh response.

The difference between horror and comedy is that comedy quickly allows us that relief, with a laugh – all safe again – while horror won't let us off the hook.

8

No Harm Meant

Why does every one of us laugh at seeing somebody else slapped in the face with a large piece of cold custard pie? Is it because we're all naturally cruel? Or is it because there's something inherently funny in custard pies? Or in faces? Or in throwing things? No, no, and no! The real reason why we laugh is because we are relieved. Because we are released from a sense of fear.

Will Hay

Based on the ideas we've come across so far, a summation of the essential elements required to make comedy might be listed simply as:

1. Expectation
2. Surprise
3. Relief

The last element is the one that marks something out as comedy: we laugh when we feel safe. If I were Aristotle, I might understand this process as:

1. Someone is strolling round the Parthenon.
2. They fall down a manhole.
3. Thank Zeus it wasn't me! I feel fantastic!

And that would get him chuckling, the Classical sociopath.

But this very basic journey from expectation to bafflement to resolution also covers way more forms of comedy than basic slapstick and Ancient Greek *Schadenfreude*. The process applies equally neatly to, say, how we might feel watching the gag-heavy disaster-spoof movie *Airplane!* for the first time:

1. This disaster movie is very exciting!
2. Oh. Everyone in it is behaving like an idiot. Have I gone mad? Have they?
3. No. It is *meant* to be silly. And my brain is working perfectly well because I can anticipate the established patterns of a disaster movie and see where they have been subverted. Phew! This is fun!

Even Aristotle might understand the basic principle here, of feeling uneasy, off-balance, surprised, ambushed by events, confused... and then realising everything is actually safe. (Provided, that is, that watching *Airplane!* didn't leave him so frightened by the very idea of air travel and moving pictures that he suffered a basic panic response, ran out into the streets of Athens and fell down a manhole.)

Comedy is an ambush to our sense of order, but it is one that resolves itself quickly as harmless. It is a grooming action, not an act of aggression, so the fear and upset with any joke is only there as a place from which we can be released. Distress is not the aim, or the principal feature. It's meant to make us feel good, not bad.

Of course, the feeling of relief with any play-fighting can be increased by tickling (or threatening to tickle) your victim more vigorously before releasing them, but that distressed feeling should not last long enough to create sustained anxiety. A quick drop from confusion to sense is fine, but a long period of worry destroys the comedy. It's why nobody laughs at a comedian who doesn't seem sure of themselves or the room seems not to like. It's meant to be relaxing. We're meant to feel safe. That's the deal. Any anxiety in the room is contagious.

WHAT DO YOU CALL A GORILLA WITH A MACHINE GUN?

Comedy being a safety signal may not seem to fit with the general perception that you can 'kill' with comedy, or use jokes to attack or damage people. Most of us have felt the pain of jokes where we're the victim. Similarly, we might hope that righteous, barbed satire might damage or shame our enemies. Surely comedy is aggressive, pointed, sharp, a hazardous tool? But that doesn't fit with observations of when we, and other primates, tend to laugh. Laughter happens when we are relaxed, and tends to vanish when we are tense.

Interestingly, there is an aggressive behaviour exhibited in apes which humans might recognise as comedy, but which other primates don't classify as comedy at all: dominance play. Gorillas are known to tease and humiliate other gorillas as a way of establishing status. But although this behaviour might seem to have something in common with certain sorts of human comedy, it is purely aggro, and rarely elicits laughter from the perpetrator or victim. For apes, humiliation is a serious business.

Similarly, chimpanzees in captivity can lure humans to come closer before throwing faeces at them: a form of crude but efficient slapstick, using anticipation, misdirection and release.

Again, though this is the sort of behaviour that would fit comic theories that involve the misfortune of others, there is no associated laughter. As with Koko, the signing and improvising gorilla who made Robin Williams crack up, any laughter seems to be social, and starts with the humans; it's not part of the aggression. The chimpanzees don't laugh when they initiate the serious dominance activity of shit-chucking, but join in as a group-bonding signal when we laugh at them for doing it.

Some scientists have proposed that teasing and bullying dominance play (which is natural to apes in the wild, and not accompanied by laughter) may be an *ancestor* of humour, without actually being it. Which is interesting, since it implies that bullying for your own amusement is to actual comedy what clubbing a potential mate over the head and dragging them to your cave by their hair is to dating. The Americans call this sort of primitive proto-humour 'roast comedy', and host whole evenings of it, dedicated to ribbing the most powerful people in showbiz, a style that has now escaped private clubs to become the default tone of glitzy awards-ceremony hosting.

This sort of comedy – which is often loved and cele-brated by highly competitive alphas on the stand-up circuit – is less about comedy than establishing status. And if you've ever wondered why some celebs 'just can't take a joke', why they're not happy to offer a toothy rictus grin in the Oscars audience cutaway shot, it's worth remembering that, in evolutionary terms, a roast gag is not a joke, it's an attack. Baring teeth has a very different meaning for most primates.

ALL IN FUN

Humour can certainly accompany aggressive behaviour, but it's not usually something that makes the *victim* laugh. A functional joke is meant to be shared, but we don't direct an aggressive joke at someone as a way of bonding with them. In fact, from the victim's point of view, it's not felt as comedy at all, but straight aggression. 'Stop it,' kids say in the playground when being teased. 'That's not funny.' Mockery defines a small tribe bonded by the values expressed in the joke, 'othering' the target, excluding them from the group. And if the victim wants to feel safe again, they may choose to force a laugh at their own expense, and join the majority. Refusing to be excluded by a joke that threatens to eject us from the laughing tribe creates a feeling of safety again, and so we can laugh too. Everyone feels safe. No harm done. It was only a joke!*

Humans may accompany aggressive teasing with a celebratory laugh. This audible signal doesn't mark the moment of danger in the comedy, but rather occurs to assert the dominant (safe) position of the aggressor and marks the rejection of any outsiders who are not laughing. The group has been homogenised and therefore soothed by the joke. Laughter remains a safety signal, separate from the aggression, a reaction to its success, one that says, 'We're fine now. We're the ones laughing.'†

A laugh and a bark can both be used to warn off outsiders. But a laugh is designed to soothe and strengthen the group, rather than simply raise an alarm. They're similar noises, but do different jobs.

ANXIOUS TITTERING

Using a laugh to declare a state of safety also explains nervous laughter. Humans might giggle in stressful situations, usually in the hope that someone will join in, and reassure us that a bigger, genuine relief laugh is coming. This is

---

* There have been few better (and funnier) studies of this than Ricky Gervais and Stephen Merchant's *The Office*, particularly the 'Quiz Night' episode, a vicious dissection of the social function of comedy.

† I'll talk about this more later, in the last part of the book, dealing with comedy's tribal functions.

using laughter's social nature to fake a sense of safety. Think of the dark, edgy jokes we exchange when we feel threatened. Soldiers and emergency crews do it all the time – it's the source of the comedy in $M*A*S*H$ – but this sort of gallows humour is about changing the declared state of the group from threatened to safe, because only then can laughter happen.

If we laugh, that means we are safe. And when we are safe, that means we can laugh. It's a reassuring loop.

We joke as an anaesthetic, to soothe pain by making the situation seem less grave, and bonding our fellow sufferers together. Dark comedy works by declaring (and thus creating) the only conditions in which it can survive: if we can laugh, we can't really be in danger. We love this trait in our fictional action heroes. Quipping while threatened is a way of nodding to everyone in the audience that we're all going to be fine. Observe how generations of children have been helped out from behind the sofa by Doctor Who not taking the monsters seriously.

HAIL TO THE EDGELORD

Agreeing on the safety of apparently edgy material is a great way to bond as a group. You may have seen a maestro like Jerry Sadowitz and thrilled to the sense of danger in the room. But as fans always say in the defence of their favourite shock comics, 'Everyone knows what he's like.' An audience knows a transgressive comic's chosen room is a magical comic space where polite social rules are suspended. And this means the audience are safe, no matter how much a comic might push them into uncomfortable areas of scabrous misanthropy. When Sadowitz's Edinburgh Fringe run was cut short in a storm of furious column inches a few years ago, the complaints – according to reports – weren't from the bulk of the audience (his tribe, who felt safe and could laugh because they had accepted the terms of the game) but from a few shocked outsiders, and notably from the young staff working in the venue who didn't feel safe. They were not part of the tribe, became anxious, and so couldn't laugh.

Significantly, that chilly moment of genuine (rather than stage-managed) uncertainty, when an audience isn't sure that a joke is really safe, is something skilled comedians try to avoid. It's why they do try-out nights for new material, and cut the stuff that knocks the audience off their stride. It's also why they pause on stage and consider theatrically for a moment when a joke proves 'too much for you, right?' If a good comic does mess about on the cliff edge where play-fighting meets actual aggression to a point where the audience isn't sure of the agreed rules, it's usually not for long. Mutual safety is necessary for the laughter to return.

And sometimes the laugh of relief that lands after a sense of safety is reasserted is the biggest laugh of all.

In his book *Don't Applaud. Either Laugh Or Don't.* about New York's Comedy Cellar (a blasphemous Mecca of comedy free speech), Andrew Hankinson quotes the owner, Noam Dworman:

> *I do have the right to tell a comedian that, for whatever reason, whether it's just they suck, or because they're dirty, whatever they're saying, 'Listen, there is a clear and evident pattern here that this is turning off the audience.' It's not about what he says. I don't care what he says. He can say anything he wants. I have to be able to tell him the audience is not accepting this.*

If a comedian's shock material does not please the self-selecting audience, even in a place where people expect to be shocked, that's not good comedy. The tribe under the Comedy Cellar's roof needs to be soothed and brought

closer by the jokes, their identity reaffirmed, their expectations fulfilled. Misread the room, and you're not a
crusading pioneer who has pushed into a new frontier –
you get gonged off, like anyone who 'sucks'.

Under all the bluster, comedy is almost always about
grooming, soothing and reassurance.

9

Play-Fighting

EDDIE: He was dead before he hit the ground.
RITCHIE: Then why did you keep hitting him with
the frying pan?
EDDIE: (BEAT) For fun.

Bottom, 'Gas'
(written by Adrian Edmondson and Rik Mayall)

Dr Sophie Quirk, in her book *Why Stand-Up Matters*,
says:

When something is 'only a joke', we allow the speaker
licence to subvert our usual standards of honesty and
decency. Joking forms a marginal safe space where this
potentially dangerous experiment may be held in safety.

In an aggressive attack, one person might laugh, like a
supervillain at the moment of triumph, because *they* feel
safe, but in play-fighting, everyone laughs. What we are
aiming for with any comedy – thanks to its origins in
tribal grooming – is the act of sharing a joke, with the
emphasis on sharing. So, good comedy doesn't just make
you laugh, it draws a little conspiracy round itself and
says 'we all agree this is funny'. Think of an audience at an
observational stand-up gig agreeing that, 'Yes, men are
just like that,' or, 'Yorkshire working-class weddings do

indeed have those things in them; well observed, sir!' Or the crowd in a hip Brooklyn cellar watching a weird cult comedian who they feel shares their sense of the absurd. And compare how we socially disapprove of people laughing to themselves. 'Share the joke with the class.' 'What's so funny?' 'Amusing yourself, are you?' 'Nobody else is laughing, Michael.'

Plenty of prank comedy or practical jokes entertain the practitioner, and can delight an audience who aren't in danger and don't identify with the victim. Of course, a practical joke's final reveal can trigger simple relief laughter. 'It was all a joke! Phew! I wasn't really in trouble!' But, if the victim of the joke feels humiliated, or struggles to shift back into a safe state after the joke's requisite period of distress, prank comedy can leave its target feeling less than wonderful. A badly judged prank gag is sometimes only comedy (i.e., a release of tension into safety) from certain points of view (that of the joker and the audience). From another point of view (that of the victim), it may be indistinguishable from an act of dominance and humiliation, and therefore lack comedy's soothing core. The insistence that a victim who isn't laughing should 'lighten up' ignores comedy's other big function: tribal bonding. This issue of inclusion and safety, and the possible ejection of the victim from the laughing group, is the difference between light-hearted teasing and bullying.

Any comedy that puts us through the distress of thinking there's a tiger, but then never gives us a hug and says there's nothing to worry about isn't comedy: it's a tiger.

WARNING! NO DANGER AHEAD!

A great example of the importance of safety to laughter was the leaked 2020 video of Boris Johnson's press secretary Allegra Stratton rehearsing her podium answers to questions about a drinks party that took place in 10 Downing Street during a nationwide Covid-19 ban on social events. In the private clip, Stratton laughs nervously about the preposterousness of claiming that a rule-breaking booze-up might have been a work meeting. She looks awkward, but finds the very idea of what she's doing ridiculous. So do her friends. 'Can we really be trying to get away with this?'

Everyone in the video is potentially in trouble, but there is a lot of giggling, because it's secret. Stratton is amongst friends, nobody can see. This situation is farcical, so she laughs. Maybe she's trying a bit of giggly anaesthetic to bond with her co-workers in their ludicrous task. By contrast, Stratton's reaction a year later when doorstepped by a hostile press pack about the same video is to burst into tears. She is about to be forced to resign. She is no longer safe. So the same subject – a secret party – is not funny now.

BLACK HUMOUR AND BAD TASTE

As we saw in the chapter on edgy comedy, although comedy is a game, it is one that is explicitly harmless for the participants.

Of course, we can all think of examples of shock humour that don't feel safe but have bonded a bunch of us together in horror that such a horrible joke was cracked.* Black comedy and bad-taste gags can confirm a group's identity by illuminating the edge of the permissible and uniting a group along lines of shared values. There is still safety, bonding and group reassurance within darkness.

---

* See the sections discussing what often feels like 'dangerous laughter' in the third part of this book.

These edgy tribal jokes often sit on the very edge of danger, dangling their naughty little legs over the precipice. That ideal joke shared between siblings at a funeral from the start of this book is certainly one that doesn't make its participants feel safe immediately. Rather, it hangs suspended for a crucial moment, building tension, flirting with the possibility of social disgrace, exposure and embarrassment, which is how it bottles its hysteria.

In his book *What Are You Laughing At?*, *Cheers* and *Modern Family* writer Dan O'Shannon observed our love of smashing our internal fire alarm when there's no fire:

> *Over centuries, we sort out the ways to give ourselves the chemical rush of relief without having to put ourselves in danger. We crave the drug.*

We love the transgressive thrill of teetering on the edge of danger while entirely safe so much that it has evolved into our addiction to the anticipation-surprise-relief beats of comedy. But what is making us laugh is the fact that we are not actually going to fall – we're just messing about on the cliff edge. Because laughter is a grooming, bonding signal, we don't make that communal social noise if we feel threatened: we scream. This 'threat' can be as literal as mock aggression from a stand-up comedian, or as abstract as whimsy and nonsense (a challenge to the assumed sensible order, or our own sanity). The moment such a threat becomes real, we run, fight and shout in distress. Conversely, if we laugh, that is the sound of a group audibly sharing the news that we're all safe.

Comedy is about surprise, but for us to laugh, the surprise has to turn out to be harmless. A tickle is never an actual attack, it is play.

It was just a joke. Lighten up.

10

Typing '5318008' on a Calculator

The computer decided that the three most popular ice cream flavours were book-ends, West Germany and pumice stone.
This was found to be due to an electrical fault.

> *The Fall and Rise of Reginald Perrin*
> (written by David Nobbs)

If comedy is play, why do we like playing silly games with our vital internal alarms? Scientific experiments seem to show that the urge to play has its roots in the same deep limbic system that helps us survive, where the brain's crucial incongruity detectors and hazard alarms lurk. And far from being pointless, play seems to serve the following beneficial functions:

- establishing social hierarchies and rules
- developing motor, cognitive and creative skills
- strengthening social bonds within groups
- helping to manage stress

All these play actions are applicable to humour (there's a lot of physical skill in delivering comedy, and even verbal comics will 'act out' their material). And while many animals engage in play activity, especially as infants, humans do it to a ridiculous extent, because we have to play if we are going to have a chance to get to adulthood.

Humans arrive in the world pretty unprepared for survival compared to most creatures, and have an extended infancy that programs our brains. One of the most important skills that humans need to learn, through play, is pattern detection and anticipation (it's the basis of almost all the games we play with babies). Our key evolutionary advantages come from cognition and language, rather than, say, possessing venomous fangs or powerful wings.

Therefore our brain rewards us for training ourselves in these cognitive skills, in the same way that prairie dogs might enjoy practising play-hunting, or a young bird might get pleasure from learning to swoop. We find things funny, and get a little laughter hit, because it does us good to play at spotting when the anticipated shapes of events and ideas are followed, and when they are broken.

In their book *Inside Jokes* (on the neurological engineering of humour), cognitive science supergroup Matthew Hurley, Daniel C. Dennett and Reginald Adams declare:

> *The pleasure of mirth is an emotional reward for success in the specific task of data integrity checking.*

Humans have taken something as dry but necessary as 'data integrity checking' and turned it into a game that makes us laugh. Renowned airborne child psychologist Mary Poppins would explain that 'play' is the 'spoonful of sugar' that makes the medicine of rehearsing cognitive processes go down. Practising pattern and error detecting is useful, so we have hardwired our brains to give us a reward for doing it, and every laugh is like being given a bike for doing well in our exams.

It may be that by encouraging ourselves to go down

TYPING '5318008' ON A CALCULATOR   63

seemingly nonsensical paths, and come back with fresh ways of interpreting seemingly mad input, comedy is a game that teaches us to keep an open mind. The pleasure hit we get from playing the game is our reward for doing a load of cognitive keep-fit. And our laugh response while in company is a social signal, encouraging others to join in the game, because mental flexibility and intuitive creative thinking are beneficial for the wider group. Comedy is a fun game for practising pattern detection in the same way archery is a fun way to practise defending your village from marauders, and Scrabble is a fun game that might help expand your vocabulary and ability to see patterns in random data.

Comedy invites us to believe 'six impossible things before breakfast', as the White Queen says to Alice, whether it's that a certain character's innate flaws will make them do illogical things, or that someone in *The Goon Show* can run to Africa in two seconds because a sound effect said so. In brain workout terms, comedy is heavy weightlifting. Comedy might be seen as the silly relation of the finer storytelling arts, but it gives your brain more extreme mental exercise, faster, than almost anything else. And that is really good for you.

THE PATTERN MACHINE

The pattern-detection machine on which we play the game of comedy is the same one we use to perceive the world around us. The trick of comedy is to run some playful 'dummy' information through all the following bits of our brain, to see what they think:

- our sensory and information-gathering system
- our pattern-detection system
- our language-processing system

- our prediction/anticipation system
- our error-detection system
- our error-correction system

Animal play activity is a safe space to practise vital social and survival skills, and similarly, the game of comedy could well have evolved from something much simpler: a pattern-recognition and error-correction training test for our brain. Any art that engages our imagination like this is, at its root, the equivalent of an old television test card, or the sheet of strange patterns you print out when you want to check why your printer isn't working. Its main use is to help calibrate the machinery that helps us explore reality. But thanks to evolution, we have started appreciating our perceptual test cards for their own strange beauty (in the same way that they now sell mugs and t-shirts of the lovely old BBC test card with the girl and clown on it).

All narrative and fiction is a way to check our machinery is working and sharpen its responses. But because comedy is evidently playful – and often comes in short, colourful, fun little bursts – it feels more like a game than *King Lear* does. It's easy to think of a cracker joke such as 'What do you get if you cross a sheep with a kangaroo?' as a short test signal used to check that our brain can get a spark out of its (woolly) jumper cables, and that's what it is. The actual truth is that both Shakespeare and crap dad jokes work the same way, sharing a common evolutionary ancestor, because they are both games we play with our human hardware.

The predictive engine in our brains is enormously important, and is otherwise employed on essential work decoding language, and even interpreting reality itself. It is meant to do very serious stuff. But that doesn't mean we can't also do silly things with it, and enjoy playing with its capabilities. If you remember sitting in a maths class with your very serious scientific calculator, then turning it upside down and typing '5318008' into it so it says 'BOO-BIES', you know the principle.

Comedy is about complex machinery with a serious purpose being hijacked for a giggle.

11

Pretty Patterns

Comedy Is Not Pretty!

Steve Martin, album title

So, we've established that humans love patterns. Being alive is a matter of guessing what's coming next, on the fly, which is hard, and so we look for shortcuts.

In his book *The Comedy of Error*, evolutionary biologist Jonathan Silvertown explains:

> *The first evolutionary step towards humour must have begun with a general mental ability to compare expectations with various sensory inputs . . . This ability would have been vital to survival.*

And humans enjoy playing with patterns and prediction more than the average beast because we have evolved language. Language processing relies on an ability to predict the next letter in a word, the next word in a sentence, the next idea in a conversation. It's a background process running in our brains all the time, and it's made us humans even crazier than most animals about pattern finding.

Neuroscientist Anil Seth, who studies human consciousness, has stated with helpful clarity that 'the brain is a prediction machine'. Seth regards our conscious existence as a real-time game we play with prediction, making best guesses based on supplied information and experience.

In the nineteenth century, German physicist Hermann von Helmholtz proposed the idea of perception as a process of 'unconscious inference', meaning that our sense of reality has to be constructed by combining sensory signals with our brain's expectations or belief about their causes. For example, we might see something in three dimensions, but that is just a conclusion our mind has reached by combining two separate images, from each of our eyes, and applying expectation to what those two sets of data might mean if put together. That's how much prediction and pattern finding we're doing all the time: even the evidence of our own eyes is assembled using patterns and prediction. We learn how to accept information from multiple sources, to sort and compare it, then transform it into an awareness of what's going on.

Conflicting data might arrive in our brains and not make sense, but we learn how to resolve those conflicts.

And by that definition, comedy is an experience that exaggerates the process by which we are aware of reality itself.

TRUTH AND CLARITY

Comedians like to say that, because jokes can expose our human frailties, comedy is all about truth. And while I don't disagree that comedy, with its use of bathos and love of undermining the pompous, is a fantastic way to expose the filthy fingerprints on our shiny public surfaces, I don't think that's a claim that comedy can make uniquely. Sure, we funny people have the bladder on the stick, and the licence to go 'ha ha' and point out the Emperor is pantless, but plenty of other art reveals our uncomfortable hidden sides too.

What I think comedy has, at its best, is not truth, but clarity. And that's because it is an art form that relies for its effects on balance, mirroring, symmetry, rhythm, contrast, pace, harmony, juxtaposition and surprise. For an audience to track the comic beats of something (alongside its narrative, verbal and visual sense), those underlying patterns have to be incredibly clear.

When comedy 'tells the truth', that's all about clarity. In good comedy, even if a character surprises us or makes seemingly illogical or wild decisions, their nonsensical actions should, on checking, turn out to be honouring some other inner truth about themselves, which – thanks to clarity – the audience will understand and accept. So, Alan Partridge will present an awards ceremony while bleeding to death from an impaled foot, rather than seek medical attention, because that is totally what Alan Partridge would do.

Comic characters are templates from which we can predict behaviour. A comic character in this sense can be a character in a narrative – one of the protagonists of a sitcom, say – or that character could be the stage persona adopted by a comedian, the in-print voice of a columnist, the house style of a publication, the expected tone of a parody, or the accepted role of a guest on a panel show.

A comic character adopts a recognisable voice and identity, with declared values and traits, and that voice helps us guess what they might do next. Are they prissy or slobby, cool or nerdy, frantic or lazy, kind or cruel? The character sets a pattern and the audience follows it. Nobody minds if that persona isn't really how the comedian is (though authenticity is always richer), because in comedy, 'telling the truth' is often simply about dealing fairly with audience expectation.

Expectation is about how information arrives in an audience's brain, one chunk at a time. Each member of the audience readies themselves for the next chunk based on what they have already absorbed. This process, essential to comedy, is all about establishing and breaking patterns.

That's why the secret of comedy is timing. You need to send the information in at the right pace: slow enough not to garble any information the audience needs, but fast enough to trip up the pattern detector. Above all, it needs to be done with enough clarity that the audience enjoys the game, and delights in being tricked, because you played fair.

PATTERN DETECTORS

A masterful example of this process is the opening scene of the feature-length comeback episode of the BBC sitcom *Detectorists*. This gentle, clever show, about a pair of metal-detector hobbyists looking for buried treasure in the Essex countryside, prides itself on breaking off occasionally to watch the clouds pass or an insect scaling a blade of grass. And yet the show dispenses its comic data at the rate of any other comedy, giving our pattern-detecting engine loads of enjoyable expectation games.

This 'cold open' scene – which reintroduces the characters after a five-year hiatus – is a wonderful example of how a piece of naturalistic dialogue in a realistically played situation, without a regimented feed-and-punchline gag structure, can still be unmistakably comedy, because of the way it sets and breaks patterns. To push a pleasing metaphor, the pattern at work here is buried pretty near the surface, the shape of the comedy lightly concealed, yet easily detectible, like the dark patches in an aerial photograph that indicate a buried Anglo-Saxon settlement.

And I'll highlight that pattern by emboldening a single word.

EXT. ESSEX COUNTRYSIDE. DAY

LANCE's bright yellow TR7 drives along the edge of an empty field and parks. A muddy Land Rover draws up. The farmer, KEVIN, gets out, as do LANCE and ANDY. They meet.

ANDY: Morning. Kevin, is it? Andy.
LANCE: Lance.
KEVIN: So, metal detectors, are you?
LANCE: **Detectorists**. Metal detectors
are in the boot all ready to go. So.
We've drawn up a contract as
discussed, outlining our agreement
that anything of any value is split
fifty-fifty between us, the finders, and
you, the landowner.
KEVIN: I'll have a look.
ANDY: We were wondering if you'd sign
that now, actually, Kevin? Best get
the paperwork in place before we get
started.
KEVIN: Oh. OK.
LANCE: So, which fields are we allowed
in?
KEVIN: Everything south of the river
is ours. Winter barley is already in
at Branford Road. Otherwise, go where
you like.
ANDY: And nobody's ever searched here
before, to your knowledge?
KEVIN: Metal detectors?
ANDY: **Detectorists**. Yeah.
KEVIN: Not that I know of.
LANCE: Well. Thanks again. Cheerio.

*LANCE & ANDY go to get their metal
detectors out of the TR7's boot.*

LANCE: Ladies and gentlemen. I give
you ten acres of prime paydirt.
Freshly ploughed. And months 'til the
crops go in.

ANDY: Bring it on.
LANCE: You're very welcome.

*KEVIN pulls his Land Rover up
alongside LANCE and ANDY.*

KEVIN: There are some guys mending the
fence down by the woods. But they
won't bother you. Just tell them
you're the metal detectors.

*LANCE and ANDY take a deep breath to
shout after his departing Land Rover.
Hard cut.*

TITLE CARD: **Detectorists**

The pattern is marked by the moments the word 'Detectorists' appears. Look at them. Evenly spaced. Each one balanced by the words 'metal detectors'. It's lovely. We hear the title of the show, and our ears naturally prick up. It happens once, and we enjoy it as a little data nugget, since we get some character detail from it: the hobbyists have a different name for their hobby than the general public, and are annoyed when outsiders mix it up. They have pride, they want respect, but they cannot demand or expect it. The actors' delivery and expressions confirm our guess that this reading is the case, so we're happy. This joke has been used in the show before, so it is a nice nod for fans, but easy to grasp if you've not seen the show before. Whether you know this thing about the characters or not, it states (or reminds you of) the 'sit' of the sitcom, and establishes the status of the protagonists within their community.

The second time Kevin says 'metal detectors', Lance and Andy correct him again. Twice now; so it's not just a joke, it's a pattern. The pained wince of Lance and Andy is doubly funny, because we enjoy having predicted it. We expect that they'll hate it, and we're right. And it tells us something about new character Kevin, which is that he doesn't listen. Our heroes and fellow hobbyists might politely request that others respect them, but they are not the sort of people who are listened to. It's all information for us to enjoy unpicking, and now it's being arranged in a lovely pattern. It's like a counting game. One Detectorists... two Detectorists... and we know what's coming next, surely; they're going to do it again...

So, when Kevin leans out of the window of his four-wheel drive and says 'metal detectors' a third time, we're primed and ready for our heroes' wounded comeback. And if Lance and Andy took a deep breath and shouted it at his departing rear headlights, it would be funny. But instead, in a stroke of comic genius, the word is cut off in the edit. And a hard cut to the title card. *Detectorists*.

We say it in our minds. We finish the pattern ourselves, which is an extra treat. And of course. It's the name of the show. We'd almost forgotten.

It's such a lovely surprise, I laughed out loud when I first saw it. What I love most about it is that even though it pokes through the fourth wall of the television screen, by acknowledging the programme's production techniques, the solid reality of the world of Lance and Andy is left intact.

On top of being a character gag, and an establisher of the situation, it's an inclusive production joke that invites you to join in and follow the show's rhythms and patterns, to enjoy a piece of craft, maybe even to join in making the show along with the team. It's generous and inclusive. You know this one. One. Two. Three, with a twist on the third. All together now...

12

The Rule of Three

I've got no sex life, I've got no frying pan, and I'm halfway through a tube of toothpaste I absolutely can't stand.

Stan, *Dinnerladies*
(written by Victoria Wood)

A theory that is often wheeled out to demonstrate that comedy follows systems and patterns is the famous 'Rule of Three'. This is the idea that audiences like to take in ideas in groups of three, which in oratory and advertising gives us 'life, liberty and the pursuit of happiness', 'snap, crackle and pop', 'work, rest and play'. It's even there in Tony Blair's 'education, education, education', a use of the oratorical Rule of Three that almost amounts to parody; millennia of rhetorical panache reduced to the bark of an Ofsted Dalek.

In comedy, the deployment of a twist at the end creates a *comic* Rule of Three. So, while Julius Caesar can rouse spirits with 'I came. I saw. I conquered', Bill Murray in *Ghostbusters* gets a laugh by pulling a tonal switch on the count of three: 'We came. We saw. We kicked its ass.'

Three is the smallest number that humans perceive as a set (a pattern that belongs together), so it's easy to spring surprises within a trio. You simply pick a member that doesn't belong, and (usually) pop them in at the end for a comedy *ta-da!* Lists of three things are funnier than lists of two, and harder to get lost in than a list of twelve.

We have brought gifts for our infant Lord. Gold, frankincense and this Lego Batmobile. . .

This idea of sets, and the fun of spotting outliers within those sets, explains how threes work in a simple list, but comedy isn't just lists (even if lists are the most efficient use of a writing room to generate comic material). However, analysing comedy as a series of beats of information reveals how three elements can form a comprehensible trail of ideas for the brain to follow and interpret as start, middle and end.

This is the shape that comedians know as set-up, development, punchline.

I suppose lesbian sex is a bit like cricket,

in that it goes on forever

and there's a lot of men watching it at home, alone, on the internet.

Catherine Bohart

That's a classic one-two-three joke. I've added line breaks to demonstrate the sections. Part one introduces what you're talking about (lesbian sex and cricket, a strong start). Part two is an idea that moves the thought on in an expected direction that is sort of interesting but doesn't necessarily get a big laugh (the comparative length of time of both activities).* But part three is a neat surprise that

---

* Little pause to appreciate the craft here, in that Bohart's second 'development' beat is warm, neat and interesting enough after the set-up that the gag could

juxtaposes a different tone. There's also space in beat three for you to fill in some detail in the comic picture, maybe using some cultural baggage you brought along yourself. It's a great audience-friendly gag.

And it goes one-two-three.

THE MAGIC NUMBER?

So is the secret of comedy. . . three? Although it would be satisfyingly Douglas Adams-ish for the answer to be a number, it doesn't take long to notice that there's loads of hilarious stuff that doesn't play out over this formalised one-two-three rhythm.

What about all those neat two-beat gags that go set-up, punchline?

Clowns' divorce: custardy battle.

Simon Munnery

I'm not addicted to cocaine. I just like the way it smells.

Richard Pryor

Life is like a box of chocolates. It doesn't last long if you're fat.

Joe Lycett

Those don't have three beats, even if you start hacking the syllables up with scissors. There's a one-two and it works fine, whether it's a pun, like Munnery's, a gag based on a comic persona, like Pryor's, or just a neat conceptual 'rhyme' like Lycett's. Does that mean there's some kind of

---

stop there, and almost work. It wouldn't feel *quite* finished, but it might get a ripple of laughter. Everything is building, in a harmonious set of ideas, to construct a pattern.

maverick Rule of Two we need to incorporate into our theory? Because that completely ruins it.

(Yes. You're right to be angry. Comedy promised us threes.)

Also, the Rule of Three, with its twist ending, doesn't explain comedy with no surprises. There's plenty of character-based comedy that warms us and delights us by being completely predictable. There's no third beat when, say, Albert Steptoe behaves in a completely Albert Steptoe way. Just a set-up (here's Albert) and then roughly what we expected (Albert is completely Albert). And it's still funny.

Go and see a good stand-up who knows how to use their on-stage 'clown' persona, and you will laugh when they behave like themselves, using certain physical tics and verbal phrasing to express a very particular world-view. When a panel game stalwart does that thing they always do, it's not a surprise – far from it. But we still laugh when Ian Hislop or David Mitchell is slightly out of touch with pop culture. Or when Aisling Bea or Rachel Parris takes issue with the perceived patriarchy in the studio. Or when Joe Wilkinson or Bob Mortimer appears to be joyously in a little world of his own. The forensic sitcom-family casting of quickly delineated clown personas in a show like *Taskmaster* is a demonstration that we love to pop comedians into little boxes and watch them confirm our expectations. There's no one-two-three waltz-time metronome behind our enjoyment of people being 'themselves' in a funny way.

In fact, so much good comedy disobeys the commonly understood Rule of Three, with its rigid rules that 'set-up, development, surprise = laugh', that the only rule it seems to establish is that we need to look for a different theory.

Maybe, for the sake of saving face, this new theory can have three elements, because us comedy nerds have spent all this time telling everyone the secret is a Rule of Three and now we look a bit silly. But let's not back down now. The last thing we want is to have to tell people that comedy is mysterious and capricious and can't be analysed at all.

Don't panic. I think there *is* a Rule of Three. But I think we've been looking in the wrong place.

But first we need to think about comedy in a slightly abstract way; not as jokes, or even as words or ideas, but as the thing with which it has most in common.

It's music time!

PART TWO

COMEDY IS MUSIC

The Rhythm of Comedy

[My novels are] a sort of musical comedy without music.

P. G. Wodehouse

You know what you're meant to do when someone asks you 'What is the secret of comedy?' You have to answer 'timing'. Preferably you should answer 'timing' too quickly, crashing into your audience's reply of 'I don't know', and that makes the joke work.

God, that joke's brilliant. And the secret of that joke? Timing.

In his terrific book on story craft, *A Swim in a Pond in the Rain*, author George Saunders dissects short stories from classic Russian literature as a way of teaching the art of human storytelling. At one point he pulls out far enough to observe 'story' itself as pure data, and it's a lovely moment of revelation, like looking back at the Earth from a space capsule.

A story is a linear temporal phenomenon . . . a series of incremental pulses, each of which does something to us.

In Saunders' refreshingly abstract model of how we respond to story, human beings are receivers, taking in information, which causes a reaction inside our brain in a fixed order. That is undoubtedly true of Chekhov and

Turgenev, but it's not a property that is unique to fiction. It could also be said of a knock-knock joke and Black Box's 1989 Italian house chart smash 'Ride On Time'.

But I'd argue that the knock-knock gag and the banging late-eighties floor-filler share one important feature in their dispensing of those 'incremental pulses'. It's an element that is slightly less crucial for Russian short stories about sad schoolteachers in wagons, but it is something we understand instinctively as crucial for both music and comedy.

It's all about timing.

B'DUM TISH

Timing is the pace of the pulse. Getting it wrong robs music and comedy of its purpose, which is to delight us with those incremental pulses, in order, to a strict rhythm. We feel it without thinking in music, and we feel it the same way in comedy. The timing of comedy and music is the throb of blood in the thing, what makes it live.

All fiction, all drama, all documentary, has a pace. I'm doing it now – look at all these bloody commas, and this is meant to be non-fiction. Without that rhythm, without that pace, this book would still make sense. It would still tell a story, it would still contain information, it would still, I hope, be interesting. I've read plenty of serious books, from crime to non-fiction, with the leaden groove of a junior-school wind band doing an ill-advised James Brown cover version, and not really minded. Good timing is welcome in all storytelling. It's helpful. But it's not essential.

But fluff the timing in comedy and your brain stops wanting to dance.

Actors often say that if they get their timing very slightly off while performing straight drama it dulls the effect, but what they are doing is still drama. However, make the same slip of timing in comedy, and what comes out is not comedy at all. The difference between comedy and drama is that unforgiving, underlying beat. Drama with a loose beat is still drama. Comedy with a loose beat isn't anything at all.

Writers talk about the 'beats' of a story, by which we mean the smallest units from which you can build narrative. Imagine you are telling a friend an anecdote. Each 'beat' is the next 'thing' that happens. And then... and then... and then. All stories are built of beats, but comedy's rhythm is unbelievably strict.

I heard a story from a film editor, with huge experience editing comedy shows, who was doing a job for a drama series. He was editing a sequence for a detective show: a long shot of a woman weeping in a car in the rain.

This editor kept trying different lengths of cut. He left it long. He cut it tight as hell. He left it somewhere in the middle. They all... sort of worked. And he couldn't decide which one was best. Eventually he threw his hands up in exasperation. 'How long is it meant to be?' he said to the director. 'If this was a comedy show, there would be one length of cut that made it funny, and the other ones would be not funny, and I'd know. But drama? There's no right length.'

And that's the difference. Comedy is either funny or not funny, depending on a strict internal rhythm. And the rhythm in which that flow of information enters the audience's brain is what determines when the twists and surprises can be dropped in for maximum effect. And if the information drops on the wrong beat, then it doesn't work at all.

In a hierarchy of art forms that depend on rhythm for their dispensing of information to the audience, comedy is near the top, above even poetry and advertising copywriting. And I would argue that it's right alongside the art form with which it shares the most features: music.

14

The Music of Comedy

I've suffered for my music. Now it's your turn.

Neil Innes

I suspect that a love of pattern and rhythm drives creative people into the fields of comedy and music equally. It can't be denied that the skill sets cross the divide remarkably often.

Kenny Everett was one of countless DJs with a gifted ear who shuffled effortlessly between comedy and music. The Goons could have formed a jazz band: Milligan on trumpet, Sellers on drums, Secombe on vocals. Even Milligan's regular *Goon Show* writing collaborator Larry Stephens was an accomplished jazz pianist. In his last recorded interview, John Lennon said he'd rather have been a member of the Goons or Monty Python than the Beatles (a band whose cultural impact, certainly at first, was arguably as much down to them being funny as anything to do with their songwriting.) Hip-hop has comedy in its bones. The single often named as the birth of rap, 'Here Come the Judge' (1968), was a tight-to-the-beat sketch by comedian Pigmeat Markham, based on a chitlin' circuit character routine, and rap LPs would pepper comedy skits between songs like a vaudeville variety bill. The genre's love of incongruity, surprise, pattern and character work demonstrates how comedy and music are different examples of the same phenomenon: an inventive game humans play with expectation, reference, repetition and juxtaposition.

It's a rarely acknowledged fact that the shift in the UK from boilerplate 'bloke walks into a bar' working-men's-club stand-up towards autobiographical and anecdotal stories from real life wasn't triggered by the alternative comedy boom in the early 1980s, but by the influx of musician-comedians from the folk scene a decade earlier, performers such as Billy Connolly, Mike Harding and Jasper Carrott. Folkies often introduce the traditional songs they play with historical context or stories of how they learned them. 'I picked this one up from a man I met in a pub in Truro, who learned it from his gran, who used to skipper a whaling ship. . .' The audience chats at a traditional folk gig are a useful way of covering while the singer is tuning their guitar, but because they are usually well-rehearsed stage 'bits', they have less in common with natural conversation than they do the tightly refined patter of stage stand-up, keeping an audience engaged, winning them over with a punchline. Eventually these chats grew and evolved into a different sort of personal, anecdotal comedy, often performed with a guitar round the neck that was barely touched. But the chat and the music were part of the same act, pulsing to the same rhythm. Folk music does love a song that starts one-two-three, one-two-three. . .

A list of successful comedians who have a music or band background would be as long as this book (I love asking, and almost everyone turns out to have an embarrassing demo tape somewhere*). I particularly love finding

---

* With the exception of the delightfully music-phobic David Mitchell, who once told me, 'I've been to see two live concerts in my life. Your band, and Dame Shirley Bassey. And neither made me want to do it again.' Which might be the nicest diss I've ever received. Happy to be up there with the greats.

out that comedians are drummers – a list that includes James Acaster, Al Murray, Matt Lucas, Mel Brooks, David Letterman, Jon Stewart, David Reed, Drew Carey, Craig Ferguson, Fred Armisen and Rosie O'Donnell. That sensitivity to pace, rhythm, punctuation and space, setting the beat for a whole room, with a natural feel for the b'dum tish of a punchline.

'DOES HUMOUR BELONG IN MUSIC?'

Music and comedy are natural companions because they appeal to similar sorts of brains, and use a blend of rote learning, craft and feel, allowing performers to deliver patterns of build and release over instinctive rhythms. In Jude Rogers' book *The Sound of Being Human*, here is how cognitive scientist David Huron analyses the human brain's response to music:

> *[There are] five response systems in our brains that fire up when music starts to play. Firstly, there is the reaction/defensive response system, which occurs when we first hear a song. Then comes a tension response system, when the brain is trying to discern what is going on, detecting disturbances in the regular flow of rhythm, or unusual cadences at the ends of musical phrases. Then come the more positive systems of prediction (wondering where a piece of music could go), imagination (opening up to ourselves the myriad possibilities of this process), then appraisal (how happy we are that we've correctly identified some patterns).*

Recognise this process? It's what happens when you listen to a joke, hear an anecdote, sit through a stand-up routine or watch a sitcom. We take a moment to settle in and work out what's happening. Next, we take in information, looking for clues, shapes, changes, patterns. Then we use that information to guess what will come next, all the time knowing that the real pleasure comes from a combination of regular surprises and the satisfaction of expectation.

Obviously all narrative forms have a rhythm, and an action movie will rat-a-tat its story beats faster than an arthouse flick where a character stares out of windows a lot in existential despair. But there is much more flexibility for loose timekeeping in drama than comedy. As we've seen, not every comedy has to make us laugh out loud on a rigid count of three – set-up, development, punchline – but if we feel there is too big a gap between joke shapes or comic ideas, we worry we've missed something. We may even get angry that what we are experiencing is 'just not funny'. It's a breach of contract.

Comedy producers at the BBC used to be trained to tick submitted comedy scripts on a printout, measuring the gaps between ticks and expecting a joke every two to three lines. If a stretch of script lacked ticks, that was something that needed fixing. Nobody would ever count one-two-three over a crime drama script, ticking the most mysterious lines, sucking their teeth, and insisting passages that were insufficiently baffling needed 'puzzling up'.

The pulse of comedy needs to be tight, either through rehearsal or feel, and the whole band needs to be locked into it, whether that 'band' is a cast of performers or the larger production team. The props, costume, lighting and design people have to be following the same beat, and plenty of comedy has failed because members of the band were playing different tunes.

Comedy writers and performers often attempt to control the pace and rhythm of their material, either by performing it themselves, designing comic printed material straight to the page, or sitting in on the sound or video edit, exerting control in any way they can on the rhythm in which audiences receive their jokes. The word '(BEAT)' in a script, signifying that an actor should wait before delivering their next line, appears in comedy scripts far more often than in drama scripts, because a pause for breath can make the difference between a joke landing safely and it crashing. Everything is about controlling the pace of delivery, and receipt, of comic information. The pulse is everything.

The comedy song is the most obvious place where you can observe the rhythm of music and the rhythm of jokes in close partnership. Surprise and anticipation work hand in hand to deliver jokes to a strict beat in the work of everyone from Victoria Wood to The Lonely Island, from Rachel Bloom to Flight of the Conchords, from Half Man Half Biscuit to Jake Thackray. The fit is so natural I'm certain it reveals music and comedy's shared neurological basis. The joy of dropping the wrong lyric in the right place, the enjoyment of contrasting tone and content, the set-up, development, punchline of comic-verse structure, the precision of pastiche. . . It's all the same pattern-making and pattern-breaking tricks that non-musical comedy uses, but with better tunes.

15

The Comedy Keyboard

This one go plunk.

'Back in the Jug Agane: Molesworth's Guide to the
Skool Piano', *The Compleet Molesworth*
(written by Geoffrey Willans and Ronald Searle)

If we want to treat comedy like music, we should think about it abstractly. The message of the comedy can be anything we want, but we need to understand the patterns underneath.

If you were teaching someone to play a song on the guitar, you wouldn't start by discussing the meaning of the lyrics. Generations of school-band guitarists don't sit their mate down and explain what 'Louie Louie' is *about*, they just teach them the three chords, and that unlocks the song. Pop songs are transmitted culturally using labelled units (in this case, the chords of A, D and E minor), so new players can follow the shape of the song. This is the scaffolding on which any meaning within the song, in the form of self-expression or lyrics, is hung.

I will happily declare that I, like most people who learned it at school, have no idea what 'Louie Louie' is about. To me the song is *about* those three chords. That music can be defined by its structural shorthand – chords, keys, tempos – is accepted so unquestioningly that classical composers title hugely expressive works after their keys, as if to head off any more detailed enquiry. 'What's your new symphony about, Beethoven?' 'D minor. I will be taking no further questions.'

It's a bit of a conceptual leap for most of us, but I think the same is true of comedy. You just need to stop worrying about the words so much, listen to the tune, feel the rhythm, and start seeing the beauty of the patterns themselves.

MEANINGLESS SONGS IN VERY HIGH VOICES

Seeing comedy abstractly as a series of patterns is a difficult habit to pick up, since most comedy criticism and fandom focuses on subject matter, not shape. We all prefer to discuss the 'lyrics' of comedy: how relatable the observations are, how real the characters seem, how surprising the ideas, how urgent the message. What we might call the 'music' of comedy – the scaffolding under the ideas – is often either ignored or assumed to be inexplicable.

But since music and comedy are very alike in how they affect our brains, we should try to come up with a way of discussing the building blocks of comic ideas in the same functional way we name notes and chords. In comedy, as in music, this structure stays the same, regardless of the message. A scorching autobiographical stand-up set or an agenda-setting piece of satirical storytelling might get attention for their content, but the 'chord patterns' that underpin comedy's most life-changing work will be the same ones used in a corny Christmas-cracker joke. It's worth remembering that Beethoven's *Eroica* symphony uses the same twelve Western musical notes as Black Lace's 'Having a Gang Bang' (to, it has to be said, less startling effect).

So, let's imagine we are making comedy on a piano keyboard.

The notes from the keyboard go into the audience's joke-processing machine, like music goes into someone's ears. Their brain then looks for repetition and change, satisfaction and surprise, just like we listen out for those things in the notes of a melody. The tune you choose to play can be as long or short as you like, and go anywhere you want. Remember: every possible comedy idea that could ever be composed comes from this same keyboard.

Sit down at your imaginary comedy keyboard, ready to make someone else laugh.

How many keys are there on that keyboard? Eighty-eight? A hundred?

Nope.

Three.

There are only three things you can do when you share comic information. Comedy is a tune played on the shortest keyboard in the world.

And that is the real Rule of Three.

INTRODUCING THE CLOWN KEYBOARD

Three notes. It's the sort of keyboard you'd give a baby (or the really stoned one in a rave act on early nineties *Top of the Pops*). Coloured stickers on the keys. Hit that one. All these others are off limits. It's that basic.

Here are your three keys:

1. Construct
2. Confirm
3. Confound

When we press each of these keys, our keyboard causes three reactions in the audience. It makes people go:

1. *'Interesting. . .'* (Construct)
2. *'Of course. . . as I expected. . .'* (Confirm)
3. *'Hey!'* (Confound)

And that's it. That's all we can do. Three notes.

Construct, Confirm, Confound is the basis of all comedy. Three notes. In endless combinations. It's so simple it's beautiful.

Pleasingly, the DNA of comedy turns out to be like the DNA of. . . well, DNA. An infinitely complex code is created from a limited number of 'letters'. It's Construct, Confirm, Confound for comedy, just as it's C-G-A-T in the case of genetics.

These minimal elements are endlessly recombined, and between them they create the huge variety of comic life.

THREE'S COMPANY

The threesome of Construct, Confirm, Confound might seem very similar to our old favourites from the more traditionally understood Rule of Three, about grouping joke elements in triples. And they do match neatly onto the notions of Set-Up, Development and Surprise, as established in classic joke structure. I suspect this is why the idea of the Rule of Three developed in the first place.

Look at how the three notes, played one at a time in that order, give us the shape of a joke.

1. Construct:
   Man walks into a pet shop.
   (We are in a pet shop.)
2. Confirm:
   He says to the bloke behind the counter, 'I want to buy a wasp.' And the bloke behind the counter says, 'We don't sell wasps.'
   (We are having a slightly odd conversation but still recognisably in a pet shop, as established.)

3. Confound:
   And the bloke says, 'But you had one in the window yesterday.'
   (The rules of the real world have been surprisingly suspended by one of the characters following a different set of rules, possessing internal but not external logic.)

But the magic of our comedy keyboard, as opposed to this rigid one-two-three form, is that it doesn't just make groups of three ideas, or little lists with a funny one at the end. Like any keyboard, you're not restricted to a set order or length of melody. And as long as the notes you play are these three notes, they sound nice together, in any order, at any length.

And that's the amazing, dumb-as-hell discovery that, remarkably, underpins all jokes' shape.

MY BRAIN HURTS

Why these three notes are always pleasurable to hear is because they represent the three types of input that our brain uses in pattern recognition.

1. Construct: new information arrives about where we are or what is happening.
2. Confirm: an echo of the Construct note. This gives us pattern-making information so we can take an educated guess where we're going next.
3. Confound: surprising information turns up, breaking the pattern (provided we understand the pattern, of course).

We like hearing these notes. Used properly, they are all in the same comic 'key', and like a musical scale, if you play a tune on them, they feel 'right' and belong together.

1. When we hear the Construct note, our playful brain enjoys taking in and storing new information.
2. When we hear a Confirm note, we are happy to be given new information because that helps us build a predictive model for what might come next.
3. And when the Confound note is sounded, something breaks a pattern, and we recognise that it doesn't belong, creating a puzzle for us to play with.

We make observations, detect patterns. . . and enjoy the surprise!

The comic keyboard's rule of Construct, Confirm, Confound is remarkably flexible. And I would argue it is the best demonstration of how our brains sort information as we invent or absorb a comic idea. And because it does not lock us into a set length or order of notes, this is a comic theory that could describe the absorption of comic information in a one-liner, a knock-knock joke, a sitcom, or (as we will see later) an entire screenplay. With this system, we're not wedded to one-two-three reveal jokes, any more than a piano player has to play the keys in alphabetical order, or stick to waltz time.

Of course, when you think of a comedian sitting down at a piano to make you laugh, you might imagine Eric Morecambe facing off against André Previn in Eric and Ernie's classic 1971 Grieg's Piano Concerto sketch. I'm delighted to report that, using this system, we will always be playing all the right notes, sunshine. And what's revolutionary about the Patented Morecambe Piano Method is that we don't necessarily have to play those notes in the right order.

But let's start with the basics and have a good look down at our keyboard.

16

Comedy Piano For Beginners

Screenwriting is constantly figuring out what no one will see coming that makes perfect sense.

David Gross
(writer, *Curb Your Enthusiasm*)

Let's start with the most basic tune. Comedy chopsticks. One, two, and a twist. Construct, then Confirm, then Confound.

Here's a quick example of this joke melody from Les Dawson (who knew better than anyone how to hit a bum note on an actual piano for comic effect).

I went to the doctor.
I said, 'Can you give me something for this persistent wind?'
And he gave me a kite.

CONSTRUCT: Where are we? What's going on? Who's in this story?

LES: *I went to the doctor...*

CONFIRM: Something that says it's business as usual. It's a story about a doctor, as expected.

> *LES: I said, 'Can you give me something for this persistent wind?'*

CONFOUND: 'What the—?' An element that does not fit.

> *LES: And he gave me a kite.*

This forces us to go back and re-examine our expectations. Usually it turns out we were using the wrong perceptual model: it does make sense, just not the sense we were expecting.

This is a classic comedy one-two-three structure. Set-up, development, punchline. (And then resolution and relief.)

ONE-TWO

But Les could happily create a one-two. (We've encountered this doorbell ding-dong of a comic tune before, when we saw some quickfire two-beat gags from Simon Munnery, Richard Pryor and Joe Lycett.) This tune goes: Construct, Confound, and works because of its speed.

> *The wife's run off with the bloke next door. Oh, I do miss him.*

The arrival of the surprise, without any time for an expected Confirm, gets a lovely shock laugh. Usually we have to reverse up mentally to spot where the joke turned left. We reward ourselves with a little pleasure hit in the brain for decoding what's going on, despite the gap in the expected data. We have solved a puzzle from limited information, and that's good practice.

NUMBER NINE, NUMBER NINE, NUMBER NINE

Les Dawson also performed expert repetition gags, hitting a note and staying on it, sometimes until the audience found themselves suspended in another world, waiting for the release.

This is a great comic shape that puts the audience in a very different state to a switchback one-two, or a classic one-two-three, and might be written as: Construct, Confirm, Confirm, Confirm, Confirm, Confirm, Confirm, Confound.

In awe, I watched the waxing moon ride across the zenith of the heavens like an ambered chariot towards the ebony void of infinite space wherein the tethered belts of Jupiter and Mars hang, forever festooned in their orbital majesty. And as I looked at all this I thought. . . I must put a roof on this toilet.

Les starts in an unexpectedly grand and literary key, which is surprising for his hangdog Northern club comic persona.* Then he slips into a comfortable, extended riff of repeated purple-prose Confirms, and one last Confound to great effect, and bingo, a huge audience laugh.

You might think of a vintage comic like Les Dawson as existing in a very different tradition from the tolerance-testing stand-up techniques of someone like Stewart Lee, Andy Kaufman or early Steve Martin. But in terms of the comedy keyboard, they're all playing the same tune here, hammering the same note again and again, making us all wait for release.

---

* In fact, a trained comic keyboardist might even say the first note Les Dawson plays here is a Confound with a Construct held under it as a bass note. Classy.

ALL THE RIGHT NOTES...

So, we can play a tune that goes Construct, Confirm, Con-found. (Line breaks added for clarity.)

> *My New Year's resolution*
> *is to get in shape.*
> *I choose round.*
>
> Sarah Millican

Or we can do Construct, Confound:

> *The other day I was thinking, 'I just overthink things.'*
> *And then I thought, 'Do I, though?'*
>
> Demetri Martin

Or we can hold a note, play it again and again. We can go Confirm, Confirm, Confirm, for minutes, and then Confound, and that's a classic, satisfying comic tune. It's Steve Coogan in *The Day Today* saying 'No one died' as a dull swimming-pool attendant, or Coogan, again, bellowing 'Dan!' repeatedly across a car park in *I'm Alan Partridge*.

A tune made of Confirm notes alone pleases audiences by proving their suspicions right about how a character might behave, whether in a narrative sitcom or when a stand-up delivers material in their established comic persona. Confirm gives us a hit of comic pleasure by reassuring us, 'You guessed right!'

Traditional comedy theory favours the Confound note above the others, because it is the final note of the standard comic tune, the memorable closing flourish.

> *Q: What's E.T. short for?*
> *A: Because he's got little legs.*

And, of course, Confound might be the most exciting note of the three as the thrilling swerve that makes an audience gasp-laugh, but all three notes on our keyboard have comic potential.

Construct

Tunes often start on a root note to indicate the key, and most comic ideas open with a Construct for the same reason. This first note lets the audience ground themselves, and sets up expectation that can be affirmed with a Confirm note or two, or subverted with a Confound.

Put the Construct beat later, and the audience floats for a moment, wondering, gathering data enjoyably before you ground them and explain what you're talking about. This trick can turn a Construct into a sort of Confound beat, and lends the Construct note a quality of comic surprise. That's what Les Dawson was doing when he started unexpectedly waxing lyrical about the beauty of the heavens. The audience leans in to listen, wanting more data. The comic's on-stage confidence and reputation mean they trust he's going somewhere, even if they don't know where.

An audience knows to expect a Construct note at the start, so if you skip it and put it later in the joke, you immediately pique their interest. That floaty feeling – where are we going? – is pleasurable, fizzy and exciting for any pattern-seeking animal, and the satisfying 'plop' of the Construct note when it does come is as enjoyable as a tune returning to its root note.

Confirm

Confirm is a note that exploits familiarity and warmth, so it can be a powerful comic tool; one that is able to create affection and loyalty in an audience, alongside the laughs.

When a sitcom pings dialogue round a room full of characters that you have come to know well, every one of them is confirming who they are, behaving in character, and we enjoy being right.

Look at this example, where prim psychiatrist Dr Frasier Crane asks a sincere question of his sexually frank radio-show producer Roz Doyle.

> FRASIER: *What do you do when the romance goes out of a relationship?*
> ROZ: *I get dressed and go home.*

If we know the show, we don't even brace for a surprise, spending a split second instead checking our preconceptions of her character. Then Roz delivers roughly what we expected, and we enjoy having used our prediction engine well. The ingenuity of the line is great, but it doesn't Confound anything. Confirm is the bedrock of sitcom character writing, and we're always happy to have been right.

This is one of the reasons we grow to love sitcom families and ensembles over time. As our knowledge of the characters deepens, we can enjoy richer Confirm jokes about them. It's also why pilot episodes are such a difficult piece of craft, because they have to get us up to speed incredibly quickly for the Confirm note to sound sweetly in our ears. As soon as we stop asking, 'Who the hell are these people?', comedy can start working its magic. It's a similar process of earning trust that we go through if we see a new stand-up for the first time.

Character needs to be established quickly, and then we relax and look for pattern matches.

Pastiche and parody are all about hitting Confirm notes that the audience can enjoy, as is comedy that relies on celebrity impressions, or exploiting recognisable stereotypes, clichés and tropes. The Confirm note is every bit as important when we make comedy as Confound.

Confound

Confound is the note that traditionally gets the most attention in comedy analysis because it's the sexy one. But Confound notes can't really surprise us unless we thought we were going somewhere else. These notes follow a logical progression, but maybe one you weren't following.

The key idea with Confound isn't to 'shock' as much as to 'confound expectation'. Which means, obviously, that there has to be expectation. And that's where our Construct and Confirm notes work in harmony with the Confound.*

When Confound is played, we feel that we have been tricked. 'Where did that come from?' Then we go back to see where on earth we went wrong. This is also where we check that the joke has played fair. For us to feel safe, reassured, happy (and then laugh), we have to discover that we had enough information from the Construct and Confirm notes to be able to guess the Confound, but realise that we chose the wrong path. (As we have seen, this is why timing is so important for comedy: so the comedian can play the bait-and-switch without being rumbled.) And we don't mind being tricked, if we had a fair chance. The fun is that we guessed the wrong pattern, not that there wasn't one at all.

And that brings us to the evil note that spoils everything.

---

* The Confound note also uses the values, expectations and prejudices that an audience brings before the joke even starts, just as our response to music depends on other tunes we've heard before. We can only be surprised satisfyingly if we think we know what to expect.

17

Confuse: The Bum Note

> '*Have you guessed the riddle yet?*' *the Hatter said,*
> *turning to Alice again.*
> '*No, I give it up,*' *Alice replied.* '*What's the answer?*'
> '*I haven't the slightest idea,*' *said the Hatter.*
> '*Nor I,*' *said the March Hare.*
> *Alice sighed wearily.* '*I think you might do something*
> *better with the time,*' *she said,* '*than wasting it in*
> *asking riddles that have no answers.*'

> Lewis Carroll, *Alice's Adventures in Wonderland*

If we have only three notes on our comedy keyboard, it should, in theory, be easy to master the instrument. We have a piano with only three notes on it, which you can play in any order you fancy without ever making a tune people don't like. It doesn't feel like a huge challenge. The problem for the aspiring comedy-keyboard wizard, however, is that there is a chance that you might, in your excitement at coaxing great melodies from such a simple instrument, mis-strike a key and produce a bum note that nobody wants to hear.

That fluffed note is Confuse.

The annoying thing about the Confuse note on your comedy keyboard is that the instrument is quite small, and the tunes are usually pretty fast, and it's easy to fumble and not play the notes properly. It looks like there are only three keys, but the crafty Confuse key is definitely there, camouflaged alongside the notes you actually want. Whatever melody you intend to play, it's ridiculously easy to flap a fat finger clumsily against the Confuse note. And every time you mis-strike the keys, the comic keyboard emits a dissonant farting noise that (unlike all other fart noises in history) is simply not funny.

The Confuse note is the thing that makes comedy hard. Because it's much, much easier to play than all the other notes.

Remember the system?

When you play Construct, the audience says, 'Ah! Here we go!'

When you play Confirm, the audience says, 'Oh, marvellous, much as I expected!'

When you play Confound, the audience says, 'How strange and wonderful!'

But when you accidentally play the Confuse note, the audience boos and throws stuff. Or worse still, goes quiet.

Confuse is the worst thing of all for comedy. It's boring.

NEVER HAD A LESSON IN MY LIFE

Learning to tell Confound and Confuse notes apart is a skill that writers and comedians hone over years of frustration. The difference is in that gut sense of what works and what doesn't. It's what live performers are learning from the awful silences that greet jokes they thought were bankers (and why they do work-in-progress shows to a hundred punters rather than to a packed theatre). When a script comes back from the producer with an unhappy question mark in the margin, that's because you hit Confuse. The art of the professional comedy maker is often simply to sift the Confounds from the Confuses before one of them blows up in your face in public.

Confound – the nice one we want – is an unexpected note that, when an audience goes back and looks at the Construct and Confirm notes, makes surprising sense. A pun is a basic Confound note: a word that might mean two things, depending on which version you're listening for. Conceptual jokes and comic imagery do the same trick. You set a scene, but reveal, at a specifically chosen point, that it's not built on one model, but another. Confound is a magician pulling back the cloth that you thought covered an egg, to reveal there was actually a dove under it all along.

With Confuse, though, you go back over the data supplied and realise you had no chance, and what the hell are they talking about? And then you worry that the problem is you, and you weren't listening, and maybe you missed something, and you check and recheck and then get annoyed with the joke teller, and yourself, and the world at large, and then you realise you've not been listening for a while because you've been trying to work out what just went wrong, and you've missed the next few jokes, which might have made sense and which you might have enjoyed, and now you're just grinding against the joke you didn't understand, like a stone in a shoe, and it's all stopped being fun.

COW TOOLS

Master gag-panel cartoonist Gary Larson published a *Far Side* cartoon in October 1982 that got so many perplexed and angry responses from readers that it made the news. Larson's cartoon showed a cow standing behind a workbench on which had been placed a row of vague, clumsy solid objects with lumpy protrusions. The caption read simply: 'Cow tools.' Larson's joke was that the sort of tools cows would make would be simpler than ours, to a degree that they would be unrecognisable. Though tool use is supposedly what separates humans from most animals, what if animals do have tools, but we can't understand them?

Readers, unfortunately, stared at the tools and tried to work out what they were for. They were looking for data in the wrong places, data that had been deliberately omitted as part of the joke. And they got confused. And went quiet. And then they got cross.

Fatally, Larson realised, one of the cow tools had been drawn to resemble a very crude saw. Readers spotted it and obsessed about the other objects, trying to find uses for them too. The 'not-quite-a-saw' had been provided to help Confirm: these are tools, not just lumps. That should have led them to the intended Confound: 'these tools are lumpy, but probably quite cow-like'. But it Confused instead. I suspect it's partly because the 'saw' sits on the far right of the tool bench in the cartoon; because Western readers scan from left to right, it looked like a punchline.

CHARACTER WITNESSES AND CHARACTER CLUES

The Confuse note upsets the smooth process of analysis and decoding. The game comes to a halt. Your audience wonders why you told them that, what it means, whether it relates to the information they've already been given. And worst of all, Confuse distracts them from taking in the next few notes properly, so they stop listening. All your careful Constructs and Confirms are wiped out.

In narrative, character-based comedy, such as sitcoms, plays and films, a joke that comes from someone not behaving 'in character' can easily be confusing rather than confounding, no matter how funny the surprise of the gag is intended to be. While Bugs Bunny can smart-talk anyone, even at gunpoint, a cowardly character suddenly delivering clever quips to a bully will usually fail to get a laugh – unless we have been led to expect them to be trying a new persona (they're drunk, they're trying to impress someone, they have received the standard comedy blow to the head).

But these sorts of character-based Confirms are part of the audience contract with most comedy, not just narrative and sitcom. A stand-up comedian can crash and burn by doing a joke that doesn't quite work for their accepted stage persona. Comics build expectation using their voice, their body language, their subject matter, their use of shock and reassurance in their jokes. A comic's on-stage 'clown' might be high or low status, sexually frank or socially timid, avuncular and welcoming or deliberately weird and spiky. And a particular joke may make perfect sense in isolation, but putting it in the wrong mouth risks Confusing rather than Confounding. A cheeky holiday-camp-style comic like Joe Pasquale can't come out on stage and say:

> People often say to me... 'What are you doing in my garden?'

Well, he can, and he did, and got rightly criticised for it, because he'd borrowed a character-based gag from lugubrious hangdog Irish comic Michael Redmond. Out of character, without that face and delivery, it's... kind of OK as a joke, but it's more Confusing than Confounding.

Crowbarring in lines that work technically but don't exploit audience character expectations is a temptation, no matter how experienced you are as a comic writer. You may feel you're gaining a joke, but you're usually killing the comedy. Worse, you lose the audience while they try to work out why, for example, a timid character whose main motivation is to get out of trouble has just delivered a pristinely crafted smart-arsed putdown to a gang of thugs. The joke – no matter how clever – now carries the information that a frightened character is actually a wisecracking, cocky Groucho Marx type and that's plain Confusing.

A common mistake in beginners' scripts (and more experienced writers' first drafts) is when everyone speaks in the same confident, clever voice, rattling out neat bits of wordplay and amusing ideas. It could be argued that any script made entirely of these sorts of gags only has one character in it: the writer. Standalone gags lack character data, and that's what the audience needs.

It's hard to admit it if you like making jokes as much as I do, but an audience isn't usually looking for jokes at all; they're looking for clues so they can make their own jokes (by guessing what a character is going to do next and being delighted when they do it). Not providing those clues, and delivering a load of nifty puns instead, is usually going to leave them Confused.

Most sitcoms demand endless rewrites in the name of clarity to ensure that characters do not suddenly lurch off the rails and do something out of character that will Confuse. It's why performer-led sitcoms are sometimes easier to make, because the star turn knows their comic persona, as does their audience, and so everyone starts on the same page in the comedy guessing game. It's certainly why coming in on series two of a sitcom sometimes feels as fun as writing fan fiction: you know these guys, and they're tagged neatly to the cast. On the page, in a pilot script, cold, their uncast voice and mannerisms still nebulous, it's easier for a character to wander off-piste and Confuse the audience.

18

The Howl of Confusion

What if there were no punchlines? ... What if I headed for a climax, but all I delivered was an anticlimax? What would the audience do with all that tension?

Steve Martin

If we're thinking of comedy as music, Confound is a harmony, in the same key as the Construct and Confirm notes, while Confuse is a discord. But just as dissonance can have a place in music, a skilled practitioner can integrate a Confuse note into the comedy soundscape. If used carefully and with confidence, the Confuse note can overload the audience's joke processor, like the distortion of an overdriven electric guitar, producing an exciting howl of comic feedback. And how much fun is that?

In the 1933 short *Me and My Pal*, Stan Laurel's Stanley is helping Oliver Hardy's Ollie prepare for his wedding to a well-connected lady.

> OLLIE: *Don't you realise I'm about to become a big oil magnate?*
> STAN LOOKS PUZZLED.
> OLLIE: *You do know what a magnate is, don't you?*
> STAN: *Sure. A thing that eats cheese.*

It's one of my favourite ever un-jokes. It seems to trust that, on hearing the unusual word 'magnate' from Ollie, most of us will probably have already guessed at a possible magnate/magnet pun coming down the line for Stan. 'Sure. I know what a magnate is. It's a thing that attracts iron filings. . .'

But clever Stan Laurel – the intelligent screen craftsman – knows the audience will have got there long before him. So Stanley – the foolish comic character – pulls away from sense entirely and leaves us giggling in the dust. What is going on in his head? Are words arranged alphabetically so the Ms get mixed up? Is that reading too much into it?

The fact that we didn't get given a workmanlike pun flatters the audience. And because the garbled logic is entirely in character, the feeling of Confusion, which lasted way longer than it would have done with a simple pun, is eventually resolved. 'It's Stanley. Of course.' We are safe again. Imagine how the same line given to more worldly Ollie would never resolve. 'Why did he say that? What's wrong with him? Have I misread his character? What does it mean for the rest of the story?' That would simply Confuse in a way that wasn't funny.

And that's the dissonant racket you attempt to rein in when you play with the Confuse note. And that's why, deployed cleverly, it can make a thrilling howl that blows your bowler hat clean off.

THE CHICKEN QUESTION

The appeal of the deliberate Confuse note is probably best illustrated by one of the most famous jokes in the English language.

Q: Why did the chicken cross the road?
A: To get to the other side.

You may feel you were born knowing this joke, it's that much of a core comedy text. The earliest sighting of it in print can be dated back as far as 1847, so there's a fair chance that it's been retold for almost two hundred years. But the punchline isn't a Confound for you to decode and enjoy. That data simply isn't there. In fact, it doesn't work at all. It's a Confuse.

An appealing theory recently did the rounds that the chicken punchline *did* make sense, that the joke had emerged from the Victorian craze for spiritualism. The 'other side', of course, was a contemporary euphemism for 'death'. How clever. The chicken crossed the road to die. I have to confess my guilt at spreading this theory around various pub tables and on some excited podcasts a few years ago, for which I apologise. It seemed so neat. Though it now strikes me that a Victorian road is less likely to be immediately associated with roadkill than a modern one, filled with motor traffic.

The problem is that this theory wouldn't explain why to this day the joke continues to be spread by non-Victorian children who don't use the phrase 'the other side' to mean 'dead'. If a joke has a forgotten meaning, it won't stay in circulation. Any reference, particularly a hidden one, needs to be recognisable and current for the audience to untangle the sense. As Jimmy Carr and Lucy Greeves observe in their book on the history of jokes, there were countless Victorian gags about seasickness, but we stopped telling them because we don't take many long sea journeys these days. Nobody passes on a baffling gag simply because their great-great-grandmother found it funny. So, why does this joke that, apparently, *isn't* about a forgotten phrase for a forgotten craze still haunt us?

The most likely explanation is that the chicken-road joke belongs to a vein of anti-humour that goes back at least to the medieval era, and was in vogue amongst the Victorians. A well-known example from roughly the same time is the Mad Hatter's riddle to Alice: 'Why is a raven like a writing desk?' And though Lewis Carroll provided a rather clunky solution in a later preface to the book, there is no answer, just the shape of a joke, containing nothing, and that's the joke.*

The gag is on us, the audience, and depends on the confidence of the teller. What's meant to be funny is that the audience overcomplicates its response by looking for clues, but it turns out that the chicken crossed the road to cross the road. The chicken doesn't know it's in a joke, and that's the joke. It's a joke about how joke shape is so rigid and formal that we follow it even if it is emptied of content. Looked at that way, the chicken gag is clever, and human, and annoying, like a precocious child (its chief intended audience).

Historian Dr Bob Nicholson, who studies the evolution of jokes, has a favourite anti-joke dating back to the eighteenth century:

Q: What is most like a cat looking out of a window?
A: A cat looking in through a window.

Human expectations are there to be subverted for the sake of a laugh, even if those expectations are about how we tell each other stuff. One of my favourite very old examples is Chaucer's *Squire's Tale*, a meandering yarn that constantly threatens to turn into a bucolic, beautiful story, but can't get started because the inexperienced storyteller keeps wandering off the point. It's a medieval anti-joke in

---

* Carroll wrote in the preface to the 1896 edition of *Alice*: 'Enquiries have been so often addressed to me, as to whether any answer to the Hatter's riddle can be imagined, that I may as well put on record here what seems to me to be a fairly appropriate answer, viz: "Because it can produce a few notes, tho they are very flat; and it is never put with the wrong end in front!" This, however, is merely an afterthought; the riddle, as originally invented, had no answer at all.'

the key of Spike Milligan, the comic ancestor of countless *Monty Python* sketches, or *Mr. Show*'s epic *The Story of Everest*. We love empty nonsense as long as we're invited to share the joke: that this is a joke about how we share jokes.*

JOKES ABOUT JOKES

We rarely tell a quickie like this in isolation, and it is likely that the chicken joke would have been delivered at the end of a series of other, more standard Victorian riddles, so the banality of its punchline would have landed even more strongly. It started with the joke-mad Victorians, and has been preserved by playgrounds full of joke-mad kids ever since. If we take our expectations of joke shape into account, the chicken joke's deliberate Confuse becomes a Confound. It's why the joke needs to be delivered with confidence. It's a character gag hinged on audience expectations of the teller.

- I have been telling jokes and I am good at jokes (Construct).
- Here is a new joke that seems exactly like the others (Confirm).

---

* To me, it's clear that the Squire's meandering Tale getting interrupted with a Pythonic 'And now for something completely different' is a blinding bit of character-based Middle English meta-comedy. But later poets such as Edmund Spenser and John Milton, treating Chaucer with high seriousness, thought the Tale was merely a fragment that Chaucer had sadly left incomplete. Spenser even had a go at finishing it in *The Faerie Queen*, which is a bit like 'fixing' the Four Candles sketch so Ronnie Corbett gets everything he wants first time. It's a perfect illustration of how, over time, and out of context, people can forget something was probably meant as a joke.

- I have deliberately not put any jokes in the joke, which is not what you expected me, a skilled joke teller, to do (Confound).

Telling this gag in its proper context is like tripping yourself over in the middle of a confident saunter to get a laugh. And it's the warmest sort of rug-pull trick, because even though the audience is fooled, it's the teller who ends up looking foolish – 'Have you gone mad? That's a terrible joke!' – so there's no actual threat to the listener. They may even cover their embarrassment at having been tricked with a loud groan, throwing any shame back on the teller.

Children acquire the chicken-road joke and play with it, coming up with their own variations, at the precise point they are learning how to construct and use humour. It's a valuable token of comic exchange with other young joke tellers, who are equally as excited about the rules, and the idea of breaking them. Mastering it seems almost to be a compulsory exam paper in the trial-and-error process of learning human comedy.

For many years, the social media account Kids Write Jokes collected examples of children trying to master the machinery of joke craft, and part of the appeal is their 'almost there' quality. And the best examples are all variations on the much-loved, unkillable, unbeatable chicken joke.

Look at this one.

Knock Knock. Who's there?
John.
John who?
John ice cream.

I mean, right now, I'm struggling to think of a better joke than that, ever.

Perhaps a successful Confuse joke like the perennial chicken gag works because it helps us learn what *not* to do. These broken jokes are the troubleshooting pages from the back of the joke-making manual. We love them because they tell us that we understand what we're doing when we're funny.

19

Shaggy Dogs

The Aristocrats!

Punchline to 'The Aristocrats' joke, Trad.

It's not just chickens that rely on the Confuse note for their jokes to work – dogs do too. A classic 'Shaggy Dog Story' is a long joke that builds to a deliberately anticlimactic Confuse ending, where none of the Construct and Confirm notes that have painstakingly been put in place end up being used at all. It's as if the bare bones of the chicken joke have been boiled down to make gallons of soup.

Lexicographer Eric Partridge traces the origin of the name of the Shaggy Dog Story to a longwinded gag about an aristocratic London family searching for a missing 'shaggy dog'. An American contacts them saying that their lost pet has been found in the USA. After a lengthy transatlantic journey, the do-gooder brings the shaggy dog to the family's Park Lane residence, where the butler takes one look at man and beast and slams the door, saying, 'But not as shaggy as that, sir.'

And that's the end of the joke. B'dum tish.

In the way they hijack and deliberately crash our brain's joke processor, the Shaggy Dog is literally the exception that proves the rule (in the original intended sense of 'prove', meaning to test). Once again, it's a joke that shows that the teller understands perfectly well how to operate the machine that makes jokes work, but they have chosen to smash it into a wall.

The climax of a Shaggy Dog Story is meant to make the audience enjoy the feeling of having its time wasted, and appreciate the teller's chutzpah. But it's also meant to make the teller's confident swagger at the excellence of their own gag seem foolish. If you've seen a great teller of anti-jokes at work, part of the fun is their deliberately cocky face as they deliver the closing damp squib. As with the chicken gag, the joke is on the listener – it is a trick – but the joke is on the teller too, the pompous twit, for thinking this thin gruel would satisfy. It's a disorienting superiority gag, an act of aggressive time-wasting, that happens best in conditions where the audience feels safe, and the intent all along was to fail deliberately.

Because the idea of safety is vital, delivering anti-comedy like Shaggy Dog jokes is the preserve of the supremely confident master comedian. The audience's incongruity alert flashes bright red, in distress and Confusion, then returns to a reassuring green. 'Oh! The clown car was meant to crash.' We need to know that the comic meant it to go wrong, not that they can't do their job. Even if it's equally unsatisfying, a Shaggy Dog feels very different from a boring, meandering anecdote told by a tedious colleague. In many ways, even though it's designed to fail, and sounds the forbidden Confuse note in the most annoying possible way, the Shaggy Dog demonstrates a comic's complete mastery of their craft.

ORANGE YOU GLAD I STOPPED TELLING THOSE JOKES?

When the respected veteran comedy writer and gag collector Barry Cryer died in 2022, many industry professionals fondly recalled their favourite jokes of his, plenty of which were anti-comedy or Shaggy-Dog shaped.* A 'comedian's comedian' is often one who takes the back off the clock to show the workings, just as Penn and Teller became the magician's magicians because they performed their magic with all the mechanisms showing. It's the connoisseur's choice. Saying you love a joke that hinges on a deliberate Confuse note is the comedy equivalent of naming Captain Beefheart's *Trout Mask Replica* as your favourite LP. It's for the real heads.

Here's one of Barry's favourites, a joke that he claimed regular audiences would often receive in bemused silence, but that fellow comedians adored. It's a trumpet voluntary on the Confuse note.

A man walks into a pub, and the landlord can't believe his eyes, because half of the man's head is half of a huge orange.

'Sorry to be nosy,' the landlord says, 'but why is half of your head half of a huge orange?'

'Well, I was tidying the loft,' the man says. 'And I found a dusty old lamp. I polished it up, and this genie swoops out of it, saying, "May I grant you any three wishes, master?"

'So I said, "I'd like to have a million pounds – and every time I take the million pounds out of my pocket, another million appears there."

'The genie said, "Your wish is granted. And your second wish?"

'So I said, "I'd like a big house with a hundred beautiful ladies in it."

---

* Barry was, of course, one of the world's foremost players of the game 'Mornington Crescent' on the long-running radio series *I'm Sorry I Haven't a Clue*, a complex and deliberately nonsensical game whose entire existence was an extended anti-comedy prank, played with commendable straight faces.

'"Your wish is granted," said the genie. "And your third wish?"
'"I'd like half my head to be half of a huge orange."'

Everyone knew Barry's reputation as a skilled comic, so expectation was always high, and breaking expectation is a basic comedy tool. A kid who's just told a dozen functional zingers is the best teller of the chicken-road gag, just like Les Dawson hammering bum notes on the piano is funny because the notes leading up to the clunker are all perfect. It's the same trick an admired technician like Stewart Lee pulls whenever his stand-up persona seemingly gets stuck in an infuriated cul-de-sac of comic frustration, unable to communicate, or move on to the next idea. Like Barry Cryer, he's playing a character who can't do the one thing he *can* definitely do, the Les Dawson of the mic stand. And as Lee's arrogant stage clown struggles to get his own material back on track, there's often a glint of manic joy in this proficient craftsman's eyes, like someone gleefully smashing an unwanted gift with a hammer.

Lee's regular collaborator Paul Putner used to do a great character turn as Earl Stevens, a visiting American stand-up whose (wholly invented) transatlantic references were impossible for any audience to follow. Performers like Andy Kaufman and Neil Hamburger made careers by emptying out all the content from their act but delivering it with misplaced confidence. Anti-comedy master Tim Heidecker performs a scabrous routine as an alpha-male circuit comic with no material that exposes how hack stand-ups use rhythm and crowd work to achieve lazy but effective results.*

These character-based acts show that the best way to harness Confusion is to give your broken gag to the

---

* Heidecker described this bleak but hilarious routine as 'Trumpian', and its echoes in empty political crowd-bait rhetoric were quite deliberate.

appropriate clown. This turns an apparent failure of comic engineering into a character note that we can predict. A Confuse (contextless) becomes a Confound (which makes some sort of wonky sense). It's why so many weird and wild jokes are bounced off the 'fool' in a comedy troupe, like Stan Laurel with his cheese-magnate.

Think of the great inexplicable jokes that belong to Bubble, Father Dougal, Woody Boyd, Coach Ernie Pantusso, Latka Gravas, Harpo Marx, Alice Horton, Trigger, Abed Nadir, Phoebe Buffay and Arthur Shappey. You can always give a Confuse gag to someone who doesn't share the rules of our universe, because it's a character gag, which makes it a Confound.

People who haven't read the hazardous material warnings are the ones who get to handle the comic dynamite, and have it blow up in their face to comic effect.

20

Sheer Nonsense

For an hour, we ran in French, which I ran fluently.

Neddie Seagoon, *The Goon Show*
(written by Spike Milligan)

Maybe the crazy rule-breaking of the Shaggy Dog is a good time to pause, and ask whether any of this abstract theorising actually helps.

'Surely some things are... just funny.'

To which the only reasonable response is:

GET OUT OF MY BOOK. YOU'RE BARRED.

Sorry. I got carried away.

'Just funny' is a problematic idea, because it's a defence that gets wheeled out whenever anyone tries to question comedy, particularly if there is an objection to the content of a joke. 'Just funny' acts as a magical invocation, a circle of defence erected around the sacred art of comedy, and what might be excusable as a healthy court jester's comic licence gets repositioned as a demand that comedy must not be analysed, or even considered as a normal creative process that humans do. It's hard to imagine music attempting the same trick.

What notes are in the tune to 'Greensleeves'?
It's impossible to say. Nobody knows. It's just musical.

'Just funny' implies comedy is a force independent of human interference. It implies that comedians are merely vessels channelling some otherworldly energy, an idea that, if true, feels like the sort of puffed-up actorly statement out of which any decent comedian should take the absolute piss.

It's an idea that insists that comedy is special. The words in *Jude the Obscure* can be analysed. The words in a joke? Off limits. As if the arrangement of shared references and assumptions that make a joke work are different from the arrangement of familiar and recognisable elements in a song, or a play, or a novel. 'Just funny' says that if something gets a laugh, there must be no further questions.

'Just funny' insists comedy magic is literally magic. Not stage magic. Not linking rings and 'Is this your card?' magic, with a learnable craft of palms and misdirection. It's real sorcery, harnessing inexplicable forces. Magic you can't write down in a book, because it would be one of those weird wizard's books with teeth and a face! It's magic with a 'k'. High Comick Magick!

We're summoning actual primal comic forces and all stars and tentacles are coming out like the end of a Marvel film! This observation I've got about how my boyfriend leaves the loo seat up? Don't look straight at it because it's a throbbing portal to a comic dimension of chaos and light that's loud as hell and impossible to explain, like the end of a Marvel film! Pop on your lead-lined clown shoes and hazmat suit, you're about to get a lethal dose of custard pie, at 200 comedy rads! This stuff? Comic uranium! We're untrained and handling fissile comic material, and it's OK *because* we don't understand what we're doing! It's fine! We don't know why it's funny. It's *just funny*!

IS EVERYTHING FUNNY?

But the idea of things being 'just funny' is the area that reveals best of all how the comedy-processing machinery in our brains interprets data and creates pleasing comic reactions. Because something being 'just funny' is demonstrably impossible.

If there were such a phenomenon as things that were 'just funny', there would be laughter everywhere. We'd be in a state of total disarray, our lives a hopeless giggly chaos. If there was no way of explaining how one thing makes us laugh and another doesn't, nothing would stop us cracking up unexpectedly at a bollard, or the colour brown, or the iTunes terms and conditions.

When arguing that some things are 'just funny', people point to jokes that seem to lack context or rely on pure nonsense. Why is it funny when Rik Mayall pulls a gormless face on stage while saying nothing and repeatedly asking the audience, 'What?' Why is it funny when Vic and Bob sing a long song about cottage cheese? Why is it funny when Tim and Eric do that thing where one of their eyelids droops while looking to camera? *It's just funny.*

I'm aware I'm slightly annoying (I won't rest until every precious comedy frog is dead), but I'd argue that because you can't initially explain something, or make it fit an instantly explicable category (pun, parody, satire, whatever), that doesn't mean it has no explanation; just that you haven't looked hard enough. We wouldn't have atomic power if Ernest Rutherford had decided atoms were way too small and that some things were 'just explodey'.

Something is obviously happening in our sober brain that turns 'regular input' into 'funny input' and makes us laugh. The exciting thing is that this mental process of 'funnification' applies to stuff in familiar comic forms (a

clever satirical takedown of a politician we dislike, a suc-
cinct and recognisable nailing of an everyday experience,
an ingenious pun, a neat turn of phrase, a precisely
observed parody), but also to mad stuff that makes us
laugh like drains, but which we cannot immediately
explain.

If the explicable 'funny' stuff and the inexplicable 'it's
just funny' stuff worked by two totally different processes,
why would they both depend on expectation, pattern,
rhythm and the attempted resolution of momentary
incongruity? It would be strange for us to have two unrelated mental games that we played with pattern analysis,
both of which exploited the way that we enjoy controlled
surprises and produced roughly the same feeling in us, but
only one of which could be studied and explained.*

I'm not a professional designer of the human body, so I
don't know, but if 'funny' and 'just funny' were different
physical processes, I suspect they'd feel more different.
Maybe you would watch *The Thick of It* and feel its
rational, enlightened satire pass through your rational
brain, after which you'd maybe vomit quietly to yourself,
to indicate this comedy was the analysable sort. Conversely, Harry Hill being ambushed by a giant strawberry
with the face of Jeremy Clarkson would be felt in your
eyebrows, making you sing a high C, to indicate this joke
was 'just funny', and sadly impossible to explain. But that's
not what happens. We know they produce the same kind
of amused feeling, with often the same accompanying

---

* Of course, this is possible. Processes as similar as smiling and laughing are two
different evolved primate behaviours that now feel part of the same one. Maybe
some research into this would reveal that there is something strange and wonderful going on when we respond to the completely inexplicable with
amusement. But I'm not a scientist. All I have is a sense that 'funny' and 'just
funny' merely reflect different degrees of surprise within the same neurological
process. But, hey, I reckon some things are 'just opiniony'.

noises, and we understand and categorise them both as comedy (whatever our tastes). So, maybe they're tickling the same bit of our mental machine. Maybe they can both be explained.

FUNNY PECULIAR? OR FUNNY HA HA?

What most things that are 'just funny' have in common is that we feel we didn't see them coming. They appear suddenly out of context, and surprise us. They don't belong, and we laugh at the juxtaposition. But not all juxtapositions and surprises are funny.

Chaotic juxtaposition is something that comedy shares with both dreams and surreal art, neither of which usually make us laugh. The dividing line is hard to define sometimes between the wildest excesses of absurd comedy and the freewheeling whimsy of dreams, or the thought-provoking inversions of accepted reality in some fine art. Freud saw jokes as waking dreams, places that illogic and the subconscious could exist while we were awake. (Typically, he was mainly interested in the mucky ones, because it fitted with his interest in suppression and taboo, the dirty dog.) Freud's groundbreaking theories led to a fascination with dream imagery and dream logic in art (and also in horror fiction, where taboos could be broken to a different but related unsettling effect).

There is an obvious common ground between this post-Freudian outburst of dream imagery employed by the surrealists and the daft leaps of logic we love in comedy. But we don't laugh out loud when we see a Magritte, even though a sketch by Vic and Bob may render us helpless with inexplicable giggles using almost identical imagery. We see a man with an apple for a head in an art gallery, and we stroke our chins and ponder our existence. But if we see a very similar-looking man with a giant onion for a head in an episode of *The Smell of Reeves & Mortimer*, we laugh at the daft vegetable bloke. Even with the crazy free associations of untethered surrealism, we know to react appropriately to someone sticking two unrelated ideas together; we are meant to go 'hmm', not 'ha ha'.

I suspect this is because context is everything. Comedy always has expectations to subvert, patterns to break, which means that even the craziest, least inhibited comedy isn't 'just funny'. With all comedy, we accept the rules, that we must pay attention to the expectations that are being established, and watch for information that matches and subverts those patterns, responding with laughter and relief, because all the weirdness was meant in fun.

Nonsense only makes sense when placed within a context of expected sense, because the pattern in comedy is as important as the breaking of it. Juxtapositions must be juxtaposed against something. The surreal Confounds of comedy only make us laugh because of the Construct and Confirm notes that support them. It is all part of a deliberate process that we accept, and is familiar to us as 'comedy'.

21

The Lure of the Brillig

Somehow it seems to fill my head with ideas but I don't exactly know what they are!

Lewis Carroll, *Through the Looking-Glass*

Lewis Carroll's poem 'Jabberwocky' is one of the defining works of English nonsense. It appears in Alice's second book of adventures, *Through the Looking-Glass*, and is delightfully out of copyright, so let's tuck in.

'Twas brillig and the slithy toves
  Did gyre and gimble in the wabe:
All mimsy were the borogoves,
  And the mome raths outgrabe.

'Beware the Jabberwock, my son!
  The jaws that bite, the claws that catch!
Beware the Jubjub bird, and shun
  The frumious Bandersnatch!'

Though large parts of 'Jabberwocky' consist of invented words you have never heard before, it is completely comprehensible, even to the extent that it can be translated into other languages.* The shape of the stanzas and even the syllables within the words themselves fall into the slots

---

* A terrific German translation was published by a friend of the real Alice's

your brain expects when presented with an epic Old English poem, so the story remains strangely clear. The mathematician and Lewis Carroll expert Martin Gardner compared 'Jabberwocky' to an abstract painting, in the sense that it alludes to its own meaning without literally representing it. Puzzling it out demonstrates that our interpretative faculties are in tip-top condition.

The poem's gibberish is a playful private language, like siblings might invent, and in fact Carroll originally wrote the first fragment of 'Jabberwocky' for his home-made family magazine *Mischmasch,* to amuse his brothers and sisters. He wrote out the verse under the title 'Stanza of Anglo-Saxon poetry'. Like much of *Alice,* it is meant to parody something familiar, in this case an impenetrable passage of poetry set by a schoolteacher. One of the things that is not appreciated enough (particularly by filmmakers trying to make overly literal adaptations of Carroll's work) is that much of the book's nonsense only seems like nonsense to us because we're not bored Victorian schoolchildren, who really appreciate someone making fun of their teachers. But if you ever remember being handed a piece of Shakespeare for the first time at school, the joke is as clear as it was more than 150 years ago. It's a joke about incomprehension, and, brilliantly, it makes perfect sense.

As Alice says to herself after finishing it:

Somebody killed something: that's clear, at any rate—

For the most famous nonsense poem in English, a lot of it *is* in plain English, and Carroll plays his Constructs and Confirms with great skill, only hitting the funny words

---

father in 1872 as spoof evidence that Carroll had stolen his poem from an earlier Germanic source:

Es brillig war. Die schlichte Toven

Wirrten und wimmelten in Waben . . .

when he's sure they will Confound, rather than Confuse. In his book *Symbolic Logic*, Carroll himself said:

> *I maintain that any writer ... is fully authorised in attaching any meaning to any word or phrase he intends to use. If I find an author saying at the beginning of his book, 'Let it be understood that by the word "black" I shall always mean "white", and that by the word "white" I shall always mean "black"', I merely accept his ruling.*

Comedy is all about sharing the codebook. Let the audience in on the joke, and you can remove all accepted sense. Even though gibberish and nonsense is the form of comedy that might seem most resistant to analysis, these jokes demonstrate how our brains are happy to take in and comprehend garbage data, as long as we are expecting it and know where to file it.

Some of it is just down to the words having a melody or rhythm that we enjoy so much that their meaning becomes secondary. We make an informed guess, pop them into vague categories for the time being, and then simply relish rolling the noises around. Carroll's contemporary, Edward Lear, played similar tricks with his casts of luminous-nosed Dongs and blue-headed Jumblies (though, improbably, these two lords of high Victorian nonsense never met). In the next century, Theodor Geisel, writing as Dr Seuss, stuffed his books with child-pleasing burbles of wild syllables that allude to meaning without ever quite possessing it. Children are assimilating new words all the time, comprehending them through context, and the same games are being played when they explore a chocolate factory bubbling with snozzcumber extract, or memorise the mock-Latin vocabulary of Hogwarts.

Nonsense words are blanks on which we project imagined value, based on clues such as their placement and the echoes of familiar syllables. The practice of replacing particular words in a poem with words whose meaning and value are unknown may have appealed to a mathematician like Carroll. 'Jabberwocky' might simply be a linguistic game for a brain accustomed to puzzling out problems using algebra.

In the same way that you might replace an unknown number with 'x' in order to perform mathematical equations, you can read a poem where some of the elements have been replaced with 'x' and 'y' – or in this case 'brillig' and 'mimsy' – and still get sense from the passage. It's not about cracking a code, or replacing abstract nonsense with a single meaning, because inserting a single value reduces the utility of the equation. The x stays x, the y stays y, just as it does in algebra. 'Brillig' has stayed 'brillig' for readers for 150 years without most of them ever thinking it means 'broiling time' (around 4 p.m., as Humpty Dumpty explains to Alice later), or ever needing to replace the unknown elements with known ones.

The fun is in pushing our brains to make sense out of abstract data, because all words are abstract data, really, and learning what to do with that is how we trained our brains to work in the first place.

NONSENSE CHARACTERS, NONSENSE BEHAVIOUR

As we saw when we looked at the art of harnessing confusion to create outrageous effects right at the edge of an audience's comic tolerance, nonsense can work beautifully as long as it is contrasted clearly with sense. No matter how stupid and unhinged something is, it will be funnier if we know which rules it's breaking, what was meant to happen, and what would normally be there in place of the madness.

One of the most inexplicable yet hilarious performances

of all time in a mainstream hit movie is Stephen Stucker's turn as Johnny, the eccentric air-traffic controller, in *Airplane!* In a film that regularly bends its own reality for the sake of a laugh, Stucker still stands out as a cannon so loose that it risks sinking the whole ship (or maybe, more accurately, crashing the plane into the control tower). His manically camp, fourth-wall-breaking theft of every scene he is in can reduce audience members to either uncontrollable giggles or head-shaking bafflement. He's having a lovely time in his own little film, only marginally connected to the one we're watching, and we've barely got a clue what he's up to. His glee is enough.

When a grizzled air-traffic controller, as tension mounts, furrows his brow and announces that the 'fog is getting thicker', Stucker leaps into shot, wobbles the nonplussed actor's belly and mugs straight to camera, 'and Leon's getting. . . laaaaaaarger!' It's one of the definitive nonsense performances of all time. It might be an in-joke for the guys behind the camera. It might be something only Stucker understood. Who knows? Even the directors can't remember.* But it is one of the funniest and most memorable moments in all film comedy.

Why? It's hard to say. But one thing's for sure: it's funny because he's the only one doing it, and it's clearly not the right way to behave in the circumstances. For nonsense to work, it helps if everything around it makes sense.

If you just watched Stucker's performance on its own, even though it would have an identical crazed energy, it wouldn't be as funny without the context. You may have watched clip montages on YouTube of these sorts of gags: 'Best crazy moments from a really funny film', and aside from acting as an aide memoire for your favourite bits,

---

* Stucker tragically died of AIDS-related complications six years after *Airplane!*'s release, so the secret of this joke may never be known. It makes it even sweeter.

they never quite work. It's counterintuitive, but montages of funniest moments aren't the best way to show someone who's never seen a film what all the fuss is about. Crazy stuff on its own suffers diminishing returns very quickly.

Nonsense performances need to be embedded within sense. The sense can be as clear as it is in *Airplane!* Everyone else in Stucker's world is trying to stop a plane crashing. That's what his mania bounces off. Or it could be as small and fragile as a bow tie. It helps that Stucker is in an air-traffic-control uniform, just like it helps that Stan and Ollie are in smart bowler hats, or Mr Bean is in a suit. Steve Martin doing mad stuff in jeans and a t-shirt would be less funny than Steve Martin in a pristine white suit. We need some Constructs and Confirms to help mad stuff stay on the Confound side of the line, and not tip over into Confusion. Mania and energy and foolishness and fluidity work best when they are pushing against solidity. It's like watching a rubber ball ricochet madly in a squash court compared to bouncing it once across a tennis court. The game of nonsense is more exciting in a small space.

It's why sketch comedy and double acts often have a straight man and a funny man. We need to get our bearings, to know the limits. Even with freewheeling comedy, reducing the amount of freedom slightly by putting walls up makes the wild and crazy stuff seem both wilder and crazier, and easier to understand.

You don't want to explain nonsense. It would spoil it. But sometimes all you need to do is explain what it isn't. And that's about putting some walls round it. You need to find a container.

22

The Bucket

I remember we had to find out what the legal definition of 'parody' was . . . But we were so close to [the original movie] Zero Hour! that we knew it never would've passed muster.

Jim Abrahams
(writer and director of *Airplane!*)

Nonsense is a wonderful delivery method for comedy because silliness is rarely aggressive, and tends to set its own foolish protagonist up as a victim rather than hurting others. Nonsense feels childlike, unthreatening. And when we feel safe, we are best able to laugh. You might see nonsense as an analogue for the classic jester's pig's bladder on a stick. 'Who could be hurt by that?' *Bonk!* And well done: you just got away with physically assaulting the king.*

Though it might only be an attack with a bladder on a stick, nonsense can still draw blood. The burbling gibberish of *On the Hour* and *The Day Today* ('Where now for man raised by puffins?' 'Sacked chimney sweep pumps

---

* You only have to watch videos of 1970s British TV stalwart Rod Hull attacking the rich and famous with a raffia emu puppet over his fist and you'll see that you can get away with turning the social order upside down as long as your weapon of choice looks like a soft toy.

boss full of mayonnaise'. . .) cushions some of the darkest and most biting satire ever broadcast. Nonsense tickles us, rather than jumping out from the shadows, and its silliness sometimes catches us with our defences down, even more ready to be surprised and delighted. That's why we often say our favourite jokes are ones that 'made me laugh, but I've no idea why'. They keep catching us by surprise in the way a rudimentary cracker joke never can.

If the best part of a laugh is the moment of bafflement and release, that drop down the rollercoaster back into safety (and laughter) gets less effective if the drop is smaller. Once we know that the dog-with-no-nose joke hinges on two meanings of the phrase 'how does he smell?', what was a crazy Big Dipper of mangled meaning turns into a sedate teacup ride.

This may be why comedians don't like the idea of explaining jokes, because it mitigates against the potential for that moment of uncomprehending freefall. That doesn't mean there is no sense to nonsense, just that sometimes, to keep the fun alive, we like to pretend our brain isn't doing its normal job, in the same way we might choose to scream on a rollercoaster to heighten a sense of managed fear. Although we do need to know a rollercoaster is *not* actually going to maim us before we can enjoy the ride, if we see that the cars will never climb higher than two feet, it's no fun either. The sweet spot is in feeling in danger for a moment, and then knowing you're not. Then we laugh.

To get that exhilarating sensation of madness, where anything might come next, but with the surprises kept under enough control to laugh safely, we need a particular tool. And this is where we come to what I like to call 'the bucket'.

WHAT'S IN YOUR BUCKET?

The bucket is whatever you are holding your daft stuff in, and it should be very clearly labelled, so it cannot be mixed up with any other bucket. Buckets work for all sorts of comedy, but let's imagine you're making some TV comedy, maybe a sketch show (remember them?) where the audience needs to know where it is and what's happening every few minutes, whenever the scene changes. The bucket's job is to let the audience know what they are supposedly watching at all times. When an audience recognises what's going on, and starts expecting what might come next, this acts as your Construct and Confirm beats, just as with any joke.

The bucket could be the titles and theme music to a cop show, or a shot of a news anchor sitting pompously at a desk, or what seems to be the start of an advertisement. It could be someone walking into a normal-seeming shop. It could be an ordinary family sitting in their front room. The audience have seen this bucket before. They know what's contained in that sort of bucket. Then they look inside, and there is the very last thing they expected.

You might want to imagine a tin can that promises to contain 'Assorted Nuts', but – *OH MY GOD!* – there's a springy snake inside. That's it. The bucket works the same way as the snake-in-a-can prank. Hardly the most sophisticated technique in the comic toolbox, but the principle of the bucket underpins some of the best-regarded comedy ever made.

So, at first glance, *Brass Eye* looks like a current affairs show. *Monty Python's Life of Brian* and *Holy Grail* are Hollywood epics. *The Onion* looks like a real newspaper. *The Office* looks like a fly-on-the-wall social documentary. *Anchorman* looks like a biopic. *Viz* looks like, variously, a children's comic, a tabloid newspaper and a supermarket-checkout-stand magazine. *Arrested Development* seems to be a soap opera of the pointlessly rich.

It's why the two protagonists of *Monty Python*'s fish-slapping dance are dressed as dignified British explorers and accompanied by light Edwardian orchestral music. Because we need to think (or pretend to think) we know what's going to happen in order to enjoy it when it gets silly.

JINGLE BELLS, BATMAN SMELLS

One of the first things that may ever have made you laugh was someone singing rude words to a hymn or popular song at school. In their book *The Lore and Language of Schoolchildren*, Iona and Peter Opie said children love parody because it is 'that most refined form of jeering, [which] gives an intelligent child a way of showing independence without having to rebel'. Children know instinctively that if the container is solid, you can put anything you want inside. It's why it remains funny when you open a school RE textbook and find someone's drawn a big hairy knob on Jesus.

As we'll see later, this sort of nonsense relies a lot on shared cultural assumptions within our tribe, knowing what you might normally expect to be carried in your chosen bucket. But that means it's the sort of comedy that's fun to share with any friends who share your culture, as a bonding exercise. Nonsense can have a tribal and social affirming function. You and your best mate both know Noddy never says rude words, so drawing a bubble with the words 'Sod off, Big Ears' over his head will never fail to get a giggle. And it's a short journey from that to *Viz* or *Team America*.

'HELLO. MY NAME IS MARTY DIBERGI. I'M A FILMMAKER. . .'

Annoyingly, one of the first things you learn as a comedy writer is that your bucket needs to look 100 per cent like a real bucket. It's as hard to make a fake advert, or newspaper, or *Game of Thrones* scene as a real one. The moments Rachel Bloom and co. burst into song in *Crazy Ex-Girlfriend* work as pop parodies because they cost almost as much to stage and shoot as a real pop video. If the (inevitably minuscule) comedy wallet available means your *Game of Thrones* sketch looks like a bargain-basement bit of studio-based late 1970s *Doctor Who*, the audience will expect jokes about Daleks instead.

Buckets are another enjoyable exercise in pattern spotting, the basic engine that drives comedy. When we made the detective spoofs *A Touch of Cloth*,* we found the most efficient way to write the scripts was to break cop drama down into its component parts. Researchers cut serious police procedurals into tiny fragments, like a forensic examiner dissecting a corpse, and arranged them under headings 'detectives lifting incident tape', 'opening morgue drawers', 'police car interiors in rain with opera/jazz/blues playing'. The writing team studied these tiny clips, divorced from narrative context, so the tropes and structural rules of detective drama became laughably obvious. Once we knew exactly what every part of the 'TV detective show' bucket looked like, we could make our own, and pour in nonsense.

The bucket is why adapting something from one medium to another is so tricky. Sometimes a funny television show won't work as a funny book, and a radio series

---

* Which we did by hotwiring the *Airplane!* team's *Police Squad*, switching it to right-hand-drive, and driving it away.

won't translate to television. Sometimes a book needs to be a book. The look, the sound, the feel, the smell of the package can be what sets your expectations up to be tripped up by the comedy. It's vital to make the bucket clear and not confusing. Our *Ladybird Books for Grown-Ups* were made on the same vintage presses that the original books had been printed on in the 1960s and 1970s, and we had to get it done in Italy, in the factory where these machines had been beautifully preserved, because that way even the smell of the paper and ink was right. A bucket must Construct and Confirm at all times, and never Confuse. This is why it needs to be diligently and precisely observed.

THE SITCOM BUCKET

The most obvious time to use a bucket is pastiche or parody. But a comic narrative of any sort declares its terms to the audience by letting them see a familiar shape from real life, inside which the most outlandish sprints of comic invention will safely be contained. Solidly drawing the boundary of your reality, deciding what is deemed possible, allows an audience to guess what's coming next, and how far you're likely to go. The bucket in narrative comedy is the contract your audience signs to establish how unlike reality you can get without them screaming 'foul'. I suspect it's more necessary in comedy than in any other narrative form, simply because comedy can do anything.

If the realistic, emotionally authentic, single-camera show *Fleabag* ended with the characters waving out of the fourth wall with goofy smiles on their faces, it would be a mistake, even though its bones (gawky posh lady running a struggling small business and talking straight down the lens about her love life) are very much shared with the contemporary sitcom *Miranda*, which ended exactly that way every week. Both shows invite you to care for their protagonists, and laugh, but slosh their sometimes similar contents into very different buckets. Punch a hole in one of the buckets, and the audience would be confused. (Was it all a meta-joke? Was this show meant to be in the tradition of Nora Ephron or *'Allo 'Allo?*)

The declared bucket Constructs for the audience. And then the contents can Confirm or Confound. And, hopefully, nobody is Confused.

So, how do we make sure the buckets in which we carry our comedy do Construct properly, and stay solid, rather than Confuse? That's down to comedy's other function. This is not about mental games, but social glue.

It's time to turn on the house lights and look at the audience.

PART THREE

COMEDY IS US

23

Laughing Together

Cheers *is filmed before a live studio audience.*

Opening voiceover to every episode of *Cheers*

Stewart Lee's magnificent books analysing his own stand-up sets are amongst the best work ever produced by a working comic on the minutiae of their craft. Lee's on-stage clown persona is a character who happily explains the technique of joke-making out loud. He then often criticises the audience for the effect that simple comic tricks have on them. If you've seen him perform, the impression is of someone who has killed so many frogs in his quest for the secret of comedy that all he can do now is throw the limp corpses at the audience, with a disdain that says he is disappointed in the audience, disappointed in himself, and, most of all, disappointed in the frogs. It's very funny.

'You liked that,' he might say to his audience,* with carefully calibrated clown contempt, after delivering a heavily signalled pun. He enjoys pointing out how elementary the joke shapes can be, despite the huge reactions he can induce with them. It's probably why he's the classic

---

* Or more accurately, to a partially imaginary subset of his audience who are defined as a sort of 'remedial set' within his comedy classroom, struggling to keep up with the bright kids, and worthy only of the disdain of the world-weary comic teacher at the front.

stand-up's stand-up, gleefully revealing the joke mechanisms that all professional comics know are there.

But because of his scorn for hack joke shapes, Lee's
books are more about the fascinating groups of humans
listening to his material, and less the rudimentary engineering behind a lot of comedy (inversion, exaggeration,
understatement, juxtaposition and so on). He's like a fine
jazz guitarist who isn't really impressed by the chords any
more, but has a load of great stories about life on the
road. Jokes can be pretty basic is the message, but *people*
are interesting. It's a fair point.

Most serious coverage of comedy in broadsheet news-
papers is similarly more fascinated by audience response
than the jokes themselves, the tribes and taboos. And
through the relentless examination of what we apparently
'can' and 'can't' say when we joke, the topic of comedy
has become increasingly fraught and toxic, just another
explosive front in the culture war.

This study of taboo and acceptability leads to an obses-
sion with surprise and shock. In technical terms, comedy
criticism can become focused on the Confound note. Critics want to know about the punchline that drew a gasp,
that made someone walk out. *Outrageous!* But I'd say
that gives jokes too much credit. Like Stewart Lee, we
should understand that jokes are fun, but it's the people
joking, and laughing at those jokes, that are interesting.
Look at the room, not the gag. Comedy is a social activity,
and we need to consider it sociologically. Which means we
need to ignore the sexy Confound notes, and examine the
functional grey notes at the beginning, before a joke even
starts to be funny. Don't look at what shocks us; look at
what we accept.

That's the tribe. That's us.

To understand the human shape of comedy, it's all
down to how we Construct.

APPETITE FOR CONSTRUCTION

On our comedy keyboard, we have two notes that give us most of our actual laughs. Confound (big laughs) and Confirm (warm laughs). Those are the sexy ones. Confound is the brassy, head-turning one. Confirm is quietly attractive and somehow irresistible, because you two just get on. But the one note we haven't looked at too closely is the boring, mousy one with glasses: Construct. But let's shake its hair down and take off those specs and realise that underneath its wallflower exterior, Construct is quite the animal. It's certainly the one that can kill you. More than Confound, even. (It's always the quiet ones, right?)

Construct usually comes at the start, and doesn't play any games with expectation at all. It just says what's going on, so we know where we are. And this is where we thrash out into some dangerous waters. Because the Construct note for a joke isn't necessarily completely contained within the comedy itself.

We arrive at any comedy ready to play with ideas, but also carrying a load of baggage. This baggage is useful. It's why we'll laugh at cultural references and archetypes and shared observations. We know what a certain celebrity is like, how someone might behave when they're drunk, what a Henry hoover is. We know what sort of person we'd expect to live on steak slices from Greggs, and who is going to treat themselves to avocado on sourdough toast from an artisanal gluten-free bakery.

Without the meat of shared assumptions, we might struggle to make any delicious comedy sausages. The Construct note includes all our expectations of what we might accept as 'reality'. This means we can start doing Confirm and Confounds to get a laugh reaction without sounding the Construct note, because within the social group sharing the joke, we all agree some fundamental things before we even begin.

YOU KNOW WHAT I MEAN?

For example, we might agree that gravity drags us downwards and dogs and cats sometimes don't get on. We accept before we even start that the Arctic Circle is cold, and that mums can fuss around their kids. Maybe we also agree that men sometimes avoid sharing their feelings, or that lawyers may be less than strictly moral, or that battered takeaway food is popular in Scotland. The queue you join is always the one that stops moving, isn't it? When people smoke marijuana they get really hungry. The middle aisle of Lidl is full of weird stuff like boat varnish and gas masks. Computer coders are a bit nerdy. Gay men tend to be flamboyant and enjoy show tunes, don't they? At Christmas, guys will want to watch *Die Hard* and women will want to watch *Love Actually*.

You know what I'm saying, right? Yeah? Yeah? And what's the deal with airline food? But perhaps we hang around with people who agree, without us ever needing to say it out loud, that Jewish people are motivated purely by money, that Mexicans like to laze around under their sombreros all day, that some people in wheelchairs are probably faking it, and that it's creepy when people talk to shopkeepers in foreign languages and you can't understand what they're saying. What is it with those guys, anyway?

And before you know it we are in an uncomfortable area that feels not quite nice. I know I didn't feel great typing the end of that riff, but it's all to demonstrate the power of shared assumptions, and the danger of the unsounded Construct note.

It seems counterintuitive maybe, but the part of a joke

that usually gets a comedian in headline-grade trouble isn't the punchline, it's the bit at the beginning, especially if they never said it out loud. The dangerous part of a joke that relies on, say, racial or regional stereotypes isn't usually the clever pun or shocking leap of tone at the end. It's the bit at the start where Moishe or Paddy or Diego walks into a bar, and you know roughly what's coming next.

The Construct note is the unsaid in all our cultural 'nudge, nudges', the 'more' in our 'say no mores'. It's what's assumed in the 'am I right?' kicker from hack stand-up. It's the tacit agreement of shared values within the locked rear of a taxi cab that can make us feel like we're going to have to nod through an unpleasant anecdote with gritted teeth.

AN IRISHMAN WALKS INTO A DISCUSSION OF COMEDY THEORY

I once saw Dara Ó Briain do a fantastic routine about shared assumptions. He would ask the audience to name any country about which they knew next to nothing, and then get them to supply a random adjective. Let's say the audience offered 'Burkina Faso' and 'feckless'. Then during the rest of the set, he'd drop a few gags or stinging callbacks that relied on the punchline, 'Typical Burkina Fasoan. You know how feckless they are!' And the audience, prepped to play a game with their own assumptions, and lacking any other better data that could replace it, would laugh. You hear 'Burkina Faso'; you know what *they're* like.

The routine would end with Ó Briain pointing out that, unless anyone learned any different about these faraway people and their legendary fecklessness, there was a chance that in a decade, tonight's show long forgotten, there might be a terrible natural disaster in Burkina Faso. And at least some of the audience, without even remembering why, would worry for the victims' chances of rescue, given the Burkina Fasoans' innately feckless national character.

The set of clever callbacks illustrated how shared assumptions, even totally invented ones, can provide silent Construct beats for jokes within a bonded social group – in this case a random comedy audience. I doff my cap to this routine, because it's one of the funniest and most inclusive stage bits about comedy theory that I've ever seen. And I don't think it's insignificant that Ó Briain's countrymen have been historically the butt of this sort of ill-thought-through assumed-Construct gag structure for centuries at the hands of the English.

NUDGE, NUDGE, SAY NO MORE

Construct is dangerous because it gives away your internal roadmap of expectation, and that's sometimes a nice way of saying 'prejudice'. When edgy comedians upset people, and defend their jokes as 'just funny', they're usually defending the solid technical flourish of the joke parts, forgetting the Construct notes they played on the way to get to their dazzling solo.

You can look at a joke again and again and not see anything wrong with it, but maybe it only got a laugh because the audience made the worst bits of it themselves. And maybe an audience who didn't start the joke with the same assumptions of 'the way things are' might see the joke differently. No joke (even a Henry hoover joke) is told in a vacuum, because we use jokes to say who we are, and who we aren't.

24

Mike is a Wanker

PETE: *You see that bloody Leonardo Da Vinci cartoon? I couldn't see the bloody joke.*
DUD: *...It's a different culture, Pete. We don't understand it. For instance,* The Mousetrap *did terribly in Pakistan.*

Not Only... But Also, 'Art Gallery' sketch
(written by Peter Cook and Dudley Moore)

We've all experienced and enjoyed jokes that absolutely kill within various social groups – amongst people who work with us, our family and friends, people from the same town, country or social background, people of the same political leanings, people who share our hobbies and passions. These jokes get big laughs because they ditch the Construct note and tickle our shared assumptions, which gives them pace and weight.

For example, if we all know Mike at work is a vain, bone-idle layabout, we don't need to sound the opening Construct note of a Mike joke when we're talking to a group of colleagues who work with him every day. We're all on the same page. So, a Mike gag doesn't need to start with, 'You know Mike? He's lazy and vain, right?' You can, provided Mike's not in earshot (the wanker), just riff on your group's shared assumptions about him. That's how jokes act as tribal glue and social affirmation. *Am I right?*

Making jokes based on these unvoiced Construct notes can be the most fun of all. Firstly, they're faster, by one comic beat, getting to the gag more quickly by leaving off the set-up. Also, we love to fill in unsupplied data to make a joke work, because it shows off our pattern skills.

Completing a crossword with most of the answers filled in for you isn't as satisfying as doing it from scratch. The more you bring to the party yourself, the more fun it is. That's why laboriously set-up jokes feel so patronising, and why a lot of well-meaning comedy that tries to include as wide a tribe as possible by taking no shared data for granted, and packing it all into the set-up, feels so awful and clunky.

There is this guy called Shmuel, which is a Jewish name, used by Jewish men. Jewish people are disputational and enjoy lively disagreement over topics they feel are important. Even gentiles in our culture understand that every aspect of life is open for debate for the Jewish community, who generally enjoy taking sides and disagreeing with one another, especially over religious matters. Shmuel is shipwrecked on a desert island, like characters in jokes from our shared culture often are, so don't worry, he's going to be fine. And he's there for ages. Eventually a ship sees a plume of smoke and comes to his rescue. The captain of the ship sees that Shmuel has been there so long that he has built three enormous, elaborate huts, with roofs and walls and stairs and floors, and even impressive palm-tree wooden towers on two of them. 'So what is this hut here?' asks the captain, pointing at the first, humbler hut. 'Oh, that's the hut where I live,' says Shmuel. 'And that one? The second hut?' 'That's the synagogue. A man must have a synagogue.' 'Right. And what's the third one?' 'Ah. That? That's the synagogue I don't go to.'

Now, you either enjoy the second half of that joke (one of

my favourites) and need to trust that the first half is unvoiced assumed knowledge, or you don't bother telling it at all. By letting everybody in, including (as I have done here) visitors from outer space, the tribal grooming function of comedy gets knackered. A joke with all its shared cultural assumptions explained within the joke itself loses the crucial intimacy that might make it as good as the joke-shared-between-siblings-at-a-funeral.

But the problem remains that we can crash and burn making jokes based on shared assumptions if we exchange these jokes within a group that doesn't in fact share those assumptions. Misread the room, use an unvoiced assumption as your Construct note that isn't agreed upon by everybody, you're in trouble. And that's because jokes aren't just a puzzle, they're a flag.

TALKING TO YOUR TRIBE

What we laugh at identifies us and bonds us, celebrating common experiences. Get the wrong reference, you lose the crowd. Misjudge an audience's tolerance for toilet humour or enthusiasm for references to French Enlightenment mathematicians, and even the best-constructed joke will die. Comedy is always the art of reading the room.

Comedy has become a very different beast on social media in recent years, precisely because of the difficulties of defining that room. We now all have a potential for our jokes to reach way beyond our customary audience of friends; suddenly we are all stand-ups, facing a crowd that we cannot quite see because of the glare of the lights (in this case of our phone and laptop screens).

When we share a funny story socially, we do a small version of any comedian's craft, judging the tastes and tolerances of the people to whom we are speaking. Imagine yourself round a pub or restaurant table with some close mates. You might make a joke using reference to some shared experience, or employ technical or colloquial language that is specific to your group. Add in a stranger to the table – maybe someone has brought their partner along who is not usually part of your gang – and you might notice them failing to keep up. You either decide then to leave them behind, playing to the usual crowd, or you moderate your references, maybe adding helpful footnotes as you go. ('Mike, you know, he's the one who's a wanker...')

But maybe the appeal of the story you were telling was totally dependent on the shared values of the group. Maybe it's a single-gender group, and the newcomer is has a different gender or sexual orientation to the rest of you. Maybe your joke relies on shared political values, and you realise the stranger is of a different opinion. You might adjust your 'material' to ensure they stay included, are not offended, to keep things cordial.

You might have a favourite crappy bad-taste Stevie Wonder gag that you love to trot out, but your new guest is blind – most of us wouldn't do it. Unless it's deliberately to get a reaction, and that's still an exercise in tribal dynamics. Are you rejecting the newcomer? Or testing them to see if they're allowed to come in? This is a natural process.

Even a purposefully offensive, I-say-what-I-like old-school comic like Jim Davidson has said he struggles to do his normal set if he sees wheelchairs in the front row, since, I assume, disabled people might be the butt of some of his gags, and he doesn't want to look them in the eye. Whatever you think that story says about him as a human being, it shows that even the most studiedly stubborn comics tailor their material to the room.

25

Laughing Together

The only other rule that I found [for comedy] is that audiences don't laugh when it's hot. A cold audience, they'll sit there shivering and they'll warm themselves with laughter.

Denis Norden

Confirm and Confound are the notes that have fun playing with the pattern-detection machine, but the Construct beat is where comedy does its second big job: social glue. The group-bonding and soothing function of comedy is partly because laughter is a contagious action, like yawning and scratching. Laughter is a Mexican wave of reassurance that spreads between members of a group, signalling that it's time to relax.

Other laughing animals do not share our ability to pass the infection along within a group, and need to be stimulated to laugh individually; more evidence that humans may have developed group laughter as a substitute for the physical grooming activities that became impractical as our tribal groups grew bigger.

The trigger for that laughter is also socially important, since a joke usually contains a token of agreement – a reference, an assumption, a common experience – that we exchange to reinforce our social group's shared values.

Jokes and the subjects of jokes unify us. The hopeful stand-up offers, 'Anyone in from Idaho?' before launching into their memories of childhood, or experiences of playing a particular place. They want to encourage a whoop that confirms that at least a few of the silhouetted heads in the crowd contain the relevant shared information to make this joke land, and send it rippling across the room. A tentative response will make the comedian erect more guides and handrails round their local references, and build their Construct beats out loud. They will need to paint some pictures to ensure consensus before they begin. ('I don't know if you've been to Idaho, but the state flag is a potato sack. . .') If the audience knows Idaho, and gives a cheer that they know the accepted potato-joke rules, the comic can have confidence not to clutter up their delivery with explanatory signage.

We're all familiar with the eagerly affirmative group-grooming mortar that holds stand-up together:

'What's all that about?'

'Am I right?'

'Have you ever noticed. . . ?'

'Who here's like me when it comes to. . . ?'

'You know what I'm saying?'

'You guys know what it's like. . .'

'Am I the only one who. . . ?'

'We've all done it. . .'

Every trusty group-bonding trope draws the tribe closer round the fire. Even a comic's choice of intro music or poster graphics can unify the room as part of their tribe, and maybe even indicate to outsiders that they may not get all the references. 'We all like the same stuff, right? This is for my people. . .'

LIFTING THE MATERIAL

A live audience – even the small group of a writers' room, or the one-on-one of a collaborative partnership – is a quick way to check that you have managed to successfully 'share the joke with the class'. As a scriptwriter, I used to think that live audiences were mainly to help the performers, giving them energy to feed off. But I've learned that a live crowd can be the writer's friend too. An audience responding with fresh enthusiasm to a gag that had gone stale for the writer can reassure you that the joke still works – you just got tired of it.

A well-wrought line that made everyone laugh when they read the script can easily die on the third run-through in the rehearsal room simply because everyone saw it coming. Suddenly there's no laugh. Has something gone wrong? Maybe it needs to be replaced? Maybe it needs to be faster? A bit more volume? How about a big, mugging expression over the top? But the moment the joke is read out loud on stage, to an audience who don't know it, the line comes back to life. An audience's authentic laughter can give a script confidence in itself.

Overexposure to, and then anxiety about, perfectly good material explains why improvisation on set is sometimes overrated as a creative tool. As Charlie Higson (of *The Fast Show*) said, 'There's a great danger in comedy that you keep changing it because you're bored with it – and you're not improving it, you're writing sideways.' There is the temptation to remember the crew laughing with surprise at a new alternative line, because the laugh at the original well-crafted gag months ago at your desk, or in the writing room, has been long forgotten.

Surely this line should be getting a laugh? And bang, it's replaced with something technically weaker that someone vividly remembers cracked the crew up on set. A technically good joke dies thanks to the affirmative and unarguable power of shared laughter within a tribal group.

CANNED LAUGHTER*

We are an estimated thirty times more likely to laugh in a group than if we are alone. If we join an audience and that social group is signalling that they are in a relaxed, soothed state by sharing laughter, we feel safe, and more prepared to laugh ourselves. Want to know why TV comedy used to have those hysterical-sounding old-fashioned laugh tracks? It's simply that. Why *wouldn't* you hear laughter when someone did something funny? It's not a trick or a way to make bad jokes seem better. It's a natural consequence of the origins of comedy in grooming behaviour. It makes sense that a joke would be accompanied by the sound of humans enjoying it.

Good jokes being delivered into cool silence, so we can make our own minds up, might seem more sophisticated, but it's new. In his dying days, Stan Laurel sadly reflected that when he saw his old movies on the TV, they seemed painfully slow. He and Oliver Hardy had left big gaps between the jokes deliberately, because they knew the audience would need a breath or two to stop laughing. Ollie would some-times even ride the audience's laugh, looking out at them directly in comic despair. But on television, without the

---

* Worth saying that canned laughter – a pre-recorded set of artificially triggered audience laugh responses laid, in post-production, over a comedy show that the audience never saw – was a briefly used technique from long ago in comedy history and one that is now almost totally extinct. Usually a laugh track is the authentic sound of an audience enjoying the show that you're watching. Oh, and they're only laughing much louder than you'd expect because laughter is social (see: this book).

additional live laugh track, Stan worried it might look like the pair's precisely timed jokes had fallen flat.

The decline of audience sitcom does seem to point to a recent acceleration in the certainty that we no longer need the group reassurance that it's OK to laugh. When we're sitting at home alone, or watching comedy on separate screens with headphones, perhaps it feels odd to engage in what is intended to be group grooming behaviour. In fact, most of us probably type the initials for the act of laughing out loud more than we actually do it. I know that the younger members of my own extended family can sit in complete silence watching comedy shows which they love deeply, feeling soothed and happy that the characters are doing their comic turns in front of them, but feeling no need to send up or receive socially affirmative laughter signals.

The pleasure hit of the comic form (the set-up, the expectation, the surprise) must still be there, or they wouldn't watch comedy at all. But comedy is now more often enjoyed like a comic novel, quietly to ourselves, in our own heads. It's odd to remember that, throughout most of human history, comedy that goes out to silence has failed. It's why a comic dying on stage makes the whole audience tense, not just the performer.

EAT YOUR GREENS

Laughter is all about bonding and agreeing, about feeling safe together, sharing our values and knowledge. The more we agree, the shorter the Construct notes can be, and the more quickly we can start having fun playing Confirm and Confound guessing games. Those are the clever, nourishing bits for the brain, the green vegetables and protein in the comic diet. The 'joke' parts of the joke contain all the vitamins and goodness that keep our processing engine on tip-top form. The Construct notes, the shared assumptions, references and prejudices? They're the carbohydrates. Comforting and heavy, making us want to sit still and pat our full bellies, satisfied and happy. Construct notes, especially unvoiced construct ones, are sugary and starchy, and we crave them because they make us feel really good for a minute. But, and this is of course my prejudice as a woke snowflake melt of the worst kind, Construct's spadeloads of comfort food are probably not as healthy for us as practising our ability to empathise and follow social cues (Confirm) or be surprised by and assimilate new information (Confound).

Construct (especially the stuff we bring to a joke without needing it to be said out loud) is the comedy equivalent of a grab bag of reassuring vintage childhood crisps. And of course we feel happy when someone gets a laugh by referring to a thing we remember fondly, or disses a group outside our tribe whom we all agree are slutty, unwashed car thieves who can't spell. And – as both the fast-food industry and the lucrative careers of shock pundits who pander to our worst prejudices prove – there's a lot of money to be made from feeding people salty, sugary junk that they really like eating, but is basically little more than dietary ballast.

Although the social bonding part of comedy is provable scientifically, evolutionarily important, and vital for the stability of our social groups, it just makes us feel nice by telling us who we are, and who we're not.

And we probably knew that already.

26

The Tribe

Laughter produces, simultaneously, a strong fellow feeling among participants and joint aggressiveness against outsiders. Heartily laughing together at the same thing forms an immediate bond ... and simultaneously draws a line. If you cannot laugh with the others, you feel an outsider.

Konrad Lorenz

One of the things it's hard to accept as a comedy writer is that most laughter is nothing to do with jokes. An incredible 80 per cent of laugh reactions in humans have no joke or comedy trigger.

Laughter isn't a signal that we've heard a clever joke. It's just something we do to make ourselves and other humans within our group feel better, safer and closer together.

Laughter signals that we are in play mode, and therefore safe to relax (there are no external threats), and that no harm is meant within the group (there is no internal threat). A laugh means we all agree that we're having a nice time, and we're happy to be hanging out together.

The evolutionary psychologist Robin Dunbar has proposed that, after humans split from our common ancestor with chimps, we used humour and laughter as a way to cement tribal relationships. The same leap forward in our evolution gave us humour, alongside increasing group sizes, each one feeding the other. Dunbar developed a theory to define the optimum size for these new human social groups. The Dunbar Number is the maximum number of active social contacts a human can usefully maintain with any degree of civility. It's roughly 150 individuals, which is, pleasingly, roughly the size of a medieval village.

The Dunbar Number is usually the membership level at which any online group (ostensibly set up to share information about the local primary-school field trip or discuss the music of a-ha) starts fighting amongst itself and fracturing into vindictive subgroups, making Dunbar the scientist who worked out the formula for the Judean People's Front from *Monty Python's Life of Brian*.*

Dunbar said that groups of primates over fifty members find it difficult to groom one another physically, so had to find a replacement. Social laughter is a noise that strokes us. The development of speech a little later meant that anyone who could use their language skills to *cause* the soothing sound of laughter became a valued member of the tribe, gaining high status, and, much later, lucrative appearance slots on TV panel shows. If we can't groom each other, we will do something else that can be done

---

* I have observed an Online Comedy Dunbar Number, which is the point at which your innocuous social media gag about how your cat's a bit fussy about their food gets marginally more 'likes' than the number of people you'd be comfortable addressing from a stage. At this tipping point, your joke will instantly start to attract furious and divisive comments from cat owners whose cats never do that, or dog owners who want to talk about dogs, or people who just want to shout at the sky. (I find myself in the same position when I see someone post that they enjoyed a film, book or TV programme and get a burning need to tell them I didn't, as if anyone gives a stuff.) We humans are always declaring our refusal of the tribe's agreed terms, splitting and flouncing out to start breakaway factions.

over a wider distance and is similarly soothing. Language, gossip and jokes all developed alongside one another to help fill the niche left by picking ticks off one another and patting each other's heads.

'WENN IST DAS NUNSTÜCK GIT UND SLOTERMEYER?'

Comedy is inherently tribal. Think about how much a comedy show that you were told you'd like but didn't enjoy makes you itchy and angry. Those aren't the jokes for your people. 'The idiots who laughed at this rubbish... did they think I was... one of them?' Comedy acts as a team strip, a declaration of values, a fire to gather around and, in some cases, a flag to wave.

The flag is our shared group identity, and that identity is reinforced by the humour we use within that group. It's why English people like to joke that Germans have 'no sense of humour', by which we mean either 'a different sense of humour', or more probably, 'a slightly different sense of humour that also includes a love of some of our own most idiosyncratically English comedy such as *Monty Python*'. Hey, we're all Saxons (we share a royal family, after all), and tribal identification gags usually target nobody more savagely than the people next door. After all, they talk funny. (As Steve Martin once observed, 'Those French have a different word for *everything*. They do it to screw you up.')

According to linguistic theory (as put forward by the likes of Steven Pinker), the human mind has both a dictionary and a grammar. Since comedy is a game played on the hardware we also use for language processing, it should share some features with language. If it does, perhaps comedy's grammar might be the stuff about patterns and shapes. The grammar of comedy is how we play with our data-processing machinery, and sharpen it with little games.

In which case, the comedy dictionary would be the agreed units, the words and concepts which we arrange in a comic order. And that dictionary will be made of things we know, stuff we agree with, tendencies we suspect, likely behaviours we assume. Comedy uses a dictionary of references, allusions, stereotypes, archetypes, thumbnail sketches (and unfortunately prejudices), and assembles them using a comic grammar.

Comic grammar is widely shared between tribes, in the same way that most languages will employ a system involving verbs, nouns, prepositions, possessives, superlatives and so on. Jokes are roughly the same shape wherever you go so we can assume that comic grammars are fairly widespread. But different tribes don't share a dictionary. And that's why it's sometimes hard to tell the same joke to different tribes. They might guess that we're telling a joke, from the rhythm and structure, but not understand the vocabulary we are using.

The dictionary of comic elements is like any dictionary: made by picking a set of tokens and agreeing what they mean. These agreements are our identity, just as they are with language. The French agree that the animal with four legs that carries cowboys around is *un cheval*, while the Germans insist it's *ein Pferd*, even though we all know it's called 'a horse', and they're just trying to show off.

In the same way, one tribe might bond using their comic dictionary by agreeing that any Polish character in their jokes is going to be a bit dim, while another tribe expects that same Pole will be a thief (the poor migrant always gets the short straw...). Or maybe one tribe agrees that pineapple should be on all pizzas. If they open a joke with a guy eating a fruitless pizza, everyone in the audience will recognise *that* sort of fool. Another nearby tribe might differentiate themselves from their pineapple-loving neighbours by telling jokes about how anyone who puts pineapple on a pizza also eats babies.

And that, in so many disappointing but hilarious ways, is how we got here.

When sharing comic ideas within a tribe, those mutual assumptions form our comic dictionary. Whether innocent or slightly toxic, they are the unvoiced Construct notes off which we can play the audience's expectations and score laughs with Confirm and Confound notes.

27

Anyone in From 1991?

When I went to Australia ... I had to go around all the supermarkets changing all the bloody names. They're buggers ... One of the punch lines [referred to] Jammie Dodgers and there's really no substitute for that ... Well, they have things called Lamington Fingers. That was all right. I coped. But it was a bit of a strain.

Victoria Wood

We joke within our class, our faiths, our regions and our nations using agreed assumptions as our starting blocks. But one of the biggest social dividers between one tribe and another is not philosophy or geography, but time.

Our cultural toolkit of shared references and resonances changes every few years, and we can be alienated completely if a joke is designed for another generation. We are all tribes in time.

The Generation X author (and *Generation X* author) Douglas Coupland said, 'There's nothing quite so micro-humiliating as making a *Brady Bunch* reference and the room going silent.' Coupland himself, a 1990s literary superstar, is probably now a niche reference that you'd trot out to get a warm nod of recognition from a crowd who came of age to the sound of Nirvana's *Nevermind*.

Maybe by quoting him here, I'm just inviting my people to gather close. But you can bet your plaid shirt and Converse Chuck Taylors that the man's right.

In the Charlie Brooker writers' room, we developed the term 'Zammo' to remind ourselves that sometimes we were only making ourselves laugh. A Zammo is a joke that kills for one demographic while whizzing meaninglessly over the heads of everyone else. It was named after the generation-defining *Grange Hill* smackhead Zammo McGuire, of whom you may never have heard, and was forged in live television fire.

A routine had been written for Charlie for an audience show that ended on the word 'Zammo'. We'd positioned this culturally freighted zinger to land at the end of the line, but when performed for a studio audience of comedy fans who happened to be a decade younger than us, 'Zammo' was just this weird noise Charlie made at the end of a sentence. He might as well have ended the line by punching the air and shouting 'Kerchow!' (Although that would at least have got a laugh from Generation Lightning McQueen.) Some cultural artefacts can have long lives – Mickey Mouse or Spider-Man, say – but nothing is more anchored in time than a children's soap-opera storyline. You either saw it, and talked about it in the playground, or you didn't.*

---

* You want scary? I recently discovered that Mrs Mangel, the grumpy old busybody character in long-running Australian soap opera *Neighbours*, was in the show for less than *two years*. Yet referencing Mrs Mangel remains a surefire joke reference for my generation. While editing this section, by total coincidence, I heard her name used as a punchline on a charity edition of *Bake Off*. Such is the peculiar tribal nature of comedy that a minor soap character from a quarter of a century ago can still act as a token of exchange, providing it's exactly the right one.

'I JUST THINK THAT THEIR APPEAL IS BECOMING MORE SELECTIVE'

Jokes can play to big or small rooms, and a joke that leaves most people cold is not a failure if it functions as essential social glue within a smaller group. In fact, these in-jokes are some of the most precious jokes of all. (We return to the start of the book and the Platonic ideal of the private joke between siblings at a funeral.) A huge stadium might warmly agree with a big-ticket stand-up that, yes, dogs and cats do seem to be very different, but a joke containing references that only a fellow fan of Rowdy Roddy Piper or *Call the Midwife* can understand will act as a much more potent tribal glue.

The online social space, for all its nightmarish flaws, can be a fantastic demonstration of how human tribes are built and reinforced with jokes. On social media, with its addictive gamifying of the normal rules of human interaction, the size of the tribes we attract and identify with every gag is represented with solid numbers. Those running totals of likes and shares are hard data, measuring the size of the crowd that gathered in response to whatever we said and thought was funny.

If we make a joke that requires some decoding (a glancing reference to a long-forgotten TV show from our childhoods, say), that joke will usually get fewer likes and shares than a joke that contains all the information for everyone to access (whether it's a self-contained gag, or connected to the day's news, so the elements are in everybody's head already). And if we're interested in comedy's tribal function, very broad gags tend to get lots of likes – a sort of gentle, warm, collective applause – but very niche jokes will often receive direct replies. And those replies can make you feel great, better than any amount of general applause. It's as if you've made a friend.

Jokes can unexpectedly leap over every expected other tribal divide, and you can find that a stranger halfway round the world, with no other shared characteristics, can decode your reference to obscure Wu-Tang Clan lyrics, and suddenly they're a new friend.

With obscure material, people want to let you know they enjoyed it, that a connection has been made. Strangers feel they can approach you and say 'I got that' or 'That really made me laugh' or 'Great joke!', with the subtext, 'We have something in common. We belong to the same micro-tribe. Let's hang out!' It's a lovely illustration of why we make jokes to each other in the first place. In-jokes are friendly ice-breakers to cross all other social divides. They identify people who accept the social offer, and with whom we might be able to bond unconditionally. All it requires is that one thing we have in common.

It's the missing information in a joke that makes it a game. A broad joke will only have a small amount of common knowledge that needs to be added – the knowledge that two words rhyme when said out loud, say, in the case of a pun. Or a joke might be based on a fairly common human experience – what it's like to be very hungry or tired, or how people interact with their pets. Mass-market joking can be tied to an agreed news cycle: something we all know (or agree) happened today, and about which we're all thinking. All those jokes require a little to be added, but will gather a large tribe, who all have access to the ingredients.

But what is beautiful about a proper in-joke – a joke that avoids directly stating all the information required to enjoy it, and maybe even delights in locking some people out – is that, at a technical level, the audience helps make the joke themselves, and so it belongs to them.

'I'M THE RUHR!'

The swapping of an in-joke is like spies exchanging two halves of a secret code-phrase. Anyone who can't fill in the missing parts to make the joke work isn't welcome in our club.

In a wonderful scene in the sitcom *Peep Show*, David Mitchell's socially awkward character Mark makes friends with a new colleague at work, Daryl. They goof off and play a game where Daryl bowls empty water-cooler bottles down the stairwell at Mark, whose inner monologue we can hear, as usual.

> DARYL: *I'm Barnes Wallis! You're the Ruhr!*
> MARK (VO): *I'm the Ruhr! And no one's actually said the word 'Dambusters'! This is bloody brilliant!*

The joy is that the Construct note was not sounded, it was merely assumed. And when that happens, we feel that we are amongst friends.

Of course, we all say we want everyone to enjoy everything, in one big happy family, all tribes as one. We've seen the Cola-Cola adverts. But deep down, in our evolved tribal primate selves, we know that a walled garden is a nicer place to hang out than an overcrowded public park full of baffling, unpredictable strangers with their annoying music we don't like. Unlike family, we all pick our friends based on various criteria, whether we admit it or not. That's just human. So we make jokes for our people, to draw them close.

And we have the power to fine-tune *any* joke. If you've ever worked for a major corporation or a children's channel, you'll have done this again and again to turn the thing you might laugh about with your mates into something you can sell to a different audience. The idea that something's 'just funny' is no use if your gag relies on you knowing all Joy Division's song titles and you're trying to get a laugh out of the under-fives. Of course, fine-tuning the gag might wreck it; perhaps the best bit of your joke is the bit that has to come out. Maybe explaining a reference or not delivering a shock wallop to our shared values takes the wind out of a joke's sails. Covering all bases can often ruin the group-bonding potential of a gag. But we can definitely try. We can take bits out that don't work for everyone in our audience, and come up with something that works better for more people.

That's probably the best definition of the daily experience of the professional comedy writer. It's not really much more than being paid to share the joke with the class. And if you're good at that, you'll probably have a career. If you suck at that part, you'll still be funny, but you might have to do it as a hobby.

GONZO CONDUCTS LIEBESTRÄUME WHILE BATTLING A CRAB

Comedy divides as much as it unites, and not everybody can laugh at everything. It's why internationally distributed streaming platforms are less keen on making comedy than national broadcasting networks are. Theirs is a business model that looks for content that plays across as many tribes as possible. Creators can struggle under those conditions because a joke that everyone likes is sometimes a joke that nobody loves. We can try to stretch our welcome across tribes as far as possible, but making *everyone* laugh is not a thing that most jokes are designed to do.

Even a silly cracker-joke pun only works if you speak the language, use the most commonly accepted accent, have a broad enough vocabulary, and maybe some cultural knowledge of the things to which the rhyming words of the pun refer. I once spoke to some lovely Swedes who told me that everyone in their homeland wonders quite what the joke is with *The Muppet Show*'s Swedish Chef because to them he's clearly speaking Finnish. Every dumb gag is a tribal token of exchange, bringing some people in closer and pushing other people away.*

In a sense, we make obscure jokes to check the credentials at the door of our party, to stop the 'wrong' people gatecrashing and possibly smashing our nice place up. The more obscure the joke, the more shared knowledge an outsider needs to bring with them in order to get in, and therefore the tighter and safer the tribe.

Jokes that use obscure references are saying, 'What's the password?' and I suspect that's a necessary part of what jokes are meant to do.

---

* In *Paddington 2*, there is a small but story-crucial joke that the treasure hunt appears to involve a hidden word, but the letter clues are actually revealing the notes of a piece of music. Very late in production, someone pointed out that musical notes only have letter names in English, while in other cultures, such as French, they are called by their sol-fa names. (Which was slightly awkward for a production being made for the French company StudioCanal.) A decision was made to plough ahead anyway, and hope that audiences in other countries had the cultural knowledge that English musical notation was different from their own. A simple gag, intended to draw children into the adventure, had inadvertently locked loads of them out.

28

The Specifics

If you'd told me in the late eighties that one day my local branch of Tandy would shut its doors to the public so that Alan Partridge could browse its electricals in peace, I'd have thought you were mad. If you'd told me that they would do this at the height of the Christmas shopping period, I'd probably have spat on your back.

I, *Partridge*
(written by Neil Gibbons, Rob Gibbons,
Armando Iannucci and Steve Coogan)

In art history, there is an appealing idea called the beholder's share, first proposed by Alois Riegl, and popularised by his disciple Ernst Gombrich. It is defined as 'That part of perceptual experience that is contributed by the perceiver and which is not to be found in the artwork or the world itself.' A vital part of enjoying art is adding some of ourselves. And in some cases, the more work we have to do, the more deeply engaged we become with the artwork, because we helped make it.

In comedy, your beholder's share explains that delightfully inclusive feeling of being allowed to 'get' a reference without it being explained, and it is one of the clues to comedy's social-bonding function. If a comedian slips one of these passing jokes into a comedy routine, a small subset of the audience will feel special that they worked it out, that this stuff is for them. A narrower laugh often goes deeper, because it provides social glue as well as the usual processing-engine workout.

The bargain of comprehensibility in comedy is the same as you'd find with any puzzle. You have to play fair, and have a feeling for what level of shared group knowledge the audience brings. As with the 'Anyone-in-from-Idaho' routine earlier, it's good manners to check that, if some of the audience do lack the common information to decode your references, you have at least given those people some clues. A reference to Shostakovich in a cartoon script for kids might work better if you ensure that the context makes clear he's a famous classical composer. Or you might judge that explaining the context will kill the social glue for the parts of the audience who do know who Shostakovich is, making them feel less part of your insider club. If you bite the bullet, strip out any clues and risk the line flying over a few heads, the reward can be a more potent reaction from its intended targets.

'MY, THAT IS SPECIFIC'

Working hard on scripts, especially with production notes coming thick and fast, you can get the mistaken idea that every joke needs to land or be cut. But, provided you put enough jokes in, people will enjoy a show where maybe only 50 per cent of your intended gags hit the whole audience. The hidden rule is that as long as your niche jokes land twice as hard with a narrow band of your audience, that audience is going to love you because they have been flattered and treated well. And a small audience that loves you might be more valuable than a large audience that doesn't mind you.

The portion of the audience who missed the reference

might not even notice they missed anything as long as a broader gag comes along pretty soon afterwards, letting them know they're not forgotten. I would point to *The Simpsons* and *Frasier* as wonderful examples of very funny, popular shows that are happy for a good slice of their jokes to be aimed solely at card-carrying members of small in-groups, because they also provide broad, bonding laughs for the wider audience. Everyone is happy, and a few people are ecstatic. That's as much as anyone could wish for.

The double whammy of puzzle solving and social bonding is where comedy is at its most effective, attacking our funny bone on two fronts. And the key feature of any joke that asks its audience to do some decoding work in return for tribal ownership is specificity. Most comedy-writing guides will tell you to use specific words rather than vague ones because that's funnier. Detail itself, the theory goes, makes your prose richer and more enjoyable.

I think this is because specificity gives the audience something to really chew on. Being made to assess the cultural weight of precise details allows an audience to flick through their library of shared information. Checking a passing reference to 'Leigh Delamere motorway services' or 'Simon Cowell's trousers' or 'Dubonnet' offers a killer combo of puzzle solving and tribal grooming, performing both of comedy's key functions at once.

SLINGBACKS

Take out the detail, and you boil out all the flavour. For example, imagine a sketch character who sits on a chair, centre stage, and addresses the camera.

> MRS CHARACTER: *Good evening. I have an interesting medical history and strong opinions on food. I don't*

> *know why I've been asked to come on television, but I*
> *became quite famous doing a charity walk in aid of a*
> *good cause. They've asked me to talk about various*
> *subjects, so I will.*

As a demonstration of how much our brains look for clues and tribal tokens, even with all the detail taken out, I suspect there's still almost enough data in there for a comedy fan to recognise who it is and be happy I've made a reference joke for us to enjoy. Feels nice, doesn't it?

Of course, it's the opening of Victoria Wood's first sketch for Patricia Routledge's menopausal force of nature, Kitty. Here's how it goes with the specifics reinstated.

> *KITTY: Good evening. My name's Kitty. I've had a*
> *boob off and I can't stomach whelks, so that's me for*
> *you. I don't know why I've been asked to interrupt*
> *your viewing like this, but I'm apparently something of*
> *a celebrity since I walked the Pennine Way in slingbacks*
> *in an attempt to publicise mental health. They've asked*
> *me to talk about aspects of life in general. Nuclear war.*
> *Peg bags.*

Victoria Wood, like similarly forensic observer of detail Alan Bennett, and her hero Joyce Grenfell, knew that it's the precision of each comic reference that makes writing sing. So instead of saying 'cat', you say 'Burmese shorthair' and leave the audience to work out you're talking about a cat. And instead of saying, 'I struggled to park my car at the supermarket,' you say, 'I left the Suzuki behind Morrisons entangled in a rusty cage of pallets, and I shall be raising the issue.' That's faux Kitty, of course. But even counterfeiting Victoria Wood's Kitty voice turns a string of information into a fun puzzle. And when your brain is dashing around trying to scavenge clues from all over, it's easier for the writer to trip it up, which increases the chances of taking you by surprise. And that is a good way to be funny.

Crucially, the harder it is to work out what's going on without bringing some knowledge from outside, the more comedy becomes a tribally targeted puzzle game that belongs completely to its intended audience.

A puzzle, plus a club. The essence of comedy.

29

These Robots Are Funny

Why should I want to make anything up? Life's bad enough as it is without wanting to invent any more of it.

Marvin, *The Hitchhiker's Guide to the Galaxy*
(written by Douglas Adams)

Specifics in a joke or routine act as lighthouses in fog. They are bright, and we look out for them. But someone without the correct codebook to decipher their flashes of light, lacking a map to help navigate using their locations, will still be lost. Maybe this baffled comic explorer was born in another country, or the wrong time. Maybe they don't share our political, social or tribal assumptions. In which case they are sunk, because we navigate comedy by the specifics. The less-important comic data between those bright points is dimmer, a sort of fog.

These bright lighthouses (with their accepted cultural weight and shared references) can even be used as a form of compressed notation. I'm not the only comedy writer who has made a quick note, maybe half asleep, or on the way to an appointment, of the bare minimum detail from which I can expand a full idea later. A whole sketch or an article or a scene might be noted down as 'pirate psychiatrist', 'canoeing funerals' or 'Welsh Batman'. One of the most successful sketches I've ever seen thrown onto a pile of submissions was Arthur Mathews' brilliant spoof vintage interview for Kevin Eldon's TV sketch show, whose pitch was three words long: 'Amish Sex Pistols'.

We used to call these ideas cut-and-shuts, like the second-hand cars built from welding two different wrecks together. Name the two or three specifics; that's enough. You can fill in the rest. The comedy happens in the gap between them, and that's where you have your fun as an expressive human. Crunching a comic idea down to its very smallest irreducible elements gives you a shorthand that resembles the way digital compression doesn't bother storing any bits of data that it can guess.

Which brings us to what robots have started telling us about comedy.

'SHE CAN'T DO FINGERS!'

The science-fiction author Ted Chiang (who wrote the story on which the film *Arrival* is based) is a writer fascinated by ideas of communication across different intelligences. Chiang published a great piece in *The New Yorker* about the rise of artificial intelligence writing tools such as ChatGPT. These bots seemed to be able to come up with accurately observed comic writing at huge speed, in response to human requests to, in Chiang's own example, 'Write an account of losing a sock in the style of the Declaration of Independence.'

What came out of machines in response to basic prompts like this seems almost indistinguishable from material you might find in *The Onion* or *Viz* or *Saturday Night Live* or *Monty Python*. It certainly feels like it might threaten the career of the professional comedy writer. But Chiang argued that bot comedy wasn't the creation of new material as much as the compression of existing culture. The results seemed familiar because the machine, like any human, was building new content out of an agreed set of cultural data (which we had specifically asked it to look at).

The bots take the sum total of human culture, as uploaded to the internet, grab the bits we've asked for and will recognise, and draw in convincing details to replace the fog between them. It's how data compression works, and what any computer does when it puts an image on the screen of our phone or tablet or laptop. The photo will usually have been compressed for easier storage, deleting the parts we probably won't notice are missing. When we ask for the image back, the machine has to take an informed guess as to what humans are likely to expect each missing block of the image to be, based on what it knows we usually expect to be there.

The illusion of comic invention in prompt-generated AI comedy writing had been created because the robo-writer seemed to be performing a basic comic move: surprise juxtaposition. But the machine wasn't really finding a comic angle, or engaging in an act of self-expression. *We'd* done that when we asked for a picture of Elton John doing a conga with some ninja ostriches, or whatever. The machine was simply lighting the cultural specifics brightly, and filling in the gaps with fog.

The illusion works because we wonder 'How does it know?' Surely only our tribe has the required cultural knowledge to make a hilarious Shirley Bassey song about West Bromwich Albion? But all this data has been provided by millions of us talking about those subjects (and every other subject) online for years. The jokes the bot makes from this huge set of shared data mean that the computer comedian passes as a human. It seems to be a member of our tribe, exchanging our tribal tokens to make us laugh. So we let it in. But that's because it has copied us.

But the bot is not a real human. We're not at a stage yet (maybe we never will be) where any of us would necessarily mistake the AI for our good friend Arthur Dent. But neither does this joking entity seem to be a machine that doesn't like or understand us, like hostile robot Marvin. It's more like Ford Prefect. A slightly annoying alien who's studied us enough to almost get away with pretending it's from Guildford by repeating jokes it's picked up about the one-way system.

The AI has no observations of human experience except what it gathers as a by-product, because these ideas and feelings are already embedded within the items in its library of human-curated material. It doesn't know that the Declaration of Independence is ponderous and important. But *we* do. And so we mistake our reflection in the screen for a human face.

The difference is that when a comedy writer takes an idea and spins out the implications, they are making something bigger out of a small idea. The computer is making something smaller out of a colossal amount of information, using our human prompt as a filter. It isn't creating at all. It is reducing. AI comedy is compression, not expansion.

But that an act of cultural data compression resembles comedy is a wonderful illustration of how comedy *is* actually an act of cultural data compression. We use jokes to signal to each other that we think alike, feel alike, belong together. And we do it by reference and allusion to a shared set of data.

What is astonishing is the way we are all fooled by the process. We don't notice that all the trees in the background of the picture the computer made for us are the same block of leaves repeated over and over again, because the important details – the cultural tokens, the shared values, the human faces, all the portions our eyes are drawn to – are so crisp.

Comedy is all about specifics, and AI-generated comedy works by nailing the specifics we ask for. And it does it uncannily well.

30

Shared Values

Comedy is very controlling – you are making people laugh.

Gilda Radner

One of the problems with making comedy in recent years has been a weakening of consensus reality. Because comedy is tribal, we need to be able to assume some sort of unity on the very basics before we can start to make jokes. Confirm gags and Confound gags don't work until you have Constructed a firm structure to bounce them off, and you can't Construct anything on shaky ground. And as our culture and politics fractures and polarises (for reasons too fiddly, insidious and annoying to go into here), it can be hard to establish your foundations. People start tutting before the first brick goes down. 'No. Not there. No. I don't think so.'

As the experienced radio producer Ed Morrish once said to me, 'Audiences used to disagree with the punchlines. Now they disagree with the set-up.'

In the 1980s, the mainstream topical TV puppet satire show *Spitting Image* could be sure that its audience, regardless of their politics, would accept that the Conservative Prime Minister Margaret Thatcher had what might be seen as a strident, no-nonsense style. The team could lampoon that in sketches, depicting her as a sort of

Nanny-knows-best vulture creature. But in recent years, comparatively toothless routines, depicting political figures in ways that probably even their mothers would say were fair enough, have raised furious online and press objections. And the objections were not about the jokes in them, but about the basic depictions of their subjects.

Because groups reject their opponent's depiction of them before they can even get to the jokes, sometimes the most effective satire can only happen when you disguise yourself as your enemy. Satire in a time of fractured consensus works best when attacking from within, exaggerating a fixed position to the point of absurdity, in the way that Jonathan Swift's anonymously published *A Modest Proposal* (1729) argued that the potato-famine-struck Irish should efficiently turn to eating their own children.

This technique of turning up to the debate dressed as the opposition is the same one that Stephen Colbert and *The Onion* employ to swipe at American conservatives. When your starting assumptions belong to the tribe you wish to expose rather than your own, you momentarily speak the same language, so you might get as far as a joke before being thrown out of the tribal joking circle. It's certainly true that in any political argument, your opponent has a better chance of hearing you if you use their agreed terms. Sticking stubbornly to your own set of rules to debate someone who doesn't share them is merely polemic, the political equivalent of shouting at a Portuguese waiter in English, increasingly loudly, and then becoming exasperated when they bring you the wrong omelette.

This issue of negotiating split consensus between different tribes is also why it's tricky to book comedy-panel or multi-act line-ups with a breadth of political views, despite good intentions. Each comic is playing to a separate tribe within the room, building jokes using a different toolkit of assumptions, and therefore the audience cannot be united in laughter. A comic relying on a set-up that they themselves accept, but the majority of the audience doesn't, won't get as far as their well-crafted punchline before the laugh jams in the breech of the comedy gun and blows up in their face.

This isn't a shortcoming of comedy, or a glitch. It's what comedy is partly for. Humans are social creatures who use jokes that rely on unspoken agreements to ensure that our groups are united, strong and stable. If the consensus splits, the tribe splits, using comedy as a tribal marker.

THE TRIBAL FIRE

To understand comedy's power as a social-bonding process, we should go back to where all this came from: a primate-grooming activity that unites social groups. Imagine jokes are little bits of kindling and we are hairy cave people, at night, in the wilderness, gathered round a fire. The fire is full of our shared observations.

Aren't these new mammoths smaller than the ones we had as kids? What's the deal with hunting party food? Cave people from the tribe of Og be all like this, but us lot from the tribe of Ug be more like this.

We gather round the warming flicker of the stuff we agree is funny, our faces lit by the glow of consensus. We occasionally find a new bit of comedy kindling that everyone agrees with. We toss it on, and we all chuckle, draw closer and say that was a good one. Nice and cosy.

Our little fire full of observations and shared jokes draws us closer, because it marks where we can all sit safely together in the vast darkness. It's our fire. Maybe, way off on the horizon, we can see another tribe's fire, belonging to those idiots from the tribe of Og. You know them? With their lunatic ideas about flint. We don't go over there and gather round their fire because it's not ours. Our fire is over here, where our values are, where we live, and its exact location, and the sort of kindling we agree burns well, marks us apart from the wild and different tribes who live in the darkness beyond. It's safe here because the fire has drawn us together, and so we have strength in numbers.

If we want to, we can take a spark, stroll off a little way and light a little joke fire further away from the middle. We might even want to light it way over there, right at the safe boundary of the group. That isolated flame, a long way from the central fire where we burn fairly safe tribal observations like 'sabre-tooth cats are different from wild dogs', might be an outlier observation that not all of us are willing to agree with. But importantly, it still acts as a tribal marker, letting all of us know how far we can assume consensus and still stay together as a group.

But the little fire of a comic idea placed on the very edge of our safe campfire has a risk attached: that if the rest of the tribe thinks it is an inch too far outside our safe clearing then it doesn't belong to us. A joke put here might make us mistrustful of the person making it, pushing them towards the heathens in the darkness who would find such a joke acceptable.

And if one of us round the fire agrees with the person who lit the comic fire all the way over there, and nobody else in our tribe does, maybe that person and the distant fire-lighting guy don't belong in the tribe's circle of safety, and they should strike out in search of another tribe.

When we light a little joke fire at the limit of taboo, there is the danger of rejection by the tribe, but also, significantly, there is a useful definition of who we are. In this way, what we choose to define as 'too far from the consensus' is a marker of our own tribal identity.

If the history of comedy is anything to go by, plenty of restless comedy types will always be looking to pull away from the lovely big fire in the middle, to stroll off and try lighting some fires a bit outside the circle, to light up more of the darkness and work out how far away from the middle we all agree is too far. Because it's a question that gives us some useful answers that can bond the group even more closely.

It's not a mistake to push boundaries: it's what comedy does as part of its essential tribal function.

31

Reading the Room

And that's another thing they don't like at the airport. Jokes. You can't joke about a bomb. Well, why is it just jokes? What about a riddle? How about a limerick? How about a bomb anecdote? You know, no punchline, just a really cute story.

George Carlin

Jokes designed for larger audiences naturally require more universal references. The sort of comedians who play colossal arenas tailor their material to please the crowd, and a character-based sitcom that plays on a mainstream broadcast channel needs to target its jokes to a wider audience than an online sketch or a cult podcast.

Watching stadium stand-ups, it can be tempting to hear their calls to the widest consensus as the sounding of a gigantic tribal alpine horn. 'Come all, from the far edges of the land, and gather to talk of the funny things kids say.' These acts rely on the power of shared reference: we've all been to a wedding, we've all seen kids bored in shops, most of us have a house full of useless crap in drawers. Comics point out what unites us, and that it looks stupid when held up to the light. It's a solid reading of the room.

Of course, the worst sort of hack arena stand-up act, buoyed by the positive response to 'Who's been on a hen do?' and 'Who remembers them Screwball ice creams?', can quickly slide towards 'Who here has got a head?' and get a stadium full of enthusiastic nodding from all the head owners in the crowd. 'I *have* got a head! He's right. Isn't he good?' But simple affirmative recognition humour is what we have comedy for at its most basic level, and it can reinforce audience bonds in a powerful and human way. Sure, specifics and cult references, and niche gags and in-jokes are deep comedy, but stuff we agree to laugh at in really large crowds can be the warmest, biggest tribal fire of all.

It's why we feel such affection for classic shows that turn up on lists of the most-watched TV of all time or why there are few nicer places to be than a huge theatre, rolling with laughter at a great stand-up who's nailed what we all have in common. It would be a dreadful curmudgeon who'd deny that the feeling of community is positive and life-affirming. A large crowd laughing in unison at its own idiocy is certainly a more benign reason to set up a PA system in an aircraft hangar than getting a crowd to bay its common desire to lock up Hillary Clinton or invade Poland.

Even if they're not starting a war with efficient crowd work, comedians have their own home turf, defined by the tribal tokens of exchange within their acts, and declarations of what 'we're like, us', compared to them over there. I've heard lovely explanations from hard-touring comics of how the various acts carve up the country: who 'owns' what region, the lines of agreed dominance drawn as distinctly as generals dividing up territory after a war. 'Michael McIntyre has everything round the M25... That's a given...'

Comedy that unites big crowds is about guessing what people will want, what their self-definition is. But it's not just hitting the major shared references and local detail that goes well in a big room. Plain absurdity is surprisingly uniting. Surreal stand-ups do well in large spaces, just as deliberately unrealistic, daft sitcoms often get a warm response from a big audience. A liberating lack of any shared references at all can be as uniting as a broad agreement on them, and unlike regional comics who lord it up on their home turf, a weirdo who doesn't belong anywhere can play everywhere. A Harry Hill nonsense routine can unite a big arena, and as long as Bill Bailey explains to his extremely mixed audience roughly who Kraftwerk are, the incongruity of the Düsseldorf pop-technologists doing the Hokey Cokey will bring the house down.

In these situations of freewheeling nonsense, provided we trust the comic's judgement, we all belong to the same tribe, and its only territory is this room. It's why silly comedy can bring people together who don't agree on anything else, and also why, if you don't trust the comedian, silly comedy can be divisive. 'I'm sorry, I just don't find them funny.' Fair enough. That was all that was required to join in, and there's nothing else to hang on to.

THE WORLD'S MOST AWKWARD PUB CHATS

The persuasive sound of communal laughter can help unite a theatre full of diverse individuals, but in a digital or virtual space, it becomes difficult even for the most expert joke maker to read a room. Online, you simply cannot know who is listening. We have evolved to sit in small groups, sharing stuff we like and giggling. Just as the lemur is designed to live in a tree, *Homo jokensis* is designed, I believe, for pub tables. In fact, the pub table may be one of our peak innovations, evolutionarily. (I don't know. I'm not an anthropologist. But I have been down the pub.)

But for the first time in human history, a ridiculous number of us have access to a colossal, noisy, indiscriminate method of distributing whatever we think is funny. We're used to cracking up four close mates over a bag of dry-roasted peanuts, but suddenly social media means anything we say could be bellowed from a Tannoy mounted in the belly of a spacecraft, and preceded by the phrase, 'PEOPLE OF EARTH. . .'

In terms of high-risk rooms to read, 'the whole of online space' is near the top. Although most of us only have a small audience online, you cannot ring-fence or even guess at the size or demographics of your crowd. It could, potentially, contain everybody who has access to the social media platform, and it's unlikely that every single one will share the required tribal assumptions.

So the imaginary pub table in which you are sharing your jokes now has a cloth over it, down to the floor, and who knows who might be lurking under there. You can see your friends sitting with you. So you judge your crowd, and share a joke. The joke relies on you all thinking ABBA are a terrible, cheesy band. (I don't want to hang out with you guys, by the way, but that's another matter.) You all laugh. The tablecloth twitches. And out pops Benny Andersson of ABBA, very upset. You've hurt his feelings. He's quite nice about it, but you feel terrible. You didn't know he was there. You wouldn't have done the shitty ABBA gag if you'd known that under your table, where you can't see, was somebody perfectly nice who might take the gag personally.

You tried to read the room, as humans have always done when attempting an act of social grooming, but you couldn't see all of it.

Comedian and actor Bob Odenkirk (star of *Mr. Show* and *Better Call Saul*) said in an interview with the *Guardian* that he had developed a 'wedding-table theory': that thanks to the free distribution of material over the internet, we are all now sharing a table with strangers and acquaintances who might not be immediately open to our jokes. This audience does not know our background, our intentions, who we are, where our limits are, and we don't know theirs. 'These things are meant to be seen in a context,' Odenkirk said, 'at a place. But the context is gone, or it's so easily erased or shifted. And it's a real problem.'

And that's where we find ourselves. And it naturally leads to a sense that you have to take everyone's feelings into consideration all the time, which can be terribly exhausting. But that's just a function of playing a very big, almost infinite room. It's hard to read a room when you can barely see the edges of it.

GUESSING GAMES

A person who can imagine what someone else might find amusing, and uses that to adjust their material, is employing something which psychologists call 'theory of mind' – understanding that others' thoughts and feelings might be different from your own. It's a basic human cognitive tool that is fundamental to how comedy works, and we'll examine it in more detail later (in Chapter 39 'Confirmation Bias'). But failing to intuit an audience reaction is what goes wrong when a joke falls flat. 'Bit obscure for you?' says the comic, cleverly shifting the blame to the audience, and moves on by adjusting their unconscious calibration of the audience's mind from high- to low-brow, and doing more fart gags.

Everybody wins.

If you can pull off a room-reading successfully, and deliver appropriate material, you perform a service: you make people around you happy. People who can engage at this sophisticated level to please others will be valued in society. They might get the protection of the group's silverbacks – even if the weedy room-readers themselves have bad cardigans, glasses, can't throw mammoth spears, and keep reciting obscure lines from old comedy shows. The astute room-analysts in the tribe will be kept around, like court jesters, protected by the muscly spear-throwing types. They may then live beyond their normal survival expectations and leave more descendants, passing on those good room-reading genes (and those terrible ones for short-sightedness).

And so we as a species will naturally evolve to become funnier – to read the room better – and more comedy writers will have glasses and bad posture than even seems possible.

I'm simplifying, but evolutionary advantage is a real thing, finessed beyond simple 'the strong survive' fascism by the human habit of gathering in tribes and finding uses for one another, even the ones who are just really good at armpit farts. Maybe this is where all those comedians come from: a long line of ape-creatures who could guess what another ape-creature was thinking, and use that knowledge to make them laugh and feel better.

32

Dangerous Laughs

Basically, for a Netflix comedy special, you've got to get all the things that you can't say, because of political-correctness-gone-mad and the woke brigade. And you put them all together. And you say them. And you find that you can say them after all.

Stewart Lee

I'm aware that this is a contentious area but I'm happy to wade into it. Because comedy's about saying the unsayable. Apparently. Comedy is about danger, I hear. And this is a book about comedy. So, I'm going to say it.

I don't think comedy is about danger at all.

Hear me out.

For me, the biggest issue with saying that every joke has a victim, or that comedy is about saying the unsayable, or that good comedy is always dangerous, or that the purpose of comedy is to take down the powerful, is that the idea is not supported by comedy's only unique and common observable features – laughter and amusement – being triggered not by danger but by its polar opposite: relief.

Comedy *can* put you in danger, of course. A joke might flag you up as belonging to one tribe and get you in trouble with another. And if that other tribe is a dictatorship with guns or a group of ideological maniacs with bombs, and it turns out they're desperately frightened of humiliation or losing status, then telling a joke can be *really* dangerous. But what's dangerous is tribalism and dictators and maniacs and guns and bombs and fear and humiliation and status. Not jokes.

JOKING ASIDE

Yes, a joke can be a tool to express dangerous ideas. But those same thoughts could be expressed by spray painting them on the side of a tank, or screaming them while charging a row of riot shields, with no comic content at all. Jokes can reflect and reinforce tribal division, but they're not where tribal division comes from. Used clumsily, a joke can make a bad situation worse, but humour is a way to help deal with a load of dangerous garbage that already exists. It's not the source of it.

If comedy and laughter are social, play-related behaviours that humans developed to replace physical grooming, then laughing is nothing to do with danger, and everything to do with danger *having passed*. It's the art form that says 'phew!' If you're talking about edge and terror and tension and danger, that's. . . you know, the other stuff. Horror stories. Thrillers. Motorsport. War.

In fact, I think that any definition or defence of comedy as 'dangerous' fundamentally misunderstands how comedy works.

DANGEROUS COMEDY

If danger made us laugh, we'd be recording sitcoms in a burning building to get the really good stuff. '*Cheers* is filmed before a traumatised studio audience. . .' And since this is a chapter on dangerous comedy, at this point I'm obviously going to have to bring in Penelope Wilton.

At an event celebrating the life of sitcom master Richard Briers, Penelope Wilton recalled how wonderful the rehearsals were for *Ever Decreasing Circles*. Every joke landed, the cast members were all in stitches. But Sunday was recording day, and as the hour approached, this team of experienced comic actors would start to get nervous. And the laughter would stop. Anxiety would reach levels where Briers would often be physically sick. But the performers were all aware that the show's comedy – which they knew was good – would fail completely if their own anxiety spread to the audience. The cast had to work out a way to seem confident. There would be no laughs, Wilton said, if they didn't somehow make the audience feel *safe*.

It's a trick every nervous novice stand-up has to master. How not to transmit your own nerves and spook the herd. Lovely Penelope Wilton, Peter Egan and Richard Briers, in a sitcom whose very soul was knitted from matching cardigan wool, had somehow let danger in. The seasoned performers knew they had to keep that danger outside the room, as if they were exorcising a terrible demon of unplayfulness, or nobody would laugh.

Of course, you might say, that's all OK if you're talking about a fairly cosy middle-class comedy.* Of course a suburban Richard Briers sitcom – or a single-panel observational cartoon about cat behaviour, or a witty pastiche song, or a knock-knock joke for children – isn't about danger.

But what about truly dangerous comedy? How about the laughs that come when we aren't comfortable?

So, let's look at the exceptions. . . The eight most dangerous jokes in the world.

---

* Which *Ever Decreasing Circles* cleverly both is and isn't, of course.

THE COMEDY OF DANGER

Dangerous Joke 1: Speaking Truth to Power

There is no denying the bravery of comics and satirists who challenge regimes and push boundaries in dangerous places. Ridicule against humourless people with too much power is usually categorised as a threat, and responded to accordingly. It can get extremely serious.

This is the very definition of 'dangerous comedy'.

But the dangerous element isn't the joke. The comedian's daring doesn't make us laugh; it makes us gasp.* We laugh, as we always laugh, with relief, that the challenge has taken place at all. The impossible act isn't the funny bit. What's funny is the relief that it was possible.

For high-ranking tribe members, a joke that threatens to overturn an established hierarchy will be felt as a threat, although the joke has the opposite intention. It is meant to *neutralise* threat, specifically the danger of excess power exerted against the rest of the tribe. The danger is not the joke – which is merely demanding safe space for expression. The danger is that joking might have to stop.

If the joke does its job of building a bubble of safety, the comic temporarily becomes the king or queen, a Lord or Lady of Misrule leading a tribe of like-minded people, drawn to the joke. We laugh at these jokes for social bonding reasons, to reassure the brave joker that they are not alone, that there are many of us, that we agree. Our laugh indicates safety, that our tribe is strong, and that the oppressor does not frighten us, even for a fleeting moment. 'Thank you for making us all less scared,' the laugh says.

Because we laugh when we feel safe.

---

* Unless it's a nervous laugh (see later).

Dangerous Joke 2: Taboo-Busting

This is what most comedians who are not working under actual dictatorships mean by 'dangerous comedy'. And, in common with speaking truth to power, when someone crosses a prohibited line of socially sanctioned behaviour, and flouts a restriction with which we don't agree, we are watching an act of daring. The warning that we must never go beyond this point *here* was stupid, and the brave jester ignored it. But we don't laugh at them running for the barbed wire and jumping. Again, that bit makes us gasp, because it's scary. ('What if the taboo was there for a reason? What if something awful happens?') We laugh when the comedian lands happily on the other side and dances about, proving that the sign saying 'Beware of the Leopard' was just meant to scare us off.

Because we laugh when we feel safe.

Dangerous Joke 3: Gallows Humour

Dark comedy is the comfort in hard times of the shat-upon. Huddling in bomb shelters and refugee camps, frazzled on tours of duty, grinding through long emergency-ward shifts, countless tense, threatened, exhausted groups use dark jokes to get through. But, again, this sort of comedy is a way of conjuring a feeling of safety out of danger, to neutralise the fear. It's a joke anaesthetic, a rousing camp-fire song in the terrifying dark.

Joking in the face of the awful helps bond and reduce isolation, strengthens resilience and reduces stress. It's a secular ritual to raise group morale. In the middle of the terror, we suddenly hear a sound that we usually only share when we are not under threat – laughter, jokes – and thus the whole group receives a reinforcing signal that they might just be OK. It's a magical act, conjuring a defensive bubble of safety against the fear. There is danger outside, but the group feels momentarily safe because they are laughing.

Because we laugh when we feel safe.

Dangerous Joke 4: Nervous Laughter

This is a version of gallows humour which uses fake laughter as a signal that we hope will be contagious and turn into the real thing. When we are anxious, we don't feel safe, but we try a laugh. Of course, we can't *really* laugh when we're tense, so it's not one that sounds like any normal laugh. But we make the noise and cross our fingers that someone else will join in. It's a message in a bottle, dropped into a frightening sea, in the forlorn hope that there's someone out there who'll send one back, and we'll know we're not alone.

You know the laugh. It sounds like the punctured squeak of a savaged dog-toy. It's the affirmation-seeking half-laugh David Brent in *The Office* sends out alongside every ill-judged gag, as a way of checking he isn't in trouble for it ('which he might be, cos, tsk, God knows these days, how can you even keep up?'). Nervous laughter is a seed-laugh sent out in the hope it will receive a genuine laugh in response, which will then spread more naturally. 'There's that sound humans make when we feel safe! So how can we be in danger?' We agree, and now we're all a gang again. Which feels nice. 'It was all a joke, yeah?' No harm done.

Because we laugh when we feel safe.

Dangerous Joke 5: Misplaced Laughter

This is a laugh that just occurs at the wrong time. Maybe you're in a subservient position, and a dominant member of the group – a teacher, a stern relative, the big boss from head office – has done something ridiculous. Sir Bernard

Business has slipped and fallen down a manhole. It's a classic! (Aristotle would have pissed himself.) And you can't hold it in, so you laugh.

Then, as Sir Bernard climbs back to the surface, covered in gunge and poo, his brows beetle and he bellows, 'Medford!' And if you're Medford, you know trouble is afoot. A sense of danger stops the laugh in your throat. But you laughed before because ridiculousness had robbed the dominant person of their power for a moment. Maybe you thought everybody would join in. But you were wrong. And you can't laugh now, can you?

Because we laugh when we feel safe.

Dangerous Joke 6: Superiority Laughter

The dominance laughter of a villain at the moment of victory, when all is lost for the hero, can seem mirthless and cruel. It doesn't seem warm or inclusive or bonding. It's hostile, thin and nasty. If some dangerous laughter is us enjoying the court jester taunting the king with a bladder on a stick, then superiority laughter is the laugh of the king later, as the jester's head plops into the executioner's basket.

Superiority laughter certainly doesn't arise from the usual affirmative and inclusive group impulses that we might expect to cause comedy. It asserts dominance, and indicates that a situation that is threatening for the victim is merely a game for the bad guy. It's a play signal, maybe to the villain's followers that they have won and that nothing threatens them now.

Because we laugh when we feel safe.

Dangerous Joke 7: Bullying Laughter

This is the laughter of a group rejecting an outsider. The laugh reinforces the idea that this sort of person would never be allowed in. The bonding laughter asserts the group's values, and so the group is now stronger, more happily self-identified, and therefore safer. We all agree those weird people over there are. . . well. . . weird. And everyone laughs, because that feels safe.

If the target is someone *within* the group who has deviated and marked themselves out as fit for ridicule, bullying laughter is the mockery that they don't actually feel they can laugh at. It's the nickname they don't like, the joke they go home and cry about, the prank that provokes them to whine, 'Oh, leave it out, guys.' It's the laugh that happens when prolonged teasing within the group hurts so much that someone dares to place themselves outside the safety of their declared group and reject the invitation to laugh. The victim says, 'That isn't funny. I didn't like it.' Because they feel unsafe, and show it by not laughing, they stand outside the group.

The remaining group then laughs, because the group is stronger and more homogeneous now, without their values and assumptions being questioned. The group heals over the hole, seals itself, and the departing victim hears the laughter behind them as they go.

Because we laugh when we feel safe.

Which brings us to the big one. . .

33

Only Teasing

It takes a big man to cry, but it takes a bigger man to laugh at that man.

Jack Handey

We've yet to cover the aggressive comic voice that is most common in our everyday lives: teasing. Mockery of others could be seen as the primal joke, the one Aristotle spotted first and the foundation of superiority theory. Teasing feels barbed, maybe dangerous, and certainly doesn't feel soothing or affirmative when we are on the receiving end. So, how does it soothe and affirm and bond? How can picking at someone's insecurities and humiliating them be a social act of calming and soothing?

Dangerous Joke 8: Teasing Laughter

We test each other within our own social groups some-times by mocking each other and laughing, which bonds us together. Hardening ourselves to this habit at school (or even in our own families) is seen as good preparation for other social situations (work, say) where teasing may be commonplace.

Highly stressed groups often use teasing laughter as a bonding tool. Just look at the nicknames that develop in the military and emergency services, all those gangs of

Taffs (Welsh), Jocks (Scots) and Bambis (crybabies). Nicknames are part of this process of teasing laughter, often
tagging members' identities to witnessed moments of
shame, physical characteristics or geographical identity.
Members are deliberately 'othered', and then welcomed,
despite their 'deviance' from a notional ideal, back into
the group, and offered safety (with the exchange of a
laugh) in return for accepting their given tag.

Teasing jokes may feel barbed or dangerous, but they
are meant in fun, to show we are a gang who can 'take the
piss out of each other' and 'handle a joke'. Nicknames,
mockery and running jokes like this are a test of belonging, a sort of ongoing initiation ceremony. But as we've
seen in animals, dominance does not tend to be accompanied by mutual laughter. The victims and practitioners
of seriously intended dominance behaviours do not laugh
along while they are in the state of high alert associated
with status disputes.

Laughter in teasing situations, again, only accompan-
ies relief, and the realisation that there is no ongoing
threat.

So, teasing creates two sorts of laughter. Firstly, the
superiority laugh of the person doing the mockery, whose
aggression has safely achieved its objective of establishing
a pecking order with them on top. Secondly, there is the
relief laugh of the mocked person, when they are told that
'no harm was meant' (so they can turn off their red threat
light). The victim's acceptance of the mockery cements
their own position in the group, that they're 'a good
laugh'. And being within the group increases their feeling
of safety, so they laugh. Both the dominance laugh of the
mocker and the relief laugh of the mocked are actually
safety laughs.

THAT HURT

The mocked person may still feel hurt. The laugh they offer may be a nervous laugh, to try to generate a feeling of safety ('We're all still friends, right?'). Alternatively, it might be a socially cued laugh, because everyone else is laughing, and it feels safer to be inside the group than outside it. We all learned as children the social consequences of responding to mockery by saying, 'That hurt,' or, 'That's not funny.' If it's not funny, it's dangerous, and that really wrecks the laughter. Marking ourselves as a killjoy, not sharing the group's values, places us in a position outside the tribe, without its protection. That's not a safe place. No wonder we can't laugh. But if we don't feel that we *want* to be safe within this group any more, because they have hurt us and don't share our values, then we reject the offer of the laugh.

Laughing at being teased shows that someone 'knows their place'. It says that others have noticed our flaws, weaknesses, differences, and accepted us despite not quite fitting some ideal template. So we feel safe, and we laugh.

This was the defence usually offered by old-school comic Bernard Manning, that he mocked everyone equally, and his teasing of the socially marginalised alongside the rest of his audience was a way of accepting them as part of society. It's an argument still heard today from comics who employ aggressive mockery as part of their comedy (such as Matt Stone and Trey Parker from *South Park*). Equal-opportunity mockery bonds the wider tribe together, because we can laugh about how we're all weird and daft and don't fit, in our own ways.

But one of the things about nicknames is that you don't get to choose your own (as George Costanza discovered in *Seinfeld* when he independently declared himself 'T-Bone' and failed to make it stick). The decision to categorise and define someone by their deviation from an agreed norm comes from the top. Someone else decides on the type of mockery appropriate for your perceived deviation, whether it's a dominant individual or the prevailing norms of society. And that's usually a big giveaway. The joke reveals the process of exclusion, even in the cause of inclusion within the group.

People are welcomed in by accepting that they will never really be on top. The laugh asserts safety and declares no challenge will be offered to the agreed terms. For example, the way that soldiers with the nickname 'Alphabet' are members of the platoon whose foreign name the others can't pronounce or spell. Nobody in a *Battle Picture Weekly* comic-strip platoon of misfits was nicknamed 'White Heterosexual English Man'. Accepting a nickname is an act of subservience, and giving it an act of dominance, both of which involve threat and danger.

Neither of those acts are funny. But we laugh to say that this is just play, because the act of dominance has passed and been accepted.

IN THE CLUB

Groucho Marx once sent back his unused membership to a sports club, saying, 'I'd never belong to a club that would have me as a member.' Thanks perhaps to its deployment in the opening monologue of Woody Allen's *Annie Hall*, the gag reads now as an angsty self-deprecation zinger, but its historical tribal edge has been lost. Snobby, racist golf clubs used to refuse membership to Jewish applicants. So, when Groucho jokes that he'd not want to belong to a club that would let him in, he is nodding to what anti-Semites would see as his membership of an institution crappy enough not to care that Jewish people like

Groucho are on the fairway. Groucho leaves the club because he wants to join the elite, a tribe that hates him and won't let him in.* I mean, it's an *incandescently* good joke.

Groucho wins because he's turned the weight of his oppression against his oppressor, and got a laugh, to show he's cleverer than them. It's a pure Jewish joke about power, like something from Ernst Lubitsch's *To Be or Not to Be*. Plus, Groucho's a major star; tearing his membership up is a loss to the club. That's a Judaeo-judo throw and a half, against antisemitic admissions policies that clearly aren't enough of an issue any longer to keep him out of the nice club rooms.

And so we can all laugh because we're all OK, because even the Jewish guy doesn't really mind. Listen, he's laughing.

Because – and I can't say this often enough – we laugh when we feel safe.

---

* Groucho was a member of the Hillcrest, the more inclusive Hollywood golf club founded so that Jewish stars and moguls would have somewhere to play. When a different club said it would be prepared to waive its rules to allow in the famous Marx family, provided they didn't use the pool, Groucho replied, 'My daughter's only half-Jewish. Can she wade up to her knees?'

34

Comic Relief

Comedy is about confidence, and the moment an audience senses a slip in confidence, they're nervous for you and they can't laugh.

Tina Fey

To me, what all the examples of dangerous or discomforting comedy demonstrate is that the parts of a joke or a comic idea that feel dangerous are not the comic part. The only element in a comic idea that belongs entirely to comedy is the crucial moment of relief, the green light.

In some comedy, the joke element might be surrounded by bad stuff, but comedy is the good part that exorcises it and makes us feel safe. Aggression, violence, exclusion, fear, anxiety, tension, othering, bullying, spite, self-aggrandisement, stereotyping, cruelty, even sociopathy, are all things that can be the *seed* of a comic idea. Incorporating them within a joke can even increase the tension and expectation that builds before the comic moment. Though ramping up the tension is not exclusively comic; it's something you can do in loads of places, from dance music to pretending you're about to throw a stick for a dog. But all the tension, aggression and stress are not the *comedy* part of the comedy. They're just regular old tension, aggression and stress.

The bullying portion of a bullying joke isn't about

comedy, it's about bullying. The nervous part of a nervous laugh is about anxiety. The superiority part of superiority jokes is about dominance. A joke that ejects someone from a group isn't funny because the person got ejected, it's funny because the rest of us in the gang agree we're stronger now, and so we feel safe. A joke that relies on beating an oppressor or breaking a taboo makes us laugh because it makes us feel brave and hopeful. It's the getting away with it that raises the laugh.

Associating comedy with danger is like looking anxiously down the list of active ingredients of a viciously chemical-looking medicine, and obsessing about the health implications of the spoonful of sugar it contains.

The sugar's not the problem. That's the bit that makes the nasty stuff easier to bear.

DON'T HUG ME, I'M SCARED

Comedians who insist comedy must always have a victim, an edge, a right to offend, a suspension of normal social rules, a need for anarchy, a set of special permissions to harm or to seem to harm, that sense of *danger*. . . they are only talking about the tension-building part of a much larger process. And, crucially, the tension is not the part that belongs uniquely to comedy.

It's like insisting that all theatre is about ice cream, because we might get a tub of ice cream at the interval. 'Ah, of course; the reason I am so fat is that I love the theatre so. And theatre, as we all know, is all about ice cream. You simply cannot have theatre without ice cream.' But you can skip the ice cream at the interval if you like. And ice cream is available elsewhere. The defining feature that makes theatre 'theatre' is not the ice cream.

These dangerous elements, the bits of the joke that are not the comedy bit, can make the comedy feel amazing, of course. That's because they ramp up the tension and anticipation before the release, like a rollercoaster climbing high before an exhilarating drop. But the comedy is in the *whee!* of the drop, not the tension of the climb.

Because the tension of the climb is everywhere, and the release of the laugh is *only* in comedy.

Maybe you're frightened and want to express that. Or you're angry and want others to feel your rage. Perhaps you're upset at some injustice. Maybe you feel threatened. It could be that you want to put someone in their place or reduce their power. You might simply want to make someone else feel bad, or unwelcome, to push them away from you.

Those emotions and intentions could all be contained within a funny idea that uses comedy to get the message across. But they could also all be contained in a serious essay, a curse, a social media post, a noisy outburst in the street, a short radio play, a manifesto nailed to a church door, a score-settling diss-single, a furious email to those responsible, a passive-aggressive Post-it note, or an infuriated ballet. The medium is not the message.

COMEDY IS THE NEW SOFT FURNISHINGS

Ever since comedy became 'the new rock and roll' (presumably because both attract artists who enjoy the reliability of Shure SM58 stage microphones and the hotplate balm of motorway food), there's been an attempt to market comedy as dangerous. But no matter how cool Bill Hicks looked with a cigarette, comedy and danger only go together in that one is the antidote to the other.

There's an unquestionably rock-and-roll moment in the TV show *Hacks*, about an old-school stand-up, played by Jean Smart, trying to reinvent her career in the modern world. In one episode, Smart's character Deborah Vance has been booked outside her usual Las Vegas comfort zone, at a spit-and-sawdust circuit joint. The venue's younger-than-her male compère, whom she has accepted as dominant in his own space, is seen offering one of the young female comics in the green room stage time in exchange for sexual favours. There is a weariness in Vance's eyes; she lived within this seedy world for decades and took its iniquities on the chin – it's the business. But Vance takes the stage and, instead of doing her usual sure-fire gags, she singles out the host as he sits in the audience, and lets him have it. It's aggressive. A dominance game.

And, sure enough, the crowd don't laugh.

It's authentic and we recognise the truth of it. We might giggle at her cojones, safely watching at home. But it's realistic that nobody in that comedy club would laugh at Vance's aggression towards the compère. Because there is danger. 'This guy was in charge. We were his tribe. What are the rules now? Are we allowed to laugh?'

Then, skilfully, Vance rearranges the room into a new tribe. It's a primal challenge for control, a pair of silver-backs circling. Then the guy backs down. Vance has the room. She has changed their accepted values. And sure enough, the tribe eject the outsider. Then, and only then, do they actually laugh. While there was danger, there was no laughter. As soon as the danger passed, and the tribe knew they were safe, the room erupted. It's a beautifully observed study, from comedy professionals, of the way that comedy exists at the moment of safety.

Otherwise the confrontation had the same tension as it would have done had the pair drawn flick-knives.

Comedy happens when we are safe. And danger stops us laughing.

When a person is said to 'laugh in the face of danger', we don't imagine them responding to danger by anxiously muttering, 'Shit, this is serious, I'm in terrible trouble, oh God oh God oh God oh God,' as their fight-or-flight response goads them into nervous action, while also some-how laughing at the same time. No, we imagine them airily *dismissing* the danger by laughing, to show they don't feel it at all. It's impossible to laugh properly while convinced that we are actually in danger. But we can use laughter as a way to make the danger feel *not* like danger.

Laughing in the face of danger renders that danger safe. We are only ever really laughing in the face of safety.

35

Woke Me Up Before You Go Go

You can't joke about anything any more.

Trad. Arr. Various pricks

One of the most contentious debates currently raging in comedy is what we supposedly can and cannot say. As I discussed earlier, the exponential broadening of potential audience size in the digital age hasn't helped. Share a joke on Twitter and the whole world can hear, whether or not they are your intended audience, with all the necessary context and references to hand. But it's also been made more incendiary by conversations about inclusion and exclusion within culture as a whole. Even if a joke is meant to bond a very specific group of people together, representatives from groups excluded from the joke (whether accidentally or aggressively) can easily hear it. And that means that they might be hurt by it.

It's worse if the excluded group has a very small voice, and you have a larger one (they might even be able to see the follower numbers next to your name). If they feel that your more dominant voice might normalise or encourage behaviour that could make their lives more difficult, that's a straight threat, so they're not going to laugh. This now-twitchy outsider group can also share the joke quickly amongst themselves in a way that, say, mothers-in-law didn't during the old working-men's club comic days when they were being picked on. The threatened group can take the bit that scared them out of context. They can say 'this isn't funny', and when other people watch it, *woah!*, it certainly doesn't seem so. And then all hell breaks loose and, would you believe it, you can't say anything any more.

PUNCHING UP AND DOWN

The defence from comedians is usually that they must be allowed to offend and hurt because every joke has a victim. The argument is that, if we think about it, when we make a joke, we are always punching, whether up or down. I hope that this book has gone some way to proving this assertion is at best a distraction. Comedy can be a lot more than a punch, and it's definitely not contingent on danger or the establishment of status. Those are separate things entirely. You can use a joke to achieve those results, but it's not what a joke is.

Because of this, I believe that any complaint about aggression within a joke is a complaint about aggression, not comedy. But when mounting a defence of a joke that's caused an outcry, the temptation is for comedians to focus on the comic elements – 'It was funny, it was a joke, no harm was meant, I couldn't help myself, everyone was laughing' – and use those as a get-out-of-trouble-free card. But of course, the funny bit was 'harmless'; that's what comedy is all about: safety.

The thing to look at, the part that caused the problem, won't be the technically competent pun, or the great delivery, or the hilarious clowning. The comedy bits will be fun and warm and safe. They are meant to defuse and soothe. The issue isn't the bit that made people laugh, it's the aggressive or toxic assumptions that wound up the tension before the drop back to safety.

It's like deliberately smuggling a bomb through airport security, causing a complete shutdown, and then saying you did nothing wrong because the hard work of the bomb-disposal squad meant the thing never went off. The whole point of comedy is to deal with danger and render it safe. And nobody is objecting to that part. It's the bulge under your coat that you're trying to smuggle through security that's getting everyone jumpy.

WHO GETS HURT

As we have seen, the common features of a joke are that:

- it plays games of expectation and surprise using our pattern-detecting system
- it returns us to a safe state, which we may indicate to others with laughter
- it forms or reasserts a social bond within a group.

The first and third features (expectation and tribal bonding) can certainly describe a joke with a victim, especially if we wish to employ expectations based on prejudice, or use the joke as a weapon to drive a victim out of our social group. But the second and third features (relief and bonding) both hinge on safety. And there is no requirement within comedy as a human social activity for hierarchies to be established, for dominance or rejection to be an essential part of the joke, or for other people to be excluded or hurt.

Don't believe me? Tell me where the victim is in this brilliant joke.

I like rice. Rice is great when you're hungry and you want 2,000 of something.

Mitch Hedberg

The third defining feature, group bonding, may be achieved by a joke that hurts someone, but that isn't a quality that belongs exclusively to comedy. Saying, 'Fuck off, Sylvia, you malingering cow,' to Sylvia at work can bond a group together more strongly if we don't like Sylvia banging on about her bloody invented allergies. But that's an insult, not a joke. 'A thing we say that makes someone else feel worse' is not a usable definition for comedy, and picking on other people isn't a quality that belongs only to jokes.

An aggressive gag, with a victim, and a strong declaration of values that excludes others, is one option for a type of joke, not a rule for all jokes. I lose count of the number of times I've heard 'all jokes have a victim' asserted, often by very clever, accomplished comics, but it's ridiculous. Insisting that all jokes have a victim is like insisting that all jokes have a banana in them, or that all films are about a mismatched group of randy British caricatures going on holiday to an unfinished Spanish hotel run by Peter Butterworth. It's descriptive of certain comedy, maybe your favourite comedy, but it's not prescriptive of all of it.

36

Raise the Right Flag

MICHELLE: ...We said it but as a joke. As in, 'We're gonna beat you up.' But like, in a jokey way. JENNY: Right. Well, the thing is, that's not actually funny, is it? Like, at all. CLARE: Well, humour is so subjective really, so.

Derry Girls
(written by Lisa McGee)

The wily medieval wizard-style comedian Alasdair Beckett-King once made an observation that I think pinpoints something that is easy to miss about comedy, aggression and the victims of jokes. He noticed that whenever there was a controversy about offence in comedy, whenever a comedian found themselves making headlines for crossing a line with their material, all the focus was on who had walked out. People became obsessed by which group had felt excluded or attacked.

The discussion would then centre on the relationship between the comedian and the targets of the joke. Was this comedian a racist? A misogynist? Antisemitic? Anti-monarchist? Islamophobic? Hostile to the traveller community? Unpatriotic? A homophobe? Can we not joke about the royal family? Are the Irish even a race? Aren't fat people fair game? Isn't it their fault for eating too many sticky buns?

Representatives of the offended group would be inter-rogated. Did they want to silence free speech? Surely there are no limits to comedy? Nobody got physically hurt; can't you take a joke? There would be calls from one side to ban the comedian from ever working again.

While defenders would make claims about the com-edian's unimpeachable past behaviour towards whichever excluded group's turn it was this week to be the butt of a shock gag within an otherwise safe room.

But, Beckett-King pointed out, it's never about who was attacked. Who walks out of the room in disgust isn't the important thing.

It's who stays.

Let's say you want to tell a joke that could be seen as racist (because you think it's just funny, or you want to see what happens, or are trying to show how racist jokes work) but you're not a racist. Don't dismiss the audience members who walk out, chuckling to yourself that they can't handle the force of your ironic testing of boundaries. Focus instead on the people who stick around.

See who's laughing their head off. See who's delighted you've decided to finally stick it to the Chinese or women or people with squints. Keep it up, and because comedy is tribal, who knows, they might decide you're their guy, and start to bring their mates.

KEEP IT COSY

The contemplative snowflake woke-brigade stand-up Robin Ince (whom you're of course welcome to ignore if you are lib-sensitive and found that description triggering) has said that the edgelord 'Cancel me, I dare you' stance of some comedians could be reframed by taking their own claim that they are pushing their audience into uncomfortable spaces, and redefining it as the opposite.

Instead of accepting these people when they say, 'Look at me, challenging my audience,' and respecting them for trying to push the boundaries of expression, we might try to see what they really mean: 'Look at me, reassuring my audience.'

The academic Sophie Quirk, in *Why Stand-Up Matters*, says that a comedian's 'basic and most necessary task is to persuade the audience that his jokes are dangerous but also permissible'. The idea of danger is a useful stage illusion that can induce the ideal hysterical conditions to make a joke land harder. If a comedian makes us feel we mustn't laugh, then, effectively, we are swapping jokes at a funeral, or in the back row of a dry physics lesson, where jokes are at their most potent.

But if we were *actually* in danger, it would be easy to stop laughing. A laugh is not like the involuntary cough that might give away an escapee's location to an armed sentry. It is a shared social signal that we are fine. No animal uses a laugh to signal that it is in danger. So if you're getting laughs from an audience, the people in that audience must feel safe. The laugh isn't separate from the values. Some jokes aren't 'just too funny' not to do, as comedians sometimes claim when they get in trouble for slipping in a shock gag they couldn't resist. Comedy is social, and a laugh comes from agreement.

The audience and the performer are engaged in a conspiracy of affirmation. Go and see a good comic whose opinions on one subject in their set are the polar opposite of your own, and see how easy it is to sit stony-faced through that bit, while agreeing that the rest of it was pretty good. I've gone quiet and waited it out when Billy Connolly got on a third-ager high horse about health-and-safety-gone-mad and how getting run over by lorries never did his generation any harm (I can't remember the details now, but a pin-sharp operator like Connolly leaving me cold was a remarkable thing to sit through).

Similarly, the BBC's Duty Log – the Beeb's internal record of public complaints – is filled with decades of *Daily Mail*-reading listeners moaning that they can't see anything funny in the lefties the Beeb keeps letting on the comedy news quizzes, who 'don't appear to have any jokes at all, for goodness' sake', and listeners who read the *Guardian* who can't understand why so many right-wing columnists get airtime when 'we all know right-wingers aren't funny'. We laugh to indicate safety and shared values, to bond and groom, not to register our disapproval. A joke that gets laughs is *not* risking the unacceptable, it's affirming the acceptable within our chosen tribe. That's how comedy works right down deep in its bones.

SHOCK HORROR!

The kindest thing that can be said of a really horrible shock gag is that it's a useful game that we play with theory of mind. Comedy at its best involves empathy, experimenting with seeing the world through someone else's eyes, and registering the disjoints and differences, whether those eyes belong to a character in a sitcom or the clown persona of a stand-up comedian. We gather clues about how someone sees the world, and imagine events or ideas from that angle, to see if that helps their nonsense make more sense. It's one of the decoding exercises we do when we understand jokes: to imagine who we'd have to be to see the world that way.

As John Fortune said of Peter Cook (quoting Claud Cockburn), a clever comedian sometimes stands 'at a slight angle to the universe' and challenges us to stand next to them.

A comedian who chooses to switch off their empathy for a joke will get a laugh. It's a brilliant trick if you can deliver shock comedy by adopting a persona of someone who's got a chip missing or didn't get the memo. Tell a sick playground-grade puppy-in-a-blender gag or try a bit of inverted-commas retro abuse of some minority group, and you might lose the room. Do it with a solid character in place, and there will be a shock reaction, as your audience recalibrates, reverses up, and tries to examine the same data through your eyes. And if your declared character fits, that might be enough to make the gag fly. To the question 'who could even say such a thing?', our brain might return the answer 'a bigot' or 'a sociopath'. And if we stand at that angle, and the data makes sense now – 'Yeah, she would think that' – the green light goes on. That's a joke. And we laugh.

A character who doesn't care about our tribe's shared values is a funny character, whether it's Rosa Diaz in *Brooklyn Nine-Nine*, Pierce Hawthorne in *Community* or Mr Burns in *The Simpsons*. In stand-up, it's how you create the imaginary comedy human 'Jimmy Carr' (as played by the real person Jimmy Carr) or the imaginary comedy human 'Sarah Silverman' (as played by the real person Sarah Silverman). Most of us have our empathy on most of the time, as far as we can, if we want to function in society. So it's liberating to switch it off. And if we're winding down after a hard day getting along with other people and considering their needs, even if we don't like to admit it, turning off our empathy in the company of a skilled comedian can be like kicking off a pair of uncomfortable work shoes.

The problem comes when we are in a crowd and the relief tips over into active enjoyment or a change of tribal values. Playing at shock behaviour is fun, as proved by the success of video games like *Grand Theft Auto*. These work, as Charlie Brooker pointed out, by acting as an urban anti-social behaviour simulator for people whose normal day jobs involve quietly fitting in. We get home and fire up a safe space where we're allowed to queue-barge at the delicatessen in a tank. The fantasy and relief of not caring is healthy, as well as sharpening the theory of mind for what it might be like to be a sociopath. Who knows, there are loads of them out there. It might be useful.

Shock comedy performs a similar function. But if we found ourselves turning off the anti-social behaviour game and then behaving like that in the street, there would be reasons for concern, particularly if we were part of a crowd of people who had all agreed to suspend normal civilised tribal rules as well. That's the issue with taboo-busting comedy: if the momentary relief of switching off the empathy turns into a normalised assertion of tribal values, if the joke becomes not a *shock* joke but just a joke (one that asserts something nasty about puppy-murder or Asian people or rape victims that we then take out into our daily lives), then we're in trouble.

WALKING OUT TO THE DISTANT FIRE

Reading the room is a two-way process. In order to perform the first function of comedy – mental games and leisure – we have to guess at the audience's tolerances, tastes and experience. And then, because jokes are tribal tokens of exchange, the jokes we tell affirm the identity of that audience. And by affirming the audience's identity, we shape them, and bond them together.

And this certainly appears to be what happens when transgressive material destabilises a tribe. Comedians who feel they belong to one community, but start to flirt with jokes that their community finds borderline unacceptable, can suddenly find they are rejected.

Sometimes work dries up. This feels like 'cancellation'. They may worry that they cannot perform any more, that censorship has acted as a threat to their living. But usually these rejected comedians are embraced by another community, whose tastes are more in line with the values expressed by the fringe extremes of their routines. Their original tribe has expelled the comedian because the jokes no longer function as a usable tribal marker. But another group will welcome them in to do the same job for them.

Go back to our image of the cave people gathering around a bonfire of their own values. Light a comic fire too close to the edge of your tribe's circle, and it might turn out to be within another tribe's safe space. Comedy that flirts just over the edges of that boundary starts to attract people in from neighbouring tribes, who recognise the unifying comic tokens of social exchange that you have on offer. Because that's partly, science tells us, what comedy is for.

We all gather to laugh under our own flags. But if you raise someone else's, don't be surprised if they start hanging around.

PART FOUR

COMEDY IS CHARACTER

37

Comedy is Fractal

One small brown pot. Containing... Another small brown pot!

Spike Milligan, *Milligan Preserved* LP, 'Auctioneer' sketch

We have seen how comedy does two things. It plays puzzles with our brains, based on our love of pattern. And it helps us gather together in groups, and establishes our values and limits. Both of these are vital for us as social, thinking animals.

If we combine both of these ideas, we can use comedy's pattern games to learn more about other people, our social groups and ourselves. So let's talk about the characters and stories we use in comedy, and hopefully we can see how they are made of the same fundamental elements as individual jokes and lines.

We've got an audience waiting to be entertained. Let's go back to our lovely little comedy keyboard, with its three notes, and learn to play some tunes on it.

LITTLE AND LARGE

One of the amazing consequences of how much comedy depends on pattern, and how it mirrors music, is that any pattern that satisfies humans on a small scale also satisfies us at a larger scale. We love the rise and fall of a short melody for the same reason we love the epic sweep of an entire symphony. The satisfaction of a well-crafted line in comedy springs from the same love of rhythm, pattern and shape that satisfies when we enjoy following the patterns of expectation and surprise within a well-crafted story, or enjoy predicting the actions of a familiar comic character. Joke. Character. Story. Scene. Dialogue. Plot. Long arc. It's all made using the same equipment, in clear patterns of set-up, expectation and surprise.

The essential storytelling model in comedy is fractal. It's all the same shapes, just bigger and smaller.

Remember those psychedelic posters of repetitive computer-generated paisley patterns that maths students used to put on their college walls? Comedy is like that. Inside every big comic pattern is that same pattern again and again, just smaller. Construct, Confirm, Confound. Forever.

The closer you zoom in to a piece of comedy, the more you'll see Construct, Confirm, Confound. And if you zoom out, those same patterns will be visible. Ideas will be introduced, habits set, and surprises will be sprung. It's the same baby game – 'I'm going to tickle you, here I come, tickle!' – being played at a micro and macro level, in all narrative, but especially in comedy. It turns out that's just the shape of fun.

Comedy creators show characters behaving in a certain way, and then tell a story, where the audience have their expectations of that character either Confirmed or Confounded. We can tell a story that either goes exactly where the audience expected (which is delightful because, hooray, clever old audience). Or we can suddenly surprise them, and then they go back and see the surprise was actually inevitable after all if looked at from another angle (which is also delightful because we enjoy learning new stuff). As long as it's possible to follow the process and learn from it, everyone has fun.

But here's the important thing to grasp regarding story: *Whether you're playing a doorbell chime or a symphony, you still only have your little keyboard and a few notes to choose from. It's still only Construct. Confirm. Confound.*

We simply apply the same rules of Construct, Confirm, Confound over a longer span. All comedy's music, no matter how long, how loud, how epically arranged, is always played using the same notes.

It's quite beautiful.

(Takes a hefty drag on the comedy bong. Gawps deeply into a brightly coloured CGI poster of the essential structure of the plot and jokes in *Some Like It Hot* that looks like an infinite cosmic tunnel of comic ideas stretching to the end of reality.)

'WE INVENTED POST-ITS'

You've probably seen images of writers' rooms, with whiteboards covered in story breakdowns and coloured index cards or Post-it notes pinned to the wall, tracking the stories within the story. The firm control of expectation through structure and plot is everything in comedy. Although the audience aren't necessarily aware it's happening, structure is key to how comedy is enjoyed, because this game is always a game of patterns.

Sitcom plots in the classic style, as you might see in *Seinfeld* or *30 Rock* (a system that has been industrially perfected in the US), will run an A, B and C plot for their characters.* The colour of those index cards writers pin to

---

* Another comedy Rule of Three that occurs fairly organically. Two plots works fine – a couple of things the main characters want, which they can clash over achieving – but you might feel you're lacking something low-stakes and plain

the wall usually indicates which story beat belongs to which character or group of characters. These storylines happen simultaneously, rather than one after the other, and the show cuts between them. We'll see a set-up for each, then a series of developments for each, then a climax, which is usually a surprise. Construct. Confirm. Confound.

A WEDDING STORY

To demonstrate this system, here's the breakdown for the classic episode of Sam Bain and Jesse Armstrong's *Peep Show*, where uptight Mark (David Mitchell) marries his long-term girlfriend Sophie (Olivia Colman). Jez (Robert Webb) is Mark's flaky flatmate. Nancy (Rachel Blanchard) is Jez's on-off girlfriend. Super Hans (Matt King) is Jez's drug-wonky mate. I've tagged each plot beat so you can see which storyline – A, B or C – is being progressed.

A plot in bold.
B plot in plain type.
C plot in italics.

Stakes and set-up
Will Mark's marriage to Sophie mean the end of his flat-share with Jez?

Story beats
- **A: On his wedding day, Mark is having cold feet about marrying Sophie.**
- **A: But the flat has been trashed by Jez, Super Hans and co. Time to move on.**

---

funny to cut away to. Four plots is impressive work (and do go and collect your prize for effort), but it can get confusing for the audience. Three seems to work best.

- B: Jez tells Mark he and Nancy are back together as a couple; things are looking up.
- B: But Nancy tells Jez she's going back to the US. Leaves to meet her father at the airport.
- **A: Jez says he knows Mark will never go through with this wedding.**
- B: Because of this, Jez has not written his best man's speech. Mark is angry with him.
- C: *Super Hans, hungover, vomits into Mark's wedding hat and shoes.*
- **A: Cold feet lead to Mark chaotically attempting to sabotage his own big day. Fails.**
- B: Nancy calls Jez. She's rowed with her dad. She wants to come back and be with Jez.
- A/B: **Jez is Mark's wedding driver,** but he wants to go and pick up Nancy.
- B/A: Mark refuses to let Jez go and get Nancy. **His awful wedding is more important.**
- C/B: *But Super Hans offers to give Nancy a lift back from the airport.* Jez is happy.
- A: Mark needs a reason to break up with Sophie. Jez tells him he got off with Sophie once.
- A: Mark goes to tell Sophie's mum it's all off. She insists a drunken snog does not matter.

(AD BREAK)

- A: Mark hides in the organ loft with Jez, still unsure about going through with it.
- B: Jez can't find anywhere to go to the toilet. He becomes increasingly agitated.
- A: Mark is so distressed he argues with Jez. He angrily dominates him.
- B: Feeling bullied and lost, Jez wets himself.
- **A: The urine floods down into the church onto the wedding guests.**

- **A: The ceremony goes ahead and is terrible. Mark and Sophie cry throughout.**
- **A: Sophie jumps out of the wedding car on the way to the reception and flees.**
- **B/C: Jez sees** *Nancy and Super Hans getting off on a bench outside the church.*
- **A: Mark, in the wedding car, realises he is utterly alone.**
- **C/B/A:** *Cuckolded* **Jez gets into the car with jilted Mark.**

Closure

The leads are back together. The question posed by the set-up has been answered. They are trapped with one another.

The A plot is about Mark and his commitment to Sophie.

The B plot is about Jez and his relationship with Nancy.

The C plot is about Super Hans and the chaos that surrounds him.

If you look, you can see that each plot has a set-up, a development of those ideas, as expected, and then a leap into a surprisingly extreme register (the usual tone of the show's comedy).

Sometimes the separate plot strands meet and affect one another. The ending resets the world and answers the original question of what will happen. The answer is that the lead characters' unbreakable and dysfunctional relationship will get in the way of any possible character progress.

You'll notice too that any moments of surprise, or Confound notes, are played off our expectations of the characters, set up by Construct and Confirm notes. To get Jez to a situation where he will literally piss on Mark's wedding, truthful character moments such as Mark's bullying are arranged so that even the shock denouement is somehow consistent with our expectations.

CUTTING AWAY

Having A, B, C plots running in parallel means you can cut away when each scene has reached its comic climax. The audience feels the rhythm of expectation and surprise, and likes to have their reading affirmed: set-up, tension, surprise, release. Now move on. Change location or focus. This pattern puts little markers in, just like I'm using paragraph breaks in this text to help steer you from idea to idea. Ready? We've finished this bit.

Welcome back. If a comedy sticks to a single plotline or character, never cutting away, it's harder to guide an audience's expectations. Multiple plots help set the strict rise-and-fall rhythm of comedy, with its quick shifts from Construct, to Confirm, to Confound. I think this shape, and how quickly it happens, helps us identify what we're seeing as 'comedy' in the first place, as distinct from drama. You'll wait ages to have the identity of a murderer Confirmed or Confounded in a drama. Comedy is built of much faster patterns, with very quick answers, to exercise that part of our brains.

When some of comedy's pacy prediction-engine workouts are imported to drama, there is a subconscious signal that this story, no matter how dramatic, is also fun. An ostensibly straight drama might adopt intercut plotlines (like a sitcom A, B, C plot breakdown) or a vividly differentiated cast of characters who behave in predictable ways (like a sitcom cast), and this makes their world a welcoming place to drop in, regardless of how tough or serious its subject. Off the top of my head, good recent examples of this comic-drama hybrid might include series like *Succession*, *Severance*, *Better Call Saul* and *Slow Horses*, all of which were made by creative teams trained in comedy, with its endless quickfire prediction games.

The A, B, C plot system allows writers to arrange the

parts of a story like a songwriter might use verses, choruses and bridges as modular sections to guide an audience through a song and make quick changes of focus over those shapes to keep things lively.

EASY AS A, B, C

Usually in any comedy, the A plot will be the main story, the B plot a smaller one that perhaps interferes with the A plot, and the C plot is often a purely comic riff* to cut away to for variety. In *Friends*, the six-character cast was mathematically tailor-made for the characters to pair off into double acts and cover all the narrative bases. It's factory-tooled American sitcomming at its most efficient.

- THE A PLOT will be the main story of the episode. The lead character wants something.
- THE B PLOT will be something that another character wants, or the main character wants as well, but separate from the A plot. A and B plots often interrupt or complicate each other.
- THE C PLOT may only get a set-up scene, a check-in scene halfway and a pay-off. It's a useful third place to go for relief once the A and B plots are up and running.

Once again, comedy is music, and the relentless beat of Construct, Confirm, Confound tends to keep things pacy.

---

* In one episode of the second season of *Community*, the sitcom-aware character Abed Nadir declares he is not interested in the A and B plots of that week's story, and says he will sit the show out. Abed in fact does not disappear as promised, and has a story of his own that runs wordlessly in the background of the other characters' scenes. He even ends up delivering a pregnant woman's baby. It's a joke about how the C plots routinely given to sitcoms' pure 'clown' characters might as well exist in their own bubble universe.

If drama is a stately concerto, comedy, even at its gentlest, has the rum-ti-tum of a manic folk dance. Even the frothiest comic story can quickly get complicated.

P. G. Wodehouse used to spend up to two years planning his comic novels, working out his plots by covering his room in dozens of index cards in a way that would be familiar to any writers' room today. But for comic plotting to work, it's not enough for a lot of complicated story strands to dance about in a frantic narrative ballet. The audience needs to know the characters so well that they can predict exactly what they will do next. And, even though they know what's coming, not be bored by it.

This is why it's often said that comedy is more about character than plot. The plots may be complex or crazy, but the audience can only follow and enjoy them because each storyline is so firmly tethered to the characters, and we feel we really know them.

In drama, characters' motives are often kept hidden from the audience, and that's what the fun is: working out what a character is concealing from us. Maybe they're a murderer, or not whom they seem to be, or holding a secret that explains their baffling behaviour. In comedy, we know everything about the characters right away, and the joy is in watching them behave as promised.

Comedy and drama teach us things about human society. Drama is tense because it implies that maybe we cannot ever really know one another. Comedy is comforting because it reassures us that we can.

38

I Haven't Learned a Thing

ERIC: Do you remember our first meeting?
ERN: I do. We decided to team up and have a go at comedy.
ERIC: We should have done that.

Eddie Braben, written for Morecambe and Wise

There is a theory that comic characters should be fixed, while dramatic characters change. At the end of every episode of a sitcom, certainly, the characters should largely reset so that next week they're back where they started and we know how they'll behave and react, so we can start playing Construct, Confirm, Confound games with them. Long character or story arcs can be added to comedy, but they tend to have dramatic shape, not comic, purely by dint of being... well, long.

The classic *Simpsons* episode 'Homer Badman' ends with one of the funniest declarations of comedy's audience contract. Homer has just been through the most stressful possible story, a tale that would forever traumatise any real person, and be a catalyst for change in any dramatic protagonist.

As the show draws to a close, he leans in tenderly, hugs his wife and tells her, sincerely:

Marge, my friend. I haven't learned a thing.

And that's what we want. Just as Tom and Jerry (or Itchy and Scratchy) can survive being crushed, mutilated and destroyed, and ping back unscathed for more adventures, a comic character normally remains fixed.

At the end of *King Lear* or *Doctor Faustus* or *Breaking Bad* or *The Long Good Friday*, lessons have been learned and the hero changed. But Captain Mainwaring is always Captain Mainwaring. Hawkeye will always be Hawkeye. Edina and Patsy, and Sooty and Sweep, and Ernie and Bert, Jake Peralta, Liz Lemon, Baldrick or Victor Meldrew will always stay the same, because that's the game we want to play: different situations with the same character dropped into them, so we can guess how they'd react. We're practising our ability to identify and predict the behaviour patterns of others, and that's vitally important for social animals.

There is a mistaken assumption that the important part of a 'sitcom' is the 'situation': the place in which the characters find themselves (a bar, a police station, a family with an elderly relative moving in, a married couple deciding to go self-sufficient). When a layperson or inexperienced writer insists they've come up with a 'great idea for a sitcom', it's usually just something like 'old people at a gym' or 'Uber drivers in space'.

But the setting of a sitcom is really just a jumping-off point. A situation comedy isn't comedy that happens in a single situation, it's a comic exercise in showing what happens to fixed elements (your precinct and characters) in different *situations*. Plural. It's no coincidence that a US factory-built sitcom like *Friends* titled each episode 'The One With. . .' That's what a sitcom is. A string of situations to test the characters out, for comedy.

THROWING BALLS AT A STICK

One of the pleasures of comedy is knowing something about characters that they don't know themselves. They blunder into trouble and we enjoy thinking, again, 'Typical!' Comedy practises the vital human social skill of predicting others' behaviour again and again, at high speed, by throwing story at characters, like a machine firing tennis balls from different angles at a fixed target, and letting us guess (usually correctly) how the balls are going to bounce off.

Because we don't want the confounding variable of a target that changes shape, size and location, the target in comedy stays still. This is why comedy characters reset after every adventure, every joke, every different angle from which balls can be fired at their sitting target, so that our predicted map of their behaviour can be calibrated and stay trustworthy every time.

There's an old comedy-writer's trick that your ensemble of characters is only ready for use when you know instantly how every one of them would react to the same stimulus. That stimulus varies from writer to writer. I used to like asking, 'What's the worst thing you could say to this person?' You can probably immediately imagine characters who might be tagged to 'You are not interesting', 'I like your sister more than you', 'You don't fool me' and so on. Or you could nail your characters by asking how each of them would react to some standard comic event – say, being pushed into a swimming pool. Anger? Laughter? Panic? Wounded dignity?

Characters' roles in the group are like evolutionary niches, and it is survival of the fittest. If two characters react the same way, maybe you need to refine them further, or lose one, since they're competing for the same laughs. You want it so you can fire an idea into a room of characters and each one will respond in a way that satisfies the audience as 'typical'.

Because comedy is about reading types.

In drama, though, change is part of the game you're following. Drama trains us to observe change in character over time, not the behaviour of fixed characters to varied stimuli. You may recognise the disorienting feeling of flicking channels, stumbling upon a random episode of a drama you've watched before, and taking a while to work out where in the characters' arcs this part of the story sits: 'Is this from before she found out her partner was having the affair?' But in comedy, the usual guarantee is that you can drop in at any point and know how Lisa Simpson or Del Boy Trotter or Kramer will react to absolutely anything at all. And the predictability is the fun.

When comedies borrow dramatic storyline shapes where characters change over time, we risk finding ourselves unmoored. 'Is this episode of *Frasier* from before or after Niles confessed his love to Daphne?' Because that changes what we anticipate Niles might say when Daphne walks in the room. Change weakens archetypes, and we need to do a bit of legwork before we're comfortable with trusting our predictions. That never happens with Charlie Brown, who can remain a melancholy, thoughtful nine-year-old for decades, in the same zig-zag t-shirt. Every time we read a *Peanuts* strip, we know the rules. That's how Charles Schulz manages to tell such richly human stories in just four simple frames.

From commedia dell'arte to the Marx Brothers, from the *Carry On* films to *Ghosts*, knowing exactly how a set cast of established characters will react to anything that's thrown at them before it even happens isn't a weakness: it's comedy's superpower. It's how comedy works, and why we love it.

39

Confirmation Bias

Because, My Lady, Ludwig was a master of disguise, whereas Nursie is a sad, insane old woman with an udder fixation. All we had to do was kill the one that looked like the cow.

Edmund Blackadder, *Blackadder II*, 'Chains'
(written by Ben Elton and Richard Curtis)

No matter how big a comic idea is, it works the same way. We understand a joke, a character, a scene, and even a whole story using the same process: looking for patterns and comparing them to what we expected. We look for pattern and shape. A pun might make no sense until you realise you were using the wrong stored template to comprehend the words. Similarly, in character-based narrative comedy, a character might surprise an audience by doing something ridiculous:

- 'I can't believe Joey is wearing all of Chandler's clothes at once!'
- 'Harold and Albert have built a wall down the middle of their living room!'
- 'Tobias has painted himself entirely blue!'

But when the audience reverses up and looks again, using a stored template of character knowledge, they should be able to see exactly why the characters did the nonsensical thing. The red light of 'this behaviour is crazy and unexpected' is replaced by the green light of 'of course they did!'.

What's interesting about character and story in comedy is the diminished role of surprise compared to processing simpler jokes. Our enjoyment of comic characters depends way more on us guessing correctly than being tripped up. Surprise is usually held up as the key to comedy, but Confirm – the pleasant harmony that agrees with the Construct note – is an incredibly powerful comic tool. In fact, I suspect that it's used in comedy as often as, if not more than, the sexy, naughty, transgressive Confound note.

Confirm rewards audiences for guessing exactly what Jerry Seinfeld or Jerry Leadbetter or Jerry Mouse is likely to do in any given situation. They behave as we predicted, and we think, 'That's so them!' An expected event delights our pattern-detecting instincts every bit as much as the unexpected. After all, anticipating another human being's likely behaviour is a vital skill for social animals.

GET INSIDE THEIR MIND

Enjoying guessing what someone will do is about practising theory of mind. This is a psychological idea that explains how we are able to guess the intentions of other people, even if they don't see the world the same way we do. The moment we acquire this skill in childhood is the crucial point at which we learn we can use not only information from our own brain, but also what we imagine might be in someone else's.

The classic experiment to demonstrate this involves a child being shown a box marked 'Biscuits'. They are asked what they think is inside. The child will reply, 'Biscuits,' (unless they are particularly annoying). But on opening the box, they find a yellow toy digger. The digger is popped back and the box is closed. Then the child is asked, 'If we asked your friend to come in and gave them the biscuit box, what would they think was inside?' A child capable of demonstrating theory of mind would be able to put themselves in their friend's shoes and answer, 'Biscuits.' Even though they themselves know there's a digger in there, they can place themselves inside a different mental landscape.

Knowing that the world doesn't see everything through your eyes, that someone else might not know there's a digger in the box, and that you should take that into account when interacting with them, is a sophisticated thought process that doesn't fully develop in children until they are around eighteen months old (and never in a surprising number of politicians and rock musicians).

Daniel Dennett, the cognitive scientist, observed that humans exercise theory of mind so much that we take an 'intentional stance' on almost everything. This means that we assume that other people and even inanimate objects have wants, desires and secret agendas. We've all caught ourselves thinking the toaster burned our breakfast because it hates us. If, like Basil Fawlty, we can be driven to thrash our Austin Maxi with a tree branch because we reckon it stalled on purpose, the same part of our brains will enjoy practising understanding or guessing the intent of characters we think we know in a funny story, and that's probably why we laugh at Basil at all: because we can guess what he wants, and enjoy his frustration at failing to get it.*

We can practise theory of mind even when the character is out of sight. In the Marx Brothers' film *Duck Soup*,

---

* If we identify too strongly with him, if our theory of Basil's mind matches our own very closely, we will fail to get any of Aristotle's 'superiority comedy' out of the experience, and this may explain why plenty of 1970s repressed middle-aged men with social-status anxiety and anger issues said they watched Basil through their fingers.

chaotic fool Harpo keeps cutting things in half with gigantic scissors. It becomes his signature move, to the extent
that when straight-man Zeppo strolls in carrying only half
of his own hat, we get a laugh from Harpo even though he
is not in the scene. We imagine a slapstick moment that
happened off stage, and we laugh twice as hard, because
we made that scene up ourselves. It all hinges on the power
of Confirm.

THE WARMTH OF CONFIRMATION

In character-based comedy, the Confirm note is king.
Reassurance and safety is, after all, a great place for laughter. Maybe the warmth we feel towards our favourite
sitcoms is a side effect of how regularly they punch the
Confirm key. It also may explain why we can watch narrative sitcom without laughing out loud, but still feel
warm and soothed. We don't need to keep making laugh
sounds to signal that we are safe, because we're not being
slingshotted between bemusement and relief. It's just. . .
nice.

The idea of a predictable 'character' in comedy doesn't
just mean the cast. A character might be an archetype
(policeman, drunk, granny) deployed in a quick sketch. It
might be a simplified, accepted version of a well-known
real-life figure who is being satirised (a cartoon of Donald
Trump or Queen Victoria). A character might be a comedian's own stage persona, or their appointed role within
the cast of a panel game.

A character doesn't need even to be a living person, or
a depiction of a living person. It can be a presentational
style or frame of reference. Character is certainly why we
might enjoy the distinctive turn of phrase of familiar columnists like Marina Hyde or Jeremy Clarkson. Character
can be the abrasive tone of a shock-jock broadcaster, or

the whimsical verbal curlicues of P. G. Wodehouse or J. B. Morton. We laugh because even their wildest stylistic excesses read as 'typical'. We know 'what they're like'.

Character might be the recognisable worldview and jargon of *Private Eye*, *Mad Magazine*, *Smash Hits* or *Viz*. A comedy 'bucket', as we've observed, can be a character too, because it leads expectation in a certain way. All of these examples depend on an audience being led to expect one thing, before those assumptions are reinforced or subverted, with reference to those exceptions.

In fact, the definition of a character for comedy purposes might as well be 'anyone or anything that we believe is about to behave in a fairly predictable way'.

'HONEY, WHERE ARE MY PANTS?'

The clear labelling of character and the management of expectation is why catchphrases work. Every time we hear their well-known turn of phrase, we know that this character has not changed. I didn't get where I am today without knowing the character-identifying value of a good catchphrase, Reggie.

And a catchphrase doesn't even need to be verbal. When suburban busybody Martin Bryce (played by Richard Briers) arrives home for the first time in *Ever Decreasing Circles*, one of the first things we see him do is untangle the landline telephone, flipping the handset round. It becomes his signature move, a grace note in Briers' motion around the set. It is a physical catchphrase that indicates that Martin needs his house just so, and every time we see him do it again, we laugh.

A catchphrase, physical or verbal, confirms that a character will never change, which is good news for us playing the guessing game in future.

4

I Wouldn't Do That, If I Were Me

I'm in two minds. Mine and yours.

Unidentified stand-up
(whom Carrie Quinlan told me she'd seen once*)

The joy of character comedy is knowing that though characters are not us, they are predictable. This encourages us to sharpen our theory of mind. We compare what we'd do in this situation with the reactions of familiar characters, measuring Confounding new input against our pre-existing models of behaviour. For this to work, characters in comedy need to be well defined and stable.

If characters change, or obfuscate their motives from the audience, that's getting dangerously close to drama. Analysing character behaviour in drama might require long, slow consideration, usually over a long, simmering plot. But in comedy, characters stay where we expect them to be, and we play games with that knowledge.

While dramatic characters can offer mystery, comic characters usually need to offer total clarity. This is because of the 'error detection, recheck, return a safe message' system that our brains perform to comprehend comedy. We see a character do something daft that we wouldn't do,

---

* If anyone knows whose gag this is, let me know in time for the next edition. It's brilliant.

pull up their record card from our internal personnel file, see a possible explanation, and understand why.

It's that lovely 'Of course!' feeling. Leslie Knope in *Parks and Recreation* is an optimist. Gilfoyle in *Silicon Valley* is a satanist. Victor Meldrew in *One Foot in the Grave* is a pessimist. Garth Marenghi in *Darkplace* is a narcissist. When we do this, we're practising living alongside other humans with different brains, and it's one of our most essential social tools.

STATUS ANXIETY

This means that in comedy, more than drama, what is needed is total, almost constant clarity.* With any character, as a writer or an audience, we need to know:

- who we think these people actually are
- who they think they are
- who the world thinks they are.

And that's all theory of mind. One of the key tools for defining these is status. Does this character consider themselves high or low status in their group? Do the other members of the group agree? And what do the audience think is the truth? By sliding these expectations around, we can make complex depictions of characters, and show the status traps into which we can all fall in real life. And that is the sort of comedy enjoyed by hyper-social tribal animals like us.

---

* Comedy writers do not get to play with mystery because there are no laughs in it. Bolt some mystery onto your character comedy, sure, in a separate register, and you can make a lovely *Thin Man* story, like *The Big Lebowski*, *Search Party* or *The Beiderbecke Affair* but you're not getting any laughs from hiding stuff. That's just plot. (More on this in the next chapter.)

A great example of status play in comedy is the question of how good (or bad) the band is in *This Is Spinal Tap*. The joke could be that the band were awful, but thought they were great. There's certainly comedy in that. But the film finds immense richness in the band being... well... pretty good. As far as heritage heavy metal goes, they're completely able to do the job, and can attract sports halls full of people who agree they're pretty good. But then the film traps the characters in the status hell of behaving like they're way better than that. And also showing plenty of people who think they're complete shit. You can read it on the poor characters' faces in every scene, that they're negotiating their own status in a dense forest of other people's opinions. It's way better than them being great (and knowing it) or terrible (and not knowing it) or any of the other possible permutations. Their cleverly established status is fertile soil for character comedy, and our love of reading minds.

LET'S PRETEND

Strengthening the parts of the brain responsible for theory of mind is, psychologists say, one of the reasons children enjoy pretending to be a doctor or a shop assistant or a postman.

Using theory of mind puts us in someone else's brain for a moment, and practising this skill with a little family of familiar fictional characters is one of the reasons comedy is fun.

We really love it when someone doubles down on who they are. When Obelix in an *Asterix* comic is super-strong or super-hungry, or Asterix himself does something super-plucky. A character exemplifying extreme features of their essential self adds a little touch of Confound under what is essentially a Confirm note, and increases the pleasure.

'I knew she was pernickety, but wow!' The audience enjoys getting to know characters, but you can always surprise them by stretching their known traits to an extreme, and hammering the Confirm note hard.

Some of the most effective sitcom character jokes contain those two notes played at once. When Del Boy falls through the open bar while flirting with the yuppie women in a bistro in the classic *Only Fools and Horses* scene, the audience laughs because it's a fall from a grand height for a character who moments earlier was telling his hapless friend Trigger to be 'cool', like him (Confound). It's also completely in character for Del to be blinded to the outside world while lost in his playboy pose (Confirm). But in addition, it's unexpected for his Mr Smooth persona to be so all-consuming, so exaggerated that he falls without even flinching (Confirm and Confound at once).

Sophisticated theory of mind means we not only know what we think about a character, and what a character thinks of themselves, but also how the character seems to those around them. We can compare these various points of view and enjoy the disjoint. As Oliver Hardy wisely observed about his own on-screen persona, 'There's no one as dumb as a dumb guy who thinks he's smart.'

The author John Higgs described this as the 'clash of perspectives' that makes comedy so rich. An audience can see that characters are blind to their own shortcomings, maybe even failing to follow social norms. But the audience also understands, thanks to theory of mind, that the characters themselves believe they are being entirely reasonable. The (comic) tragedy of Alan Partridge isn't that he's a pompous prick, as much as it is that he doesn't know we can all see it.

Laughing at comedy characters is a social psychological workout: it practises empathy, runs checks on our pattern-observation software and sharpens our theory of mind.

41

A Dramatic Pause

It is as if children know instinctively that anything wholly solemn, without a smile behind it, is only half alive.

Iona and Peter Opie

Of course, the pleasure we feel about guessing motive, anticipating behaviour and enjoying story drawn from character in comedy is also true of drama. We like character consistency and predictable narrative sense in drama too, but we don't need that same speedy check and relief we expect in comedy. In comedy we want answers, even if they're stupid ones. In a dramatic story, we're happier to stay puzzled for a bit.

A character in a drama might do something we don't understand, and because we accept the pace of reveal in dramatic narrative, we know to wait 'til later to find out why. In fact, if we don't get an answer, we'll lean in closer, hunched over our popcorn, with one more reason to keep watching. The more puzzled we are by a character's behaviour, the better. We park our concerns and think, 'Well, that's something we'll find out later.' Chekhov can place his famous rifle in full view in Act One, knowing we'll wait for the end of the story for it to go off. That's drama.

But when a comedy character does something confusing and it isn't immediately explained, we just get confused. 'That's not what Liz Lemon would do. Who wrote this shit?' I find when a comedy character does something inexplicable or out of character (provided I have confidence that the writer knows what they're doing) I subconsciously file it in the 'drama' section of my brain and assume it's part of a longer plotline, not a gag. The data is stored in a different box, to be checked later. Withholding answers is *not comedy*, and you can feel it in your bones.

Comedy plots are so tied to character that, usually, if there is a beat of action that isn't what we expected from that character, and if that beat on second inspection still leaves us mystified, it's not read as good storytelling, but as a missed opportunity. 'That part simply wasn't funny. It didn't make sense.' The contract of swiftly confirming expectation of character (and thus returning us to safety) is broken, and we can completely lose faith in the story.

QUICK AND SLOW

Drama drags its mysteries out; comedy gives quick answers to let us know we were right. A whodunnit that was built on comedy's framework would reveal the killer a beat after the murder, just so we knew it was the person we expected and the writer hadn't screwed up. In drama, we have learned to wait for answers, because that's what drama does. It's got another purpose: to train our brains to follow cause and effect over longer stretches of data-gathering. I wonder if drama pleases the patient, observant part of the human brain that evolved to watch the slow patterns of migrating animals and the changing seasons, while comedy delights the bit of us that sat around the fire at night, with the rest of the tribe, laughing at one another's foibles and differences when the hunt was over. A comedy drama might blend these two threads, but if you tease them apart, you'll notice that nobody's laughing at the long story arc. That's doing quite a different job.

Comedy is constructed in antic little loops of question and answer. 'Why did that character do that? Oh, yes. Of course.' It's why it suits improvisation so well: as long as the consistency of character and motive is there over every short sprint into the ridiculous, the audience are happy to play a string of fun puzzle games at machine-gun speed. Comedy's workout for our pattern-detection engine is cardiovascular, not for building stamina.

By contrast, drama's long-haul contract is so well understood that we will happily keep the red light of puzzlement on from the initial 'what the—?' beat of a drama for hours, or weeks, or years of watching. In fact, drama series with a mystery at the heart often make audiences furious when they finish with a straight answer to who-actually-dunnit or answer what-the-bloody-hell-was-going-on.

COMEDY DRAMA

Of course, the combination of the quick-release tease-and-reveal character work of comedy with the slow burn of a drama can be great, as proved by our love of comedy dramas, and long arcs within continuing sitcoms. Stable, recognisable, easy-to-read comedic characters might act out a lengthy mystery or a will-they-won't-they romance for us over a long stretch. The unbreakable structure of fixed characters reacting predictably to new situations allows swift-release gags within a longer narrative, and that's really entertaining. It's drama software running on comedy hardware.

There is a wonderful moment in the first season of the comedy-bones TV spy drama *Slow Horses* where a thrilling car chase is ruined because one of the spies has forgotten to fill up his car with fuel. Within the longer thriller arc, with its unanswered questions, we have a sitcom-style character beat. Only a scene or two earlier, hapless spy Min Harper sat for ages on the forecourt of a petrol station. But we realise he got distracted thinking about food and sex (a solid character note). In comic thrillers, we love a quick gag about established traits within the longer flow of the drama, so that we can say 'typical'. It may be why detectives always used to have wacky, stereotype sidekicks, to play these quick gags off.

All a writer is doing by sounding both comic and dramatic tones at once is tickling our pattern-detection engines at two different speeds in two different registers. It's a slow, pulsing dramatic bassline with quick birdlike comic melodies trilling away on top. What our brains are doing is the same thing (looking for patterns), so we don't have to switch on some different machinery. We just have to be alert, and enjoy hearing a bit of counterpoint.

Iconoclastic theatrical whirlwind Ken Campbell once memorably said that any drama with no jokes in it should have its funding removed, since the purpose of drama was to hold a mirror up to life, and life had loads of jokes in it. I think it's a good rule for any writer to follow. Jokes don't derail drama, because they're running on the same bit of human brain hardware, just at a different pitch.

And humans enjoy the combination of drama and comedy just as much as they enjoy two voices in harmony, or two musical instruments playing together.

42

Patterns of People

Comedy is unusual people in real situations; farce is real people in unusual situations.

Chuck Jones
(*Looney Tunes* animation director)

Because comedy needs us to know what its characters will do before they do it, it can take a while for any new comedy to bed in. You know the feeling when a new show only seems to 'get good' after four or five episodes? The art of a great pilot episode (or a great bunch of opening scenes in a comedy film, play or book) is acknowledging that the audience can't employ pattern prediction yet, and then doing everything possible to get round it.

It's the same blockage we might get when we first see a new stand-up comic, maybe at an open-mic night. We don't know what they are likely to say yet, so how can we be delighted or surprised by what comes out when they open their mouth? It's why most new stand-ups learn to dress and even stand a certain way to create some minimal immediate audience expectations. It's also why so many of them open with a joke about audience expectation, based on their own appearance, often a variation on 'I know what you're thinking. [Celebrity X] has let themselves go' or 'I know, I know, I look like a supply teacher for the Taliban. . .' or similar. Get that opening line right, so it establishes a character straight away, and it can be a new comic's first banker.

It's not just self-deprecation, it's the first clue as to how they see themselves or are categorised by others. Technically it takes the unspoken Construct note of what they look like, and delivers a quick Confirm/Confound gag. This opening joke can demonstrate minimal competence to the audience, get a laugh, and be exchanged for a few moments' grace to add more detail to their simple thumbnail sketch. The opening of a new stand-up's first routine has the same structure as the first scene of the pilot episode of a new sitcom: it's all about getting to know people.

GETTING TO KNOW YOU

Without an ability to confirm or confound expectation of established character behaviour, comedy has no real meat to feed on and ends up relying on sugary filler. You don't need to establish character to use puns,* or unmotivated slapstick, antic action, unfocused comic energy, mugging, simple parody, unmoored pop-culture references, obscenity, comedy dancing, invective, broad-as-hell shock gags, or character jokes that are bounced off pre-existing expectations of off-the-peg archetypes, like nuns, gangsters or vegans.

Some of these elements can, of course, create excellent comedy, but they won't get as many rich laughs as they would if they were attached to something more substantial, and (unless in the hands of incredibly charismatic performers) they won't get you much love. You can't even

---

* Plenty of great stand-ups rely on nothing more than elaborate puns, but after a handful of these, provided the gag work is really single-minded, we know them as 'the pun guy', and that becomes the character we're watching.

do something as seemingly route-one as farce, cringe or embarrassment comedy unless you know what the characters have to lose, whom they might want to impress, what they consider normal behaviour and where they draw their moral limits.

If you study US sitcoms, you can see the hard-learned character-set-up skills that arise in an industry that, thanks to 'pilot season', produces and rejects an almost infinite number of first episodes as part of its normal process. Sitting through the opening five minutes of the average American TV show is like watching a crew of storm-weathered roustabouts erect a big top at practised speed. They're amazing at it. The poles go up and the whole structure is in place before you know it. I'm often tempted to applaud.

When I've got round to rewatching the early episodes of a sitcom I like, I sometimes realise that there were lots more jokes in episode one than I had remembered. Of course, those jokes were always there, but I couldn't see them properly, because they were about a bunch of characters I'd barely met.

HAVE WE ALREADY MET?

The challenge for any writer is to get the audience feeling as if they've known these characters for ages, even though that's not true. But nobody on their sofa wants to sit through Construct, Construct, Construct beats, because then the first few minutes of your comedy won't be funny. Laughs come easiest when we Confirm and Confound. So we need jokes.

But we can't make jokes about characters nobody knows. So we're back where we started.

A clever trick is to ensure that the first thing we see a character do feels somehow completely true to their essence, although we've never seen them before. We might have a set-up beat to show that a character is grand, or schlubby, or wacky, or greedy, but we should do it so fast and simply and clearly that even that first clue about them should feel not like set-up, but like a great confirmation gag. 'Typical!' The advantage is that, with an empty slot in our brains for character data, whatever is shown to us for that character gets filed eagerly. And that means we might take it in so quickly that we file it too fast and mistake new Construct data for established Confirm data. And that means we might laugh with recognition, while we're actually just being briefed.

It can be handy for characters to introduce themselves with a simple move or piece of dialogue that is so indicative of an accepted 'type' that we slot them into a mental category before we even notice. A prissy person dusting a chair with a tiny handkerchief before sitting down, say (which is how we first 'get to know' Niles in *Frasier*).*

When you think about establishing character fast, think of American TV-sitcom title sequences, where they freeze-frame, and the actor's name comes up on screen, over some trademark moves for their character.

I've always liked how *Brooklyn Nine-Nine*'s opening titles are edited from the most archetypical action each character does in the pilot episode (Jake playing with toys, Rosa smashing a computer, Terry overwhelmed on the phone, Amy's precise finger guns, Boyle clumsily stepping on food, Gina crazy dancing, Captain Holt implacable as a statue). That's the sort of behaviour you want your audience to see straight away from every character, filed so

---

* Actually, that piece of sublime physical comedy is a slightly later beat within Niles' introductory scene. The first clue to his character comes over a black screen where we overhear him meticulously recounting every detail of an argument with Yoshi, his gardener, about the gravel in his and Maris' Zen garden. Even typing that makes me happy; every word of it helps us get to know Niles.

quickly that they think they always knew it. Then you can start confirming their expectations and getting laughs, so they stick around, and you can supply more information, to help get more laughs.

Just to show it's not only the former colonials who can do it, a personal favourite character establisher is by Dick Clement and Ian Le Frenais, in the opening scene of the 1976 film version of their *Whatever Happened to the Likely Lads?* sitcom. Geordie social climber Bob Ferris greets his old schoolfriend Terry Collier, who is fishing from the harbour wall at Tynemouth with a tin of Mc-Ewan's lager in his hand. There is a bit of 'Alright, kidda', a short, characterful chat about Bob's wife's bruised toes, and then Terry says:

Want some coffee? I'd offer you a beer, but I've only got six cans.

And Terry takes a swig. Boom! That's who he is, and who Bob is, and who the pair of them are together. Even if I'd blundered into the cinema not knowing this sitcom at all, I can now enjoy the rest of the film. You could do any joke you like about Bob and Terry after that, and I would know when they were being themselves and when they weren't, and probably be able to work out why. All set up in a couple of seconds: the whole history and state of their friendship.

The start of the story meant my brain was ready to take in that information at express speed, and it would have been delighted that it was able to use that compressed packet of character data to play some prediction games almost immediately.

43

Character Pieces

Calvin's personality dictates a range of possible reactions to any subject, so I just tag along and see what he does.

Bill Watterson
(creator of the comic strip *Calvin and Hobbes*)

Humans are social animals, and the better we learn how to get to know each other quickly, in a safe environment, the smoother our lives will be (unless we are a dictator or a hermit).

Comedy is a terrific simulator where we can practise these skills.

A double act might show us how two people (work colleagues, siblings, life partners, best friends, superhero dynamic duo) can get on. A three- or four-person comedy can be a good analogue for a whole family. And a large ensemble can act as an educational demonstration of how we might follow the motives and needs of a broader tribe, maybe our workplace, school or home town. Guessing what might happen next, in real time, with a lot of conflicting players on the pitch, is the most rewarding game of all. This is the 'big precinct' model that fuels hit shows like *Cheers*, *M*A*S*H* and *Scrubs*, and provides the framework for all those hit vintage Jimmy Perry and David Croft sitcoms like *Hi-de-Hi!* or *Are You Being*

Served? If you are a fan of the *Asterix* comics, it's the pleasure you feel when you see that familiar Gaulish village on the opening map page. 'I know these guys.'

Sitcom-writing gurus repeat the mantra that you need to 'build your family' before starting. If the only rule were for the funniest characters to be put together, there would be no need for them to work as an analogue for anything else. But we read character and story much more easily (and therefore exercise our pattern and prediction software best) if the cast are interconnected by bonds that we understand already.

If the setting of a comedy is domestic, the metaphor is pretty clear: the sitcom families in *Outnumbered* or *Roseanne* or *The Simpsons* are meant to be read as our own family, or families we know. But we can test our prediction abilities on any group that delineates a group of characters as separate and conflicting personalities, and then watch them interact.

So the crew of *Red Dwarf* are also a family (starchy dad, soft mum, anxious kid, selfish kid) and they slide into these recognisable roles as easily as did the grotty students in *The Young Ones*. Bigger ensembles simulate bigger social spaces. *Motherland* is a set-up that demonstrates a range of different parenting styles; not one mum, but a demonstration suite of approaches, just as *Modern Family* illustrates all the variations of, well, a modern family.

ONE OF THOSE NOVELTY CHESS SETS WHERE IT'S THE SIMPSONS

Comedy ensembles are like chess sets. The pieces need to be instantly recognisable and move in agreed shapes, so we grasp the rules quickly and can think a few moves ahead, but these pieces should be able to perform an infinite number of games. We've been using comedy as a safe space to watch and learn about human interaction for so long that some of the games have become classics, and we play them again and again. These are the comedy set-ups that we recognise as familiar, maybe even without being able to articulate why.

In a chess set and a comedy cast, your pieces occupy well-defined positions, with immediately recognisable differences in behaviour. For the game to work, we all agree to stick to the rules, so pawns move like pawns, bishops like bishops, and everyone playing the game knows what to expect. The skill and fun of chess is predicting the moves. That's why it isn't permissible to replace your king with an action figure of Optimus Prime and knock all the other pieces over. As generations of kids have learned after trying this classic move ('The Optimus Gambit'), eventually nobody will want to play the game with you because that's not playing fair.

Each piece is fixed and predictable, and their character can't suddenly swap or change, except (like chess) over a long period of time, following strict rules. In chess, of course, it's permissible for one of your pawns to become a queen by advancing up the board to the last row and, against unimaginable odds, winning an honorary promotion. This is the chess version of a sitcom will-they-won't-they romance that ends in a wedding episode.

The clearer the characters and the distinctions between them, the faster the audience will join in the game. It's useful to avoid having two characters who are too similar, because if you do, the audience will start to obsess about finding differences between them. If there was an earlier prehistoric version of chess where there were several pieces that all moved like a knight, we've forgotten it, because what's the point of that? We lost the donkey dude and the giraffe jockey, and we kept the horse guy, and so here we are.

AVENGERS, ASSEMBLE

I'm going to keep saying 'sitcom' as a shorthand in this section, but the same rules apply to the Bash Street Kids, the news team from *The Day Today* or Marvel's Avengers. Anywhere you want to build a group of characters to generate jokes and story energy, and expect the audience to be able to guess how each character will behave, you're making a little sitcom.

You may have noticed that when they started hiring sitcom-trained people to make Hollywood's superhero blockbusters, the first thing that happened is the heroes began gathering in little clumps where we knew exactly which one was going to deliver which snappy comeback. This vastly increased the potential audience outside comics fandom, because you didn't need to be familiar with the characters to join in the fun. It was like *Scrubs* in spandex, and for a while the sitcom-with-explosions became the most successful entertainment franchise format on the planet. These things work because humans are wired up to like playing this game, in whatever guise you want.

As we've seen, a lot of comedy writing is the craft of setting up expectation and then paying it off. When a lavish cake appears in your story, you – and your audience – should know which character's eyes will bulge greedily, which character will pretend not to want any even though they do, and which character will waspishly disapprove of the extravagance.

There are plenty of books and theories about this, but in the next two chapters, I'll run through some well-used set-ups that audiences tend to grasp quickly thanks to familiarity, and I'll talk about them in increasing order of size.

44

Double Act

He let Judge Nutmeg pick away at Vic's confident façade, and I suppose in that simple dynamic, the seeds of a double act were born.

Bob Mortimer

Two's company, and a double act is a perfect way to set up a comedic character dynamic. The trick here is often to have a pair of opposites. Split a functional character in half, maybe, and give one set of useful traits to one of your heroes and the missing bits to the other. This bonds them as a pair. Together they would form an integrated entity. With their soul fractured, all that's going to happen is chaos, conflict and frustration. Which we'll all enjoy watching. Hurrah for existential terror!

Maybe have an anxious person stuck with someone who's irritatingly devil-may-care. That dynamic gives you most of the classic flatshare-from-hell set-ups: *The Likely Lads*, Sid and Tony in *Hancock's Half Hour*, Felix and Oscar in *The Odd Couple*, and, one of my personal favourites, fretful Arthur Dent and immediately annoying Ford Prefect in *The Hitchhiker's Guide to the Galaxy*.

A good refinement of the *Odd Couple* dynamic is the pleasing pop-culture/pop-psychology theory that if you imagine yourself as part of *The Muppet Show*, we are all either a Chaos Muppet or an Order Muppet. The universe is in balance, with Kermit, Sam the bald eagle and Scooter on one side, Gonzo, Beaker and Animal on the other. That's how the Muppets' show-within-the-show gets put on, that's how the comedy dynamics within the sketches work, and it's certainly a good way to write a comic duo. *Sesame Street*'s sacred central double act of Ernie and Bert is endlessly useful as a template when inventing a comedy pairing. Outside the Muppets, in the extended puppet comedy universe of our collective childhood cultural unconscious, Sooty is order and Sweep is chaos, just as *Rainbow*'s George is order and Zippy is chaos. It even works for humans. Mark in *Peep Show* is order, Jez is chaos. They'd work brilliantly in felt, with googly eyes. It's a great formula.

If you want less contrast, with your double act feeling more like a united front against the world, try two upbeat idiots, but very slightly different upbeat idiots. Again, your double act combines two halves into a single whole, but the parts are less in conflict with one another. That's how you get Laurel and Hardy, Romy and Michele, Bill and Ted or Ant and Dec.

In this case it's sometimes good to have one character believe they're leading the other, occasionally falling into the roles of *the idiot who knows nothing* and *the idiot who thinks they know everything*. The character versions of Eric Morecambe and Ernie Wise perfected by scriptwriter Eddie Braben play a delicate dance with this arrangement. Eric and Ernie slide up and down in their mutual pecking order, each sometimes playing the high-status character, sometimes the low, but always clearly having one another's back. It's a warm and appealing double-act dynamic the team admitted was borrowed from Laurel and Hardy. These duos might bicker, like siblings, but they form an unbreakable alliance against outsiders, with the unspoken rule that they might tease or even slap each other, but nobody else is allowed to lay a finger on their best friend.

This alpha and beta double-act dynamic, based on status, is something audiences grasp very easily. We're so attuned to watching for clues to status that we can follow it even if it flips back and forth from scene to scene like Eric and Ernie's, Pete and Dud's or the Two Ronnies'. Remember the way Winnie-the-Pooh would lead Piglet confidently into adventures he didn't quite understand? Neither of them know what's going on, but they have agreed on their roles for the day. There's a great gag on this trope in *Romy and Michele's High School Reunion* where the best friends argue almost to their deathbeds about which one is the Mary and which one the Rhoda, referring to the hierarchy of the best-friend archetypes in *The Mary Tyler Moore Show*.

Defining characters' status is vital in a double act. Often in clown duos, that's the extent of the character work you need to do to give the audience enough clues to make comedy. Simply decide who thinks they're in charge and who's following behind. And if you're sticking to rigid statuses – one canny, one naive, say – it's always fun to flip those over. The master–servant inversion, with the wily servant outwitting their social superior, was a key comic trope in Roman theatre, and it definitely ain't broke. It turns up everywhere from Jeeves and Wooster to Wallace and Gromit. If the person who's supposed to be comfortably on top is actually sitting on the shelf below, there's immediately a comic energy. This is the key to the complex social comedy simmering in *Dad's Army* between the frustrated middle-class Captain Mainwaring and his number two, the airily born-to-rule Sergeant Wilson. The topsy-turvy chaos of war has misfiled them in the wrong ranks.

That's how to work a duo. Now let's look at some bigger groups.

45

Marge & Dorothy & Velma & Ringo

You haven't got a sister, Rick. You're the classic example of an only child.

Vyvyan, *The Young Ones,* 'Bambi'
(written by Ben Elton, Rik Mayall and Lise Mayer)

So what happens when we move from the double act into group dynamics with three, four or more characters? ·

COMEDY'S SACRED THROUPLE

A venerable three-way set-up from traditional clowning that turns up in lots of sitcoms is Whiteface, Auguste, Tramp. The arrangement is:

- Whiteface: the leader of the group, middle-aged, often a social climber
- Auguste: a magical, often childlike character; a holy fool
- Tramp: the 'character' slot in the troupe, usually old, with disgusting or extreme tastes.

The system works because it gives your troupe three clear age slots, with the appropriate visual clues corresponding to three outlooks on life. That's really easy for an audience to read. The two outlier clowns (young idiot and old idiot) can also wreck the aspirations of the central Whiteface, who is often the one carrying the plot (or, in a circus, the ladder).

You'll recognise this dynamic from *Only Fools and Horses* (Del, Rodney, Granddad or Albert) and *Father Ted* (Ted, Douglas, Jack). *Absolutely Fabulous* has Edina as the Whiteface, Patsy as our (secretly ancient) boozy Tramp, and silly Bubble as the daffy, young Auguste. In *Blackadder the Third*, Edmund Blackadder takes the role of the hard-working Whiteface, Prince George is the childish Auguste, and Baldrick the filthy Tramp. The same arrangement occurs, with some classy tweaks, in *Frasier*, where Frasier is the fretful, aspirational Whiteface lead, Niles the unworldly sprite-like fool, and Martin Crane the earthy old man who drags them both down. It's also how the Three Stooges and, to a lesser extent, the Marx Brothers operate (Harpo is the textbook Auguste).

Interestingly, this classic threesome was how the original line-up of characters for ensemble sitcom *Dad's Army* was imagined, before the cast became larger and more complex. Private Pike was the 'stupid boy' Auguste, Captain Mainwaring the pompous Whiteface middleman, and Corporal Jones took the silly old man slot. Jimmy Perry and David Croft said they borrowed this dynamic from Will Hay's classic British film comedies, such as *Oh, Mr Porter!*,* where Hay would play the Whiteface lead,

---

* Will Hay was a music-hall star who'd trained under the great Fred Karno (the impresario who'd launched the careers of Charlie Chaplin and Stan Laurel). *Oh, Mr Porter!* was a railway-themed film outing for Hay's classic clown trio. It was based on a 1920s stage play, *The Ghost Train,* written by Arnold Ridley, who would eventually go on to play doddery Private Godfrey in *Dad's Army.* Which is rather pleasing. Arnold Ridley's great-niece Daisy plays Rey in the *Star Wars* films, a franchise whose story was kicked off in 1977 by the comedy pairing of a fussy, socially anxious Whiteface robot and a baby-burbling innocent

Graham Moffatt the soft youth and Moore Marriott the peculiar old man.

Dad's Army left its clown trio origins behind to become one of the defining big-ensemble comedies of its time. So how might these more complex groups of funny characters work?

THE FAB FOUR

And so we come to Matriarch, Patriarch, Craftsman and Clown. This mystical-sounding formula for building the ideal sitcom cast was popularised by Mitch Hurwitz, creator of *Arrested Development*, though he makes no claim to have invented it. The dynamic probably goes back much further, most likely to the archetypes used in Renaissance theatre and the commedia dell'arte.

Whatever its origins, it feels instantly familiar, instantly *right*.

The idea is that any network of comedy characters can be mapped roughly over a classic sitcom family of 'mom, pop and two kids'. Imagine your gang driving along in one of those classic station wagons with wood panelling up the side. Putting your justified criticism of stereotyped gender roles to one side, this means you have the dad (driving), the mum (in the passenger seat in charge of snacks and tissues) and two competing siblings (squabbling for space in the back).

These characters play the following roles:

- Matriarch: the cautious carer; a safe place, where other characters come for comfort
- Patriarch: the flawed driver, pushing the plot forward

Auguste robot, owned by a strange, wizened old hermit. There. *Oh, Mr Porter!* to *Star Wars* via classical clowning theory.

- Craftsman: the diligent, soulful one, striving to better themselves
- Clown: a force of raw energy, chaos and selfish will.

Because I said imagine a family in a station wagon, you've probably already noticed this is the perfect description of Marge, Homer, Lisa and Bart from *The Simpsons*, and in that order. But it's so many more. The genders and ages aren't fixed, and it's not just for foursomes. The dynamic doesn't describe a fixed cast. It's about the conflicting forces within a group that seem to generate the maximum comic energy.

Here are some examples (because working these out is fun):

	MATRIARCH	PATRIARCH	CRAFTSMAN	CLOWN
The Young Ones	Neil	Mike	Rick	Vyvyan
Roseanne	Dan	Roseanne	Becky	Darlene
The Good Place	Chidi	Eleanor	Tahani	Jason
The Golden Girls	Rose	Dorothy	Sophia	Blanche
Seinfeld	Elaine	Jerry	Kramer	George
30 Rock	Liz	Jack	Tracy	Jenna
Friends	Rachel	Ross	Chandler	Joey
Fawlty Towers	Sybil	Basil	Polly	Manuel
Scooby-Doo	Daphne	Fred	Velma	Shaggy
The Incredibles	Elastigirl	Mr Incredible	Violet	Dash
Star Trek	Bones	Kirk	Spock	Scotty

Peanuts	Charlie Brown	Lucy	Linus	Snoopy
Porridge	Barrowclough	Fletch	Godber	Mackay
The Beatles	Paul	John	George	Ringo

I've stuck to the key foursomes if there are larger casts, and gone with Hurwitz's divisions for shows he discussed himself (he makes fairly convincing cases for his picks). I've also done the Beatles. Because it's impossible not to. Obviously you can argue the toss about some of these, and I hesitated before popping a couple in their relevant boxes, but that's the game: to consider what 'comic energy' is coming off each character. Because that's what an audience will be looking for when they try to predict behaviour.

Even a drama series like *Star Trek* can use these dynamics because it has a sitcom energy in its core cast. As well as the week's exciting space plot (and all that boldly kissing green space ladies whom no man has boldly kissed before), the audience enjoys guessing what a small precinct of fixed characters are typically going to do in any situation.

My favourite non-comedy example here is the Beatles. When Peter Jackson's *Get Back* documentary reconstructed archive fly-on-the-wall footage of the band as if it were modern reality TV, it turned out that stories, conflict and humour arose as organically as it did for the fictionalised Beatles we had seen in their films and cartoons. Maybe that's why so many people loved them, and why we felt we understood them. It's certainly why they're funny: we can guess what each member will do. The group often said themselves that they weren't really the Beatles at all until they found their Clown and popped him behind the drumkit. All four energies were needed to spark this family into creative life.

Bigger ensembles can have a couple of each archetype. The *Friends* cast has a spare Craftsman (Monica) and a spare Clown (Phoebe), and they clearly differ from the other characters in those roles, while sharing a similar energy.* In *The Good Place* there is another layer of the dynamic above the central human characters, where Ted Danson's immortal Michael acts as a spare dad, and D'Arcy Carden's all-knowing problem-solving Janet could be seen as an odd sort of bonus robot† Matriarch.

And sometimes characters can even be a blend of the types, or move into and out of their appointed roles. This is useful if a character who normally carries one of the vital energies within the group is absent for some reason. Maybe they're simply not in this plotline or scene, or involvement in their own story stops them performing their usual function. In the sitcom *Ghosts*, when Alison, the owner of Button House, is away dealing with her end of the plots, Pat, the late scoutmaster, usually steps in as Matriarch to care for his fellow ghosts' wellbeing. And when Pat needs comfort himself, Robin, the gruff caveman, slides into the Matriarch role, offering soft, timeworn wisdom, and producing some of the show's most touching moments.

ENERGY, ELEMENTS, HUMOURS AND OTHER COMEDY WOO

At the risk of going a bit woo, it's not about fixing characters in stone; it's about respecting their 'energy'. By having characters channel clear and varied energies into the

---

* It's sweet that the Matriarch and Patriarch in *Friends* are drawn together as a couple, because opposites attract, and so are the two Craftsmen, because they understand one another.

† Not a robot.

comedy, they will always fulfil our expectations. This means that, though the situations can change and the gags can be a bit crazy, something in the comedy will always be predictable, safe, comforting and reassuring: the energies emanating from our cast of characters. And that will make us happy. So every new situation, each exaggerated testing of the characters' reactions either reinforces things we already knew, or reveals further clues about their inner unchangeable essence.

If you enjoy the hey-nonny chic of medieval-sounding clown theory like this, you could connect Matriarch, Patriarch, Craftsman and Clown to the ancient concept of the humours in the human body, four essential fluids that need to be in balance. Or you could consider the four comic roles as the four classic elements in nature. Imagine a sacred foursome of Earth, Air, Fire and George Costanza. A healthy comedy will have a set of energies within it, and hold them in some sort of balance for the audience to comfortably negotiate what's going on.

I suspect that character formulas, like most writing theory, should only really be ways of troubleshooting when something goes wrong. Writers should write whatever we feel is real, makes us laugh and tells an authentic story. But if something in your comedy feels dead, it's useful to check you have wired it up properly to all four comic forces. Cutting off the supply of one energy isn't a disaster, but changes the comic tone, so make sure that any shortfall is deliberate. As comedy writer Sarah Morgan observes in her lecture on this system, Sharon Horgan and Rob Delaney's sitcom *Catastrophe* lacks almost all Matriarch energy, which gives it a distinctive, bitter flavour. Without a comedy mum, there's no big Dan Conner or soft Marge Simpson to wipe away tears in their world, but that helps tell stories about adulthood sometimes being weird, lonely and hard.

'I'M CRAFTSMAN, WITH MATRIARCH RISING'

Writers and fans love to feel like we've stumbled upon some primal code that unlocks story, and maybe even humans. Remember how excited I got back there about Chaos Muppets?

There's a thrill of the alchemical to Matriarch, Patriarch, Craftsman and Clown. Maybe if we study the scrolls from the Wizard Hurwitz, we will be able to summon a sort of whoopie-cushion demon in our basement to help with our pilot script. I've seen people attempt to bolt Matriarch, Patriarch, Craftsman and Clown over their real-life groups of friends. And when I say 'people', I mean 'me'.

But I think that's reassuring, because it confirms the central idea of this book: that humans are pattern-detecting creatures. Comedy is a game we play to sharpen those essential skills. Putting people in boxes is a trick that helps us navigate all that complex, baffling human behaviour, and do it at speed, often after only meeting people briefly. (Any laugh in the first couple of pages of a sitcom script is a demonstration of how effectively this can be made to work. We don't know these characters, but we somehow *know* them like we do our own family and friends.)

Personality categories help us navigate social situations. We can better guess how to make people happy, whom to befriend, whom to avoid. Labelling people is a social habit that can go toxic, of course, pushing people out of our tribe, but it's also handy for recognising different sorts of human, exercising theory of mind and developing empathy. Expectation doesn't have to be the same as prejudice.

There are loads of these rows of identity boxes into which we quickly pop people for convenience, and we use them almost without realising we're doing it.

Think about signs of the zodiac ('I'm such a typical

Aries'). Geographical identities ('I speak as I find, coming from Yorkshire'). Myers-Briggs psychological profiles ('I'm staying in bed; I'm an introvert'). Pop-psychiatric diagnoses ('Julian, you're such a narcissist'). Jungian archetypes ('I can't really work for anyone, I'm a rebel'). It's how we design our avatars for video and role-playing games ('I'm chaotic neutral'; 'I'm sniper class') and even define unofficial roles in groups at work and elsewhere. ('Watch out for Rob, he's the joker'). If you've ever filled in one of those 'Which Character Are You?' quizzes about some popular TV show, you're part of this process. It's about imposing order and logic and systems on messy real life, and I like things like that because I'm such a Miranda.

The comic archetypes in Clown groups work because they were evolved by comedy creators to help audiences guess how characters might behave. So when a writer decides that this character is a classic Matriarch or Craftsman type, this will be understood by an audience who don't necessarily know the categories by name, but are used to looking for exactly these clues. We've met these guys before, more or less, not only in real life, but in comedy. This guy's a Kramer, that one's a bit Bert, or a classic Trigger, pretty much your basic Karen Walker, completely Lisa, pretty damn Larry David. The transmitter and the receiver of the comic character information are sharing the same human codebook.

When analytical Abed breaks his cocky friend Jeff Winger down into a cocktail recipe of other sitcom characters in *Community,* it's not only the show's habitual gag of allowing writers'-room chatter to be heard by the audience, but voicing what our brains did in the pilot episode when we first met Jeff.

10 per cent Dick Van Dyke, 20 per cent Sam Malone, 40 per cent Zach Braff from Scrubs. *And 30 per cent Hilary Swank in* Boys Don't Cry.

There's no dark secret here. We're seeing the categories we made ourselves. What we do in creating and enjoying comedy, when we predict and file human behaviour based on interpersonal dynamics, social status, self-image, group role and outlook. . . that's just who we are.

PART FIVE

COMEDY IS STORY

46

Building the Clown Car

Of course in comedy, nothing works unless it's pretty much perfect.

John Cleese

The balance of sense and nonsense in comedy is felt nowhere more acutely than in the issue of comic storytelling.

A comedy that tells a good story, but lacks jokes is no use. But just as bad is a load of jokes that aren't anchored to any story. Story tells us what characters want, who they are, when they feel they've won and lost, which makes it easier for an audience to guess what those characters might do next, and have those expectations Confirmed or Confounded: the basis of comedy.

So if we want to be funny, we're going to have to learn the same storytelling techniques that are used by the people who make all those stern-faced dramas, heart-rending tearjerkers and gripping thrillers.

SOME IMMEDIATELY DISMISSABLE HORSESHIT FROM ROBERT MCKEE

In his book *Story*, legendary screenwriting tutor Robert McKee says:

*Comedy allows the writer to halt Narrative Drive ...
and interpolate into the telling a scene with no story
purpose. It's just there for the yucks.*

Which, I should like to point out, is a colossal dog turd of
a piece of advice.* Stopping to add some comic business
with no narrative purpose hasn't been a good habit since
the late sixteenth century, when Shakespeare got bored
giving the troupe clown some 'business' between the
action, and started putting the funny guy in the middle of
the story. Look at the difference between an early Shake-
spearean comic-relief scene (audience prepares to have a
little puzzle break spotting allusions to cuckoldry) and the
integrated roles of the Fool in *King Lear* or Dogberry in
Much Ado About Nothing.

'Interpolate a scene with no story purpose', as McKee
advises, and the moment you need to lose ten pages to
tighten your script, you'll find those clutch-down 'just-for-
the-yucks' scenes end up in the screenwriting program's
trashcan folder (or even worse, on the cutting-room floor,
having wasted everyone's time and money on set). The
best sort of comic business in a plot is funny *and* narra-
tively driven, the comedy providing a fun counterpoint to
the action, without getting in its way or stopping its
momentum. Remember those wisecracking sitcom-style
superhero films I mentioned earlier? That's how they perform their box-office magic.

That's how to make drama better by making it funny, but
what about straight narrative comedy, such as a romcom
or a quirky character study? McKee's fellow Hollywood
screenwriting consultant Steve Kaplan (who has a proper
track record in comedy) has pointed out that whereas in a

---

* Maybe it's worth pointing out here that McKee says that he bases most of his
writing theories on Aristotle, a man who, as I mentioned earlier, mainly laughed
when other people in Ancient Greece fell down a hole and he didn't.

drama, a character stopping to muck about would be a distraction from the story, in comedy the character's behaviour, however ludicrous, *is* the story. If a comic scene tells us things about the character that we can use to play guessing games about them, it is 100 per cent necessary. And, in comic terms, that counts as 100 per cent part of the story.

A film like *Withnail and I* or *When Harry Met Sally* might contain very few scenes of McKee-esque 'Narrative Drive', but nobody would say that those films' carefully arranged comic set pieces didn't tell a revealing and engaging story about their characters. *Withnail* is at heart a quasi-military survival drama about two under-resourced men lost in hostile territory, comically applied to a pair of sensitive actors. The plot itself is pared to the bone, to enable the rich character comedy room to breathe, but it's still basically a journey into and out of the woods, fending off threats, in a classic dramatic shape.

So, learning more about the characters is everything. The story is just there to give us more tools with which to play our prediction games. In drama an externally driven plot can have its own momentum. Think of some basic plots that can propel drama. Off the top of my head:

- looking for treasure
- staging a rescue
- achieving a position of high status
- looking for Mr or Ms Right
- getting revenge
- winning a contest or battle
- trying to escape
- unmasking a killer
- working out what the hell is going on in this weird place.

In a drama, you are following a long story. You look for narrative clues to help you guess where you're going. It's a sustained exercise in information gathering. But in comedy, although these same underlying plots might help push the story forward, it's the character-revealing incidents that happen along the way that are where your prediction engine is getting its fast-paced workout.

Under those conditions, watching how a character reacts to or incites any action at all, no matter how dumb, is exactly what we came here for. Nothing in a comedy script is 'just for the yucks'. And if it is, you should try to think of something more useful for your characters to do. Just because what they are doing makes you laugh, that doesn't mean it's a waste of time. Do you learn something about them? Then that bit's earned its place.

Provided the ridiculous action reveals more about what characters might do next, it's the central business of your story. Everything that happens in a comedy script gives you fresh data that helps you play the next bit of the game. That's where the 'yucks' come from in the first place.

THE TEST DRIVE

I have come to think of plotting comedy as building a car and taking it to a test track. I can enjoy myself in the design phase, go crazy. My story-car can have fins and a wacky paint job. It can sport a forest of racoon-tail aerials and a corkscrew neon flagpole. I can give it bat wings, luminous cow skulls on the grill, and a ten-foot exhaust pipe that blows bubbles and plays 'Oh Carolina'.

But once the car is put in motion, barrelling towards the finish line, it will become clear which bits actually help it move and which bits drop off when it hits a bump.

And experience in the field has revealed that a good comedy story needs wheels and an engine more than it needs a pair of prop-synchronised firework launchers and a chocolate windmill. This doesn't stop me endlessly trying to add fun accessories to plots that don't help and are just dead weight. It will never stop me hoping against all good sense that I might be allowed to swap the perfectly functional back wheels of my comedy car for this pair of enormous Dairylea cheese triangles. Every bloody time. Plenty of storylines have, once I set them going, been revealed to be like the clunky Homermobile from *The Simpsons*, bristling with ugly protrusions. And of course, like Homer, I never learn a thing. But thinking of your story-car as a car – a machine that needs to do car things – is a good way to save time, and grief, over repeated drafts, desperately trying to make the damn thing roadworthy.

CUTTING ALL THE JOKES OUT

One of the awful truths of comedy writing is that, if a script is running long, the first thing that gets cut is jokes. It's almost impossible to remove a beat of plot to save time, because then the thing doesn't make sense. 'How did the characters get out of the locked room? Where did the ski instructor come from?' But you can always end a scene earlier, or trim dialogue.

Guess what? That's exactly where your favourite jokes and maddest ideas will probably have been placed. It takes work and skill to integrate jokes into the story so they can't be snapped off. Every gag needs to carry valuable narrative and character information that will earn the line its place in even the tightest edit. It's why writing comedy is hard.

A lot of the most enjoyable gags are the flags and aerials and fins on your comedy clown car. Any comedy creator wants to try to keep as many of them as possible, because that's where you really cut loose. But to make that work, you're going to have to design your story-car's maddest accessories to be streamlined, and maybe even functional. They may have to help the car move too.

Unfortunately, the silliest parts are usually the bits that catch audiences by surprise, when they laugh loudest. So when the production pit crew come to inspect your vehicle (insisting you need to lose excess weight to achieve sufficient story speed), your dumbest, funnest shit needs to look as integral as possible. Loath to lose your favourite balloon-animal dispenser? You need to make it work as a passenger airbag. Wedded to the fart machine? Hide it inside the engine.

THE IRISH JOKE

One of my favourite jokes I've ever seen attempted in a mainstream, realistic sitcom was in Emma Fryer and Neil Edmond's short-lived but lovely BBC sitcom *Home Time*. Fryer's character Gaynor returns to her time-capsule 1990s teenage Coventry bedroom twelve years after failing to make it on her own. Her mum, a domineering and selfish woman with a thick Dublin brogue, fusses and patronises Gaynor, while her dad, a hangdog Midlands taxi driver, watches with glum acquiescence. Mum is Sybil Fawlty big, hogging most of the dialogue, until we really know the monster squatting at the heart of this sitcom family. We get a quarter of the way into episode one before Gaynor is alone in her dad's taxi and gets a chance to ask something casually.

> GAYNOR: *How long has Mum had an Irish accent?*
> DAD: *A few months...*

It's a fantastic surprise gag. Of course. Gaynor's mum, narcissistic and weird, desperate to create her own fraudulent maternal mythology, isn't Irish after all. It's a wonderful, almost *Simpsons*-esque leap into the absurd, but it tells you something strange and essential about the mum character. It also anchors the weary relationship that Gaynor and her dad have with the mum's noisy excesses. Maybe this sort of thing is the reason Gaynor left home and is so wary of returning, in which case it's a daft joke that might be the key to the whole show.

A couple of savvy producer friends flagged that joke up as something they'd have cut for breaking the audience contract, which it certainly risks doing. But I love it, and would hold it up as an example of how, if you keep your favourite funny ideas integral to character and story, you can have the best of both worlds. It's a colourful fin on the roof of the car, but it makes the whole thing go.

The need to keep your clown car moving is why the best jokes 'come from character', regardless of how tired we all are of hearing that. If a line is just a pun, or a whimsical idea, or a bit of idle wordplay, it's going to fall off when the story hits a pothole. Some jokes are the nodding dogs on the clown car's back window, and some are the spark plugs, the fuel tank, the steering wheel. You want to have as many of those as possible. Then if the car drives in a straight line and doesn't fall to bits, it can also have room for your beloved fluffy dice and the belt-fed hotdog cannon.

47

The Shape of Story

I always fight and argue like hell about the structure when people want to make changes. . . Then we finish the show, and they say: 'God, we're ten minutes too long,' and immediately I go: 'Cut that out. Fuck the structure.' . . . Structure's important until you're ten minutes too long.

John Sullivan
(writer of *Only Fools and Horses*)

Pattern processing is about matching or not matching expectation, and that's as true of a story as it is of a joke. Audiences learn to anticipate the pace of any story from their previous exposure to other stories. Just like the theories of character dynamics, I suspect that a lot of highfaluting theories of mythic structure are simply observations of human habit. The stories humans enjoy most get retold the most, and we start to expect those patterns to repeat, just like Western ears expect Western tuning in music, or Americans happily swallow their strange vomit-flavoured chocolate.

The story patterns with which we are familiar become a handy crib sheet for comprehending anything new. That doesn't mean everything always has to run strictly on the same rails; as we've seen, our pattern-detection engine benefits from a varied diet, because it is nourished by surprise. But we rely on patterns and prototypes because we want our entertainment to Confound not Confuse.

For example (and with a spoiler warning to anyone who's been trapped behind a rock fall since 1960), it's exciting when the protagonist fails to last the course in *Psycho*, because that's not what normally happens, and the switch to watching the antagonist instead is beautifully pulled off by a master storyteller. Because this radical variation is executed with panache, and we are guided through it in a way that keeps us entertained, we're Confounded, not Confused.

If another story uses this hero-killing shape in future, we are more ready for it. But stories tend to work best when they surprise us with their details rather than their fundamental structure. Following the standard accepted pattern of storytelling isn't boring, because we enjoy the feeling of being right too. Remember: to Confirm is as much fun as to Confound, because both sharpen our pattern-spotting engine.

HOW LONG IS A JOKE ABOUT A PIECE OF STRING?

Any story is a balance between artistic expression and audience expectation: the audience marches to whatever pace you set, and you mustn't trick them or trip them up. The opening of any tale you're telling sets the pace for the rest of it. The audience subconsciously absorbs the rate at which you are dropping information into their brains, and then adjusts the points at which they expect to be given new information.

This sense of expected story shape is so innate that it's impossible to create a one-hour show by sticking two half-hour shows together (even in a culture where we now often binge-watch episodes of television back to back). TV execs sometimes try this trick of bolting two episodes together to fit a slot, and it is almost always disastrous. The rhythm feels wrong, without an audience quite being able to articulate why. The truth is that you can't cut story to length like carpet because narrative is not an unending roll; it has a sensed shape.

This means there is an opening section of most stories where the audience is provided with the information they will need to follow the action. This 'receive phase' – you might think of it as a story's Construct note – will be a percentage of the full length of the story. It's a few minutes of establishing beats in a twenty-two-minute sitcom. Or ten minutes, at most, of introductory scenes in a ninety-minute film. 'Who is in this story? What do they want? Where are we? What questions are we asking?' Imagine you are unpacking a toybox, getting all the figures and furniture out so you can set up a doll's house. We can only start to play once the toys are unpacked.

ONCE UPON A TIME. . .

Think of how a fairy story begins. Here's one I liked when I was small, 'The Gingerbread Boy':

> *Once upon a time, there lived a little old man and a little old woman, and they lived on their own in a little old house. They didn't have any little boys, and they didn't have any little girls.*

Great start. Got you. That's all the pieces in play. Can we start the story now?

And sure enough, on the next page the story starts, when the little old lady proposes baking a surrogate gingerbread child, like a sort of godless confectionery Frankenstein. That first page feels like the unpacking of the box of toys and the next page is when we start playing with them. New elements can be brought in later, of course, just as you might add a few more toys to spice up a game when you've exhausted the play value of your initial set-up. But we know that first page is for us to take in Construct data, and the next part will be doing something with it.

In this case the elderly couple's childlessness leads to a beat that makes solid fairytale sense. Baking a novelty cake, even one shaped like a person, is a Confirm note: lonely old ladies do bake cakes to keep busy, and sometimes they make them in funny shapes. If she were explicitly aiming to conjure an enchanted magical child from cake ingredients, we'd wonder why the Construct page hadn't included the fact that she is a witch. But it's just a cake: so, it's a Confirm.

Now the magical part of the story can begin when the gingerbread boy comes to life, in a lovely fairytale Confound. That is the last thing we were expecting! But, check the data, and it sort of makes sense. She made a wish. A wish has come true. And she and her husband react appropriately with surprise. Even a fairytale, where anything can happen, has all the data required, dispensed at the right pace for the audience. No child is going to stop their parent and protest that they don't know what's going on.

CONSTRUCTION TIME

The length of the opening Construct section is instinctive. Though perhaps, more accurately, you might say it's learned. I sometimes describe our sense of the shape of story as 'the weight of the rest of the book in your right hand'. You know roughly how long a story is likely to be, and how much further there is to go, all without quite *knowing* how you know. It's a vague narrative proprioception, caused by a sense of the weight of data to come.

Our brains sense roughly where we are – at the start, or the middle, or the end – and what sort of information is likely to be coming in. And that enables the storyteller to deliver as expected, or surprise us. It's why sitting through an unexpectedly long, meandering film can feel so much less satisfying (or comforting) than sitting through three crisp episodes of a TV show back to back, with their fixed lengths, episode breaks and regular narrative rise and fall. The length of time on the sofa is the same, but the shape of our expectations is completely different.

As a writer, you can feel the crucial opening Construct phase of a story nowhere more keenly than in the room at a test screening of something you've written. The audience, who have been happily paying attention, almost palpably shift in their seats once they sense the toybox has been fully unpacked. Now any new information is not processed as part of the set-up, but as development of what they've already been given. Your audience closes the toybox, turns their attention to the doll's house they've just filled with exciting stuff, and wants to start playing.

ENTER, PURSUED BY A BEAR

The most remarkable example of this that I've seen was working on the film *Paddington 2*, where there was a lot of set-up to get into the start of the story. The first film had to introduce the bear and his bear family, and say how their wild existence related to the human world; then we could send Paddington off on his adventures. But the sequel had all the characters from the first film to get back out of the toy-box – the bear plus his new adopted human family and local nuisance Mr Curry – plus a previously unseen community of interacting neighbours (so the locals could be upset by the removal of the bear later). And we needed a quick recap of what everyone was like in the first film, a sketch of how they'd changed since, and some clues for the audience as to what the characters wanted now. Plus there was a new plot that needed to start running in the background while we were doing that.

Getting all this set-up going took so long that the arrival of Hugh Grant's theatrical antagonist Phoenix Buchanan kept happening quite late in the film's running time, dangerously close to the 'no longer listening' marker in the audience's collective attention. We hoped against hope that the sheer size of the performance would mean it wouldn't matter. If you've seen the film, you'll know that Hugh Grant arrives in that film like a glorious meteor of delicately spiced ham. Surely people would pay attention, even if they were a bit tired from taking in all the preamble.

But preview screenings revealed something crazy: audiences didn't notice him. Grant's first plot beat came after the audience had thought we'd got all the toys out, so his arrival was categorised as a pleasant celebrity cameo, not an important part of the story. And then when his character reappeared a few scenes later, carrying the entire plot, it was confusing. The audience got lost.

The story needed to have all its essential toys out of the box earlier. There were two solutions: editing in Grant's first appearance earlier (which was tricky because it was attached to a specific location) or cutting the other introductory material to the bone, so that it was over more quickly. This was director Paul King's eventual solution, meaning the character's arrival was pulled just back inside the line marked 'set-up'. Now the audience was still in 'getting out the toys' mode, and not 'playing' mode when Phoenix Buchanan turned up, and they all knew instinctively where to put him.

Nobody watching the film at any of those fidgety previews would have written 'antagonist arrived too late after initial set-up phase' on the forms that the studio collected

afterwards to help gauge audience response. They would
have just felt confused, or not enjoyed the film.

'What was it like?' 'It was. . . OK. . . The bear was cute.
Not as good as the first one. . .'*

This sort of innate structure is subconscious. We don't
know what's wrong; we usually just feel that we've stopped
having fun, that the story is hard to follow, that we don't
care. It's why editing is such an important part of creating
stories, because the order and pace of events can always be
fine-tuned to fit an audience's unconscious expectations
better, and the effects on our enjoyment of the story are
profound.

---

* I dropped Paul King a line to check it was OK to share this story, and he sadly
informed me that he was currently repeating the same mad process on his current
film, tearing his hair out trying to get the stupidly overambitious number of set-up
beats essential for the story in before the audience-fidget line. Every single time,
we build our unwieldy Homermobiles again, and we haven't learned a thing.

48

The Straight Story

*If a comic laughs at their own jokes, I don't like it.
They shouldn't find it funny. They should seriously
believe in this stupid thing they're saying.*

James Acaster

If we need to have a simple story behind our jokes, we're
going to have to figure out the best way to structure one.
So let's park the funny for a bit, and talk about story structure. After all, if your jokes depend on subverting or
confirming expectation, you need to manage that expectation. Any lack of storytelling clarity will really get in the
way of the guessing game, because your audience can't
play properly if they're Confused.

And the big problem is that comedy is really busy.
There are patterns being set and broken all over the
place, at the level of words, lines, jokes, character, scenes.
Good comedy has loads going on. The hardest pattern to
establish, therefore, is extended plot, because it's the last
thing your audience has got its eye on if you're doing your
job properly.

So the clearer your overarching story can be, and
the more simply it can be told, the better.* Will these guys

---

* This is particularly the case with a long fictional narrative, but applies to any
extended structure, such as the shape of a one-hour stand-up show.

fall in love? Will they get the thing they want? Will they escape? It's usually a good idea to keep this central story clear and simple because the audience's focus should be elsewhere, with any luck, enjoying all the lovely comic detail.

It's a matter of taste, but I don't think anybody should come to a comedy for the intricate dramatic plotting; they can get that somewhere else. That's not to say that a comedy can't have a satisfying, emotional story – in fact, that helps, because a strong, engaging story is easier to follow. But the unique value of comedy is in its prioritising of laughs. Comedy is the funny one. So be funny.

And to be funny, your story needs to be clear. But the perhaps unexpected corollary of that is that your story doesn't have to be funny.

PLAY IT STRAIGHT

'Hang on,' you might say. 'If comedy is for laughing... why should the story not be funny? Shouldn't everything be funny?'

The glib answer? No. Jokes are short and stories are long. Story made its choice when it decided to take its sweet time. It's not a joke. It's too long. So it's something else.

Take it as permission to have a break. You can't use a crazy, fizzing switchback form like jokes and make a solid structure out of it, any more than you can build a house using only soft furnishings. They're different things. This is all about that clown car on the test track. If it hasn't got real wheels, a proper engine, it's not going anywhere.

So the surprising discovery is that if you're doing a detective spoof, make it a real murder case. Every plot in *Police Squad* is one Columbo might try to crack. *Wacky*

Races? The cars are crazy but it's still a real race. *Annie Hall* is a real love story. The producers in *The Producers* are, as far as they're concerned, caught up in a real drama of Broadway funding. Jack Lemmon and Tony Curtis's jazzers in *Some Like It Hot* are really going to be murdered by the Mob. Sure, they're in drag, and there's comic mistaken identity that arises from that, but the threat and the direction of the story are believable and real. The crime stories in *The Ladykillers* and *The Lavender Hill Mob* and *The Big Lebowski* alike are played absolutely straight. Real robbery. Real kidnap. Real danger. It's the funny details and characters strung along that serious storyline that give them comic flavour.

There's an old writer's rule that the audience will usually suspend disbelief for one crazy idea – a teenager with spider powers, say – but will get exhausted if asked to accept two, three or more – and he travels through time, and everyone in his city has a talking condiment set as a sidekick, and we view the action from inside his head, where his emotions are controlled by a cartoon octopus in a top hat. A good story should play out the honest implications of its best idea, not keep adding comedy spins until it's simply confusing.

It's a good habit to carry across into plotting a comedy. Come up with an idea that has comic potential, and then, playing it as straight as you can, see what happens if. . .

'AND DON'T CALL ME SHIRLEY'

A good comic plot can hinge on a single funny twist. Here are some great ones:

- A hustler director tries to film a star vehicle without the star knowing he's in it.
- A man wakes up in a time loop, and uses it to get the girl.

- North London slackers hide from the zombie apocalypse down the pub.
- An ordinary man in biblical times is mistaken for the Messiah.
- A cocktail-toting fast-talking flirty married couple solve a murder mystery.
- A young man obsessed with death falls in love with an old woman obsessed with life.
- Two best friends finish their school history project using a time machine.
- A struggling actor drags up to get a job and becomes a star.
- Two producers try to stage the worst musical of all time but it's accidentally a hit.
- Two friends go to a school reunion pretending they're successful businesswomen.

The jokes that are pulled at story-beat level in these classic comedies are minimal, exploiting their single comic element with integrity, and following where it goes. Sometimes the comic twist is merely a matter of switching the expected casting (*Shaun of the Dead*, for example, is a fairly straightforward zombie horror film, with real emotional stakes and thrills, but the protagonists have been swapped in from a slacker flat-share sitcom). Otherwise, the story engine in a good comedy is as propulsive as any drama, with the same solid character-rooted beats you'd expect if played straight.

Even sketch-based comedy films tend to string their routines along a straight plot, often borrowed from a familiar genre. Comedy writer David Quantick calls this 'Oxbridge plotting', from the way that the university-revue-trained comedians like the *Monty Python* team or Pete and Dud would peg sketch material along the washing line of a pre-existing story (Arthurian epic, *Boy's Own* adventure serial, Sherlock Holmes mystery, the Faust legend, etc.). It's a way to turn sketch-writing into big-screen storytelling, by borrowing someone else's engine. Oxbridge-revue-trained Richard Curtis even gave away the secret string-of-sketches formula in the title of his first big hit, *Four Weddings and a Funeral*. Assembling sketches over a strong, straight shape is a way of keeping a story on the rails while building it from funny modular units. Even a freewheeling sketch-based comedy like *Anchorman* has a straightforward showbiz documentary structure underneath. And how many sincere underdog sports movies have had their skeleton borrowed by that same American goofy sketch-comedy factory?

A non-joke plot is easier to be silly over the top of, because it provides clear patterns for audience expectations. It's distracting if you're cracking gags at every level. That's like a song where every instrument is playing a solo. There's a place for free jazz, sure, but don't expect to have your music requested much at weddings. A simple story, honestly told, can support the wildest comic invention. Remember: the characters (and the audience) really want the plane to land safely in *Airplane!* and that's the most stupid film ever.*

CIGARETTE-PACKET STORYTELLING

I remember once running into *Peep Show* and *Fresh Meat* writers Sam Bain and Jesse Armstrong at a launch party. They'd recently returned from LA where they had been working alongside the crème de la crème of British writing talent, coming up with a plot for a new star-vehicle comedy

---

* The makers of *Airplane!* borrowed those edge-of-the-seat beats from *Zero Hour!*, a real 1950s airborne-disaster movie whose script they followed so slavishly they had to buy the rights. They later said the biggest mistake they made was to try to make their follow-up movie, *Top Secret!*, without sticking their jokes over an existing dramatic plot.

movie. 'How did it go?' I asked. 'Almost impossible. So hard,' they replied. 'So is it a tricky plot?' I said. 'No. You could write it on a cigarette packet. But if you go to the cinema and think "that plot is ridiculously simple", then we've all done our jobs.' A world-beating international Brains Trust had been assembled to come up with a story so basic, so obvious, and therefore so clear, that the comedy would be free to work over the top. That's the aim.

If your character and gag patterns are beautiful, imaginative and complex (which is how you are going to make clever jokes that will take people by surprise, and also deliver satisfying confirmations of character), you don't also want a crazy unpredictable pattern pulsing away in the background. Because then you'll just give people a headache.

Sometimes the best place to hang a load of brightly coloured pictures is on a plain white wall.

49

The Big Questions

Drama is intention and obstacle. Somebody wants something. Someone is standing in their way of getting it... In a courtroom, the intention and obstacle are clear. The stakes are high. There are two opposing sides. The formality of the argument, that each gets a turn.

Aaron Sorkin
(writer of *The West Wing* and *A Few Good Men*)

There are endless books on story structure, some of which are superb, and some of which are plain confusing. The growing popularity of the idea of a narrative monomyth, some innate human story we are compelled to retell, means writers can find themselves wilting under the onerous weight of their duties as an eternal bard. But getting a Sharpie and a whiteboard and trying to make your story fit Buck Clusterfuck's Narrative Octagon of Potential, marking points where the hero *transcends the wildwood* or *envelops the witch* feels a bit silly as soon as you remember you were meant to be writing a ten-minute under-fives cartoon called *Wobbles the Pirate Potato* (which is what most of us actually find ourselves writing to keep the wolf from the door).*

---

* 'The wolf at the door' is almost certainly beat twelve in Buck Clusterfuck's classic Ascent of Story Mountain system. I imagine.

BUT STORY IS HARD, SO WE MADE IT SIMPLER

The best, practical roll-the-sleeves-up writing tool to fix story that I've ever come across is Trey Parker and Matt Stone's storylining system for *South Park*. It's great, and it demonstrates that what the human brain is looking for in a story is the same thing that it's looking for in a joke: pattern.

Parker and Stone's method is to write down their story, as loosely as you would do if you were telling an anecdote to a friend. Then you go back and make sure that none of the beats of your story are linked by the word 'and'.

Yup. It's as simple as that.

If one beat is separated from another by the word 'and', they're not connected. It's like building a Lego wall by grabbing random coloured blocks out of the box and snapping them together. It kind of works, but it lacks a pleasing pattern. It's the way that an overexcited five-year-old might tell a story (or build a Lego wall, for that matter). It's fun, but usually too chaotic to really please our pattern-loving brains.

> *And we went to the zoo and I've got a bear at home and the stone in my shoe hurt and Maddie had more ice cream than me and Mum broke a fingernail taking the wheel off the car.*

This sort of 'And'-based storytelling is somehow both tantalising *and* boring. As Homer Simpson memorably says, 'It's just a bunch of stuff that happened.' If this story were a string of musical notes, it would be jumping about all over the place, creating a 'challenging' melody that might get some hipster chins stroked, but nobody's going to whistle it.

Parker and Stone's genius was to work out that the connecting words you need are 'But' and 'So'. Something happened *BUT* something else happened. Something happened *SO* something else happened. Now each event is connected to its neighbour by a link of causation or obstruction.

Let's try the kid's story again with a bit more 'So' and 'But'.

> *So we said we'd spend all day looking round the zoo. But I love bears. So we went straight to the bear enclosure. But it was a long way. So it took ages. But I had a stone in my shoe. So we stopped for ice cream. But Maddie and me had an argument about it. So we had to go home. But the car broke down. So Mum tried to phone the repair van. But they took ages to come. So she took the wheel off herself. But she broke her fingernail.*

I love the 'But' and 'So' method, because it's simple and practical, and – because nobody in comedy writes character-based storylines faster than the *South Park* team, with their insane weekly topical turnaround – it's battle-tested. They needed to develop a factory production line for story, and they came up with one that's Henry Ford good.

You might notice that the system doesn't proscribe what goes between the 'But' and 'So' connectors, leaving you free to pick any subject matter or treatment (which is handy for a freewheeling show like *South Park*). 'But' and 'So' help make your story strong and clear enough to support your ideas and jokes. The audience can follow where you're going, and trusts you, because your story has purpose, revealed by its pattern.

THE BIG QUESTION

So we have a formula for linking our story beats. But we don't have a story.*

---

* 'So' and 'But'. See? It's brilliant. Works every time. Now we're motoring.

Obviously it's not hard to make up a story. 'Can Wobbles the Pirate Potato steal Captain Carrot's treasure?' is a functional story. And then we can put things in Wobbles' way (doors, crocodiles, outbreaks of whatever maritime illness vitamin-C rich potatoes get instead of scurvy). That way it's not just 'And', 'And', 'And.' Obstacles and consequences are all in place, a sense of pattern, and we get a nice 'But' and 'So' rhythm going.

> But the treasure map is in the parrot's nest. So Wobbles climbs the tree. But his peg-leg falls off . . .

The only problem is that I've written loads of these, and they're sometimes not very exciting. A story like that has a direction and a rhythm to it, a pattern, even, but nobody really cares. (Except pirate potatoes looking for treasure, and they're not your intended audience.)

One elegant solution is to realise that a good story isn't a destination, but a question. So the art is in finding the best question. You want one that your audience (and you, importantly) want an answer to. Then the thing catches fire.

This idea of 'story as question' is hard-earned writing advice that I picked up from a splendid lecture by comedy-writer-turned-modern-horror-supremo Craig Mazin (*The Hangover*, *Chernobyl*, *The Last of Us*). He proposed that the reason people really loved big hit movies was that these films didn't just tell a story (which could meander all over the place if you weren't careful) but rather posed a question to which we might want to know the answer.

Mazin used the example of family-favourite fish flick *Finding Nemo*. Looking at it carefully, the story wasn't 'Can Nemo's dad find Nemo?' as you might expect from the title. It was 'Can an anxious parent learn to trust their child to be independent?' When you think about it, a story about actually *finding* Nemo would be little more than a dramatised game of hide-and-seek, or one of those lift-the-flap books that satisfy pre-schoolers but are rarely optioned by big Hollywood studios. 'Is he in the rock pool? Nobody there!' But framing the story as an urgent question, with wider resonance for the audience, gave each scene in the story a reason to be there, creating both structure and significance.

I think this Big Question system works because it means the audience has a reason to follow the story, but it also gives you, the writer, a reason to write it in the first place. It's a rare practical storytelling tool that's not replacing inspiration with a mechanical system. It increases our engagement with the story we're telling, because if your story is a question you want to explore, it won't bore you. And if it doesn't bore you, you'll enjoy writing it, and then it won't bore someone else. Of course, that means a good story-inciting question should be something you want to know yourself, and then the story you write is you puzzling it out.

If you already know the answer, why bother? Writing takes *ages*.

50

Is This the Right Room
For an Argument?

*If I start on a film and right away know the structure –
where it's going, the plot – I don't trust it.*

Pete Docter
(writer and director of *Monsters, Inc.* and *Up*)

So the theory is that all good stories need a central question. But how best to answer it? Because I like patterns,
since I am a human being, I started to wonder if maybe I
could work out a pattern of answers to the core story question (like *South Park*'s delightfully practical 'But' and 'So'
system) that would make fixing story beats easier when I
got stuck or lost.

So I followed the patterns of answers in some of my
favourite stories. And I found that they were doing something really satisfying. These stories answered their stated
question by looking at the question from different angles
in successive scenes, and changing their mind based on the
evidence. And the pattern they made was so simple it was
hilarious. The question was stated at the top of the story.
And then, wherever I looked, the story beats went. . .

Yes. No. Yes. No.

*Can men and women be friends without sex getting in
the way? Yes they can. No they can't. Yes they can. No
they can't.*

It was screenwriting by Irving Berlin. The *Annie Get Your Gun* system.

I'll stress that I don't think it's how stories are *written*. No good writer is listlessly flicking a mechanical switch forwards and backwards. (Though being aware of this rhythm certainly won't be a hindrance if you're trying to work out the beats of a story for the first time.) Storytelling is organic and should start from the gut, with honesty and self-expression, and an interest in human interaction.

But I do suspect it's how stories are edited and fixed, whether the people fixing them know it, or not.

Whether you're refining drafts, cutting an edit, or simply retelling an anecdote you've told many times to friends, you take out stuff that doesn't move the story on. If you're cutting to the chase, that chase needs movement. Answer 'Yes' to your core question in a scene, and your audience aren't looking for another 'Yes'. They will be waiting for the counterargument. Give the same answer twice and the audience's attention will wander. But you can maintain their interest by constantly saying, 'On the other hand. . .'

Also, if your story answers 'Yes' or 'No' three times in a row, it will seem like you're coming down hard on one side or the other. That will feel like you've reached a conclusion, and your audience will expect the end credits soon, and a chance to go for a wee. So writers naturally keep flipping from 'Yes' to 'No' to keep the story alive. It's a courtroom drama. If the debate is over and one side has won, we're done here. To maintain narrative drive, you want to keep stating one side, leading the audience one way, and then stating the other.

A good story gets its energy by not answering its own questions straight away. Why? Because that's what the story is there for in the first place. Story should be a process, not a conclusion. When you really love a story, you'll notice that a sense of not-knowing is somehow there every time you return to it, even if you know the ending.

I suspect it's why spoilers often don't actually spoil something (and why much-anticipated endings of long stories often disappoint). The destination is... fine. It's nice to have an answer. But the journey, the uncertainty, is the fun.

With a good initial question, and a satisfying uncertainty about the answer, we can rewatch favourite films and reread favourite books. We put ourselves back in that satisfying *yes, no, yes, no* space again. The story retains its energy because it doesn't know the answer, even if we do.

And then at the end, a moment of resolution. Yes or no. The final verdict. 'Yes! They did it! Hurrah!' Or 'No, they failed. Everyone died; how sad.' And in the case of plenty of very influential and popular stories (especially in the less commercial, artier end of storytelling), the creators will stop their to-and-fro debate with the question still unresolved, and leave you to make your own conclusion. 'It was never a ghost at all . . . or was it?'

NO FURTHER QUESTIONS, M'LUD

West Wing writer Aaron Sorkin said he always treated story as a court case, and his much-admired plotting tends to follow the to and fro of prosecution and defence around a central argument. It's a back-and-forth rhythm Sorkin learned from his lawyer parents.

The shape of legal argument works for drama, but can also be used to firm up the structure of a book, or a sketch, or even an article or a blog post, to give it rhythm and shape, and keep it moving. In emulating the shape of newspaper prose to structure spoof press articles for *Viz*, I noticed one day that I was always following this pattern of back-and-forth debate.

Even if the central proposition of a gag piece was as idiotic as whether a cryptozoological monster was actually Bungle from *Rainbow*, or if psychic Uri Geller could produce dogshits on demand, the best structure was for the reader to think alternately that the headline's ridiculous claim was credible, and then not. I suspect it's why newspaper headlines often have a question mark in them.

So to tell a good story, we ask a question. Then argue it out.

- Can two women in the youth-obsessed fashion industry resist the inevitable passage of time?
- Can a man with anger issues ever succeed running a hotel?
- Can two likely lads stay friends when one of them gets married?
- Can a man's independent spirit survive in prison?

Those keep a bunch of classic sitcoms going very well. How about some classic films?

- Am I going to stay alone on this boring farm, or make a load of cool space friends instead?
- Can a good girl and a greaser rebel sustain their love with their schoolfriends watching?
- Does a man's life mean nothing if he stayed in Bedford Falls and never travelled like he promised himself?

You'll notice that even if the setting of these stories is alien to us (prison, the planet Tatooine, hospitality), the questions are about human relationships and have outside resonances. That way your audience are going to stick around to find out the answer. Because it might be useful.

BACK ON THE OLD JOANNA

So we could label those alternate story beats 'Yes' and 'No'. And there are certainly echoes of *South Park*'s 'But' and 'So'. It's a pattern in a couple of colours. Which is very satisfying.

And of course, if you're hunched over the familiar comedy keyboard, working out your 'Yes' and 'No' beats, you'll find you're back playing a melody on the two basic notes that underpin all comedy: Confirm and Confound.

Oh, and before we can answer the question, we have to set up a world where there is a question to be answered. Which means the first note of the story's pattern is a Construct.

And if we're staring at the comedy keyboard it's worth remembering that if we connect two beats with an 'And', people get bored and lost. That's because the 'And' beat is a Confuse. 'Why did that happen? It just did.' Any time we use 'And', it's not anchored to the central question we're following, so everyone gets lost.

Construct. Confirm. Confound. And never Confuse. It turns out that's not just jokes. It's story too.

A story's core question will usually be related to the protagonist's worldview. They enter the story with an expectation of the answer to come. *Of course men and women can't be friends without sex getting in the way.* Then a 'Yes' note will Confirm that view. They were right. A 'No' will Confound it. They were wrong. And that's our tune. Three notes, one of which you play at the start, and the other two which you alternate to maintain interest.*

Driving story with a Sorkin-esque legal back-and-forth is fascinating because that's exactly the process we saw when we were talking about theory of mind with regard to comic characters. It's a point-of-view game that gives

* I first observed this Yes-No shape happening in a bunch of my favourite audience-pleasing blockbuster movies, and it's appropriate that the ultimate blockbuster storytelling technique should also be the theme tune from *Jaws*.

our empathy and perspective systems a workout. What if we look at the question from a pessimistic stance, then an optimistic one? Maybe two characters could take a side each? How does it look if we think the answer is 'Yes'? How does it look if we're convinced it's 'No'?

I love finding these simple instruments that can produce satisfying and profound stories. It's like discovering you can play *The Lark Ascending* on a Swanee whistle.

KILLING THE BEAR

Asking a question and answering 'Yes' and 'No' is such a powerful story tool because it simplifies things that other theories of storytelling insist on calling by much more arcane and mythical-sounding names. The Call to Action? That's a 'Yes'. The beat where the hero Refuses the Call? That's a 'No'. The hero's Death and Rebirth? Sounds like a pretty big 'No' then a great big 'Yes' to me.

In the two *Paddington* films (and I still feel a mixture of pride and horror about how well these bits work) the loveable bear is 'killed' on screen near the end, once in an air vent and once in a submerged train. It's a version of the 'hero's death' beat from classic storytelling. There's a fun mythic bonus (if you like that sort of thing) because the bear is overcome respectively by the elements of fire and water. But it's really just a big penultimate 'No'.

The audience holds its breath. The question in those films is 'Can a refugee rely on the kindness of strangers?'* and at both of these near-death points, Paddington is alone and nobody is looking after him. So the answer is

---

* One of the best moments writing those films was realising (in a final edit-bash a couple of weeks before the premiere of *Paddington 2*) that the underlying question of the story had been alluded to by the little bear's iconic luggage tag all along. *'Please look after this bear. Thank you.'*

'No'. But, it's a kids' film, so a few seconds after the 'No' gasp, friendly hands appear and rescue him, returning the verdict 'Yes'. In the first film the hands belong to his adoptive family, and then in the second film it's the tattooed fists of society's most mistrustful and wounded outcasts. Judging by audience response, both these moments of 'Yes' feel wonderful.

Deploying climactic, almost melodramatic 'Yes' and 'No' beats is such a powerful tool that you can change the meaning of your whole story by stopping on 'Yes' or 'No', or choosing to leave the case unproven. Snap that last victorious 'Yes' beat off, so your argument ends on a 'No', and you've got a tragedy. Leave the answer ambiguous and the audience can take the argument home to settle themselves. Maybe you want to let the jury decide. End on a massive 'Yes' to a question that people privately worry to themselves might be a 'No', and you may have written the feelgood hit of the year.

So all we need is a good, satisfying question to start. Then 'Yes' and 'No'. The two notes of a good story. Back and forth. An unsettled melody that makes a beautiful, basic pattern. One note then its opposite. Up and down. For as long as you like.

It's such a simple tune.

An Incredible Story

The easiest way to build a story is not to use your imagination, but to simply apply logic.

Nell Scovell

Because this was all inspired by Craig Mazin's revelations about *Finding Nemo* (and because Pixar is a studio whose practised method is famously good at coming up with clear narratives that audiences of all ages love), let's look at another of the peak-period Pixar films. Brad Bird's *The Incredibles* manages to be a family comedy with an action-movie pulse, and, like the best stories, its central question is something its creator wanted to answer for himself.

The Incredibles was inspired, Bird says, by his own midlife crisis about work-life balance. Could someone give focus to a time-consuming, obsessive job (as, say, a superhero, or one of the world's top animation directors) and also be a good parent? Your family audience are going to want to know that too, so we're away.

If you're relying on this basic-as-hell two-note Yes-No story keyboard for your structure, the central question needs to be compelling enough for the audience to stick around to hear the possible answers. Even a simplistic mission-based story like a James Bond film isn't really asking 'Can 007 stop the evil Doctor Craphat stealing the moon?' That's the plot. The story, the central question, is more like 'Can a man balance his lust for pleasure with his sense of duty?' It's a bloke fussing about work-life balance again, making Bond the perfect franchise for the working-dad audience. In that sense, *The Incredibles* didn't just lift its musical score from the suave superspy.

So let's ask the same question *The Incredibles* did, and see how each beat of the story answers it. Once you spot the pattern, it's quite exhilarating to watch it streak by like a precision-engineered Incrediblemobile. In this story, Pixar really knows what it's doing.

The Incredibles: Yes-No Beat Breakdown

PRELIMINARY SCENES
The story so far. . .

THE QUESTION: *Can we balance our need for success and self-expression with our responsibilities to our family?*

1. Superheroes are interviewed about their tricky split identities. NO.
2. We see Mr Incredible at work. He is brilliant at it. YES.
3. Mr Incredible meets Elastigirl. She tells him he needs to be more flexible. NO.
4. A big superhero adventure breaks out. Mr Incredible saves the day. YES.
5. Mr Incredible arrives late to his own wedding to Elastigirl. She cautions him. NO.

Elastigirl whispers the film's central quandary to her new husband. . .

ELASTIGIRL: *To make this marriage work, you have to be more than Mr Incredible.*

ACT ONE

We set up the world: basically 'Marvel's Fantastic Four are a sitcom family'.

THE QUESTION AGAIN: Can we balance our need for success and self-expression with our responsibilities to our family?

6. The superheroes' colourful antics have seen them banned. Mr Incredible has a dull job. The family are settled but frustrated. Nobody is themselves. NO.
7. Mr Incredible and old super-friend Frozone do some secret hero work. YES.
8. Elastigirl tells her husband he is ignoring family life. 'You are missing this.' NO.
9. Mr Incredible's superheroic side explodes at work, doing what he is good at. YES.
10. The incident is covered up for him but he loses his job. He can't keep doing this. NO.
11. Mirage, a mysterious woman, asks for his help. 'You can still do great things.' YES.
12. Mirage's exciting superhero-mission-briefing message explodes, wrecking the family home (and nailing the central theme of the film). NO.
13. Mr Incredible lies that work is sending him to a conference. Maybe he can have both lives, career and domestic, after all! YES.

And so on. . . Yes, No, Yes, No, back and forth. I've continued the breakdown for the whole film, which I'll put in an appendix (pages 350–56) for anyone who wants to play the game right to the end, but trust me, it works. Yes, No, Yes, No. All the way to the penultimate *Nooooooo!* where all seems lost. Then, don't worry, we get a climactic *Yessssss!* to send us home happy, punching the air.

Sometimes a 'Yes' or 'No' beat will be made up of a

string of smaller scenes (for example, the wonderful 'Yes' montage of Mr Incredible getting back in superhero shape and being a great dad at the same time). And sometimes a beat will merely be a brief flash of triumph or impending disaster (such as the tiny heart-in-mouth 'No' moment when Elastigirl is convinced Mr Incredible has been caught in a romantic clinch with the flirtatious Mirage). But we still feel that uncertain swing, propelling the story on towards an answer. This gripping narrative tennis match – Yes, No, Yes, No – is the drive that keeps everything moving.

If you imagine the classic coloured index cards on the writers' room wall, tagged to 'Yes' and 'No', we'd see one colour, then its opposite, in a pleasing chequerboard. The 'Yes' and 'No' makes a regular, satisfying pattern to follow. And we do love patterns.

THE QUIET QUESTION

So, if the story is a series of answers to a question, how do you ask that question so the audience hear it clearly, and therefore can follow your pattern? There's a neat trick that I've observed in countless stories, and it really works:

- Find a quiet place, near the start of your story.
- Lower your voice. So the audience lean in.
- And then you whisper your question.

Look back at the Yes-No breakdown for *The Incredibles* – there's a point, at beat 5, where the theme is stated by Elastigirl at the altar:

5. Mr Incredible arrives late to his own wedding to Elastigirl. She cautions him. NO.

Elastigirl whispers the film's central quandary to her new husband. . .

ELASTIGIRL: *To make this marriage work, you have to be more than Mr Incredible.*

Nobody shouts it. It's not on a mission briefing on a huge wall screen. It doesn't come in an exploding briefcase. It's almost a whisper. A little intimate warning out the side of her mouth. But the important point is: it comes exactly when we, the audience, are listening.

Looking for this beat in stories that I loved, I noticed that the best place to pop the question appears to be right after an absolutely wonderful bit where you've fulfilled every promise to your audience. If it's a romcom, we should just have enjoyed some fizzy banter between the leads. If it's a thriller, we should be calming down after a car chase. Everybody in the audience is well fed, happy and completely on-side.

Then pause.

And have someone say what your story is about.

It doesn't matter what else your characters think they're doing, whatever mission they're on, whatever their declared aims. What they say they *want* isn't important. But what they *need* in your story is to be able to answer this one Quiet Question.

And you don't need to know what your question is going to be before you start writing (though well done if you do). Often making a story work is just a matter of discovering you've asked the wrong question, or that you've accidentally asked two questions, or three. Or that you had one question, but asked it at the wrong point, when it was too noisy, or too late, or too early, and nobody heard.

But it's all about making sure the question is heard, and then answering it.

LOUD STORIES OFF QUIET QUESTIONS

The Incredibles is a huge, brassy, superhero epic. But its central question isn't about giant robots, or saving the world from baddies, or a crystal mitten that will cause the end of the universe. It's about something small, relatable and simple: being a good dad.

And it's *whispered*.

I started looking for these tiny, mumbled questions elsewhere and was surprised that even if I looked at some of the biggest blockbusters I could think of, they were still tied to a simple Quiet Question. You know that tug on your heart at the beginning of *Star Wars* when Luke stares at the two suns? That's the Quiet Question happening. 'Will I ever be more than a lonely small-town hot-rod nerd?' That's the core question that lonely small-town hot-rod nerd George Lucas cared about more than 'Can I blow up a metal planet?' (Yeah, sure you can, but who cares? Don't you want to be so cool that you're friends with a princess, actual Bigfoot and the Space Fonz? And then they stand in a row so we can all see? THE END!)

Quiet Questions are a beautiful trick to keep stories anchored. Which helps them mean something to an audience.

What surprised me was how many popular hit stories were driven, not by their loudly declared plot aims, but by character-based Quiet Questions. I found two great examples in a pair of Steven Spielberg classics that I'd loved since I was a kid, where the heroes didn't get what they said they wanted, but the films still felt exhilarating and triumphant.

In *E.T.*, ten-year-old Elliott wants a friend. And he finds one. And then at the end, his friend leaves, never to return. And we all feel happy. Hang on. That's a sad ending, right?

He loses his best friend. Why do I want to stand and cheer?

But there's a quiet moment round the kitchen table, after his first encounter with E.T. in the yard, where Elliott makes a snarky remark about his absent dad being 'in Mexico with Sally'. The comment visibly hurts his mother. His brother asks (quietly, of course), 'Why don't you think of anyone but yourself?' Bang. There's the theme: 'Can lonely, hurting Elliott learn to feel for someone else other than himself?' And at the end we see Elliott has learned empathy.

Question answered, so the alien can go. The answer to the Quiet Question was what we wanted settled, not the more loudly declared goal of 'I must be forever friends with a squidgy goblin I found in the shed'.

In *Raiders of the Lost Ark*, Indiana Jones doesn't get the Ark at all – his eyes are closed when the prize is opened, so he doesn't even get to satisfy his academic curiosity – but we still feel like he's won at the end. Because the quest for the Lost Ark is just the plot. Which begs the question: what's the story? Why do we feel satisfied, when Indy fails by his own declared terms?

Of course, the Quiet Question the audience is waiting to have answered with a big, crowd-pleasing 'Yes' isn't the treasure hunt mission, it's a more subtle moment near the start. And it's not about the box at all. After the exactly-what-we-came-for temple chase with the big stone ball, Belloq, the smug French archaeologist, steals the golden statue Indy just snaffled and whispers meanly, 'There is nothing you can have that I cannot take away.'

You'll notice that the Quiet Question doesn't necessarily have to be phrased with a question mark. It just needs to sow a question in our minds. And sure enough, Indy loses the Ark of the Covenant at the end, but he gets the girl. Resourceful, brilliant Marion Ravenwood is, it turns out, something Belloq couldn't take away (even with the promise of a nice-but-impractical dress and a bottle of his family's best eau-de-vie).

Quiet Question answered. Story done.

The daftest comedy needs this simple clarity as much as the biggest blockbuster. Because comedy plots should really be straight plots with jokes hung on them. The audience wants to be able to follow what's going on, and know when the hero has won or lost. And for achieving that, the Quiet Question is a wonderful tool. Look for it in stories you love. And steal it. It's an amazing trick.

Plot vs Story

I wanted Hitch-Hiker's to sound like a rock album. I wanted the voices and the effects and the music to be so seamlessly orchestrated as to create a coherent picture of a whole other world – and I said this and many similar sorts of things and waved my hands around a lot, while people nodded patiently and said 'Yes, Douglas, but what's it actually about?'

Douglas Adams

The idea of the Quiet Question reveals something that I'd never been able to quite articulate before: that plot and story are different things. The loudly declared aim is plot (get the treasure, beat the baddie, escape the trap, win the contest, dude, where's my car?). And the quietly stated question is your story (Is there something more precious than money? Can we learn to work together? Should you trust your feelings? But why did you lose my car, dude?).

The plot is declared openly, and is needed to get things moving. But what we are actually watching, and what we really care about, is the story.

Alfred Hitchcock, talking to fellow director François Truffaut, shared a famous explanation of why plot is often little more than a load of antic bullshit to keep your characters moving. He called the plot motor in his thrillers 'The MacGuffin'.

> *[The MacGuffin] is the device, the gimmick, if you will, or the papers the spies are after . . . So the 'MacGuffin' is the term we use to cover all that sort of thing: to steal plans or documents, or discover a secret, it doesn't matter what it is.*

I like how this lines up with the idea of plot and story being different. The MacGuffin turns our plot into a little cart on a track. It gathers speed along the rails, while our characters sit in the back chatting about something more interesting: the story. Here's Hitchcock again:

> *And the logicians are wrong in trying to figure out the truth of a MacGuffin, since it's beside the point. The only thing that really matters is that in the picture the plans, documents, or secrets must seem to be of vital importance to the characters. To me, the narrator, they're of no importance whatever.*

Which is what the MacGuffin does. It's the declared aim, but if we, the storyteller, start to mistake it for the actual *story*, we'll miss a chance to do something more interesting. Which is a good habit for a thriller, but for a comedy, it's absolutely essential. Separating plot and story means we have loads of opportunity for subversive little character games and unexpected gags without ever losing momentum, or getting waylaid.

If you check out the appendix for the full *Incredibles* breakdown, you'll notice that the film's wonderfully realised supervillain Syndrome barely appears in our Yes-No storyline. On paper, it's a superhero story with a great supervillain, but it turns out he's all plot. He's just there as an impulse to push the heroes towards another 'No' or 'Yes' beat in the actual story of Mr Incredible's midlife shambles.* The question isn't 'Can Mr Incredible beat Syndrome?' A fictional hero beating a fictional baddie has no resonance beyond the fiction itself. But the story – 'Can a heroic career thrive alongside the needs of family?' – is what we came to find out, because the answer to that might be useful to us puny humans after we leave the cinema.

THEME FROM A QUIET PLACE

Teasing plot and story apart is a real writer's skill. I suspect that what a writer needs to think of as 'story' – the essential underlying question being answered by your writing – is what many people talk about as 'theme'. In everyday usage, 'theme' has slightly pretentious associations: a chin-stroking bonus for critics and students to chew over. But your 'theme' is what we are addressing with your Quiet Question. Every 'Yes' and 'No' beat then becomes a restatement of the central theme of the story, and an exploration of it, and that creates strong, urgent, focused writing. Having a solid theme is just good manners, and means you're not wasting your audience's time. You have a clear aim and are inviting them to join you for the ride.

Theme, when it's tethered to your Quiet Question, is not an optional layer you consider while sucking the arm of your glasses. Every beat of the story refers back to it, answering 'Yes' and 'No'. It's the fundamental scaffolding that holds the whole thing up. Without something urgent that you are asking, and for which you need to find an

---

* Because it's a great script, he's also a place to drop some thematic stuff about the very idea of super-talents, but that's just more lovely texture, and it's surprising how much it doesn't interfere with our main story.

answer because you don't yet know, telling a story is merely going through the motions. And people can tell.

IT'S JUST A BUNCH OF STUFF THAT HAPPENED

While both plot and story have motion and stakes and shape, you might say that plot centres on action, and story centres on emotion. That may be why a lot of fiction aimed at getting a complex emotional reaction can get away with fairly basic plots (at least compared to the average whodunnit, say), while thrillers will often go easier on the emotional story and focus instead on elaborate chains of complicated, maybe even hard-to-follow events.

In certain sorts of drama, for instance a chase thriller like *The French Connection*, the plot (catch the bad guys) and the story (can a rough street cop outwit some classy international criminals?) run side by side, like a car chasing a train. It's hard to tease them apart.

In comedy, though, running your plot and story in lockstep is less useful, because your hopefully stripped-down, easy-to-follow plot will just stop your story being very interesting or funny.

In most cases, the plot *is* just a bunch of stuff that happens, while a good story can be a lot more than that. The plot might simply be the lead character's job. If they're a detective, it's the case they've got to crack. If they're a teacher, it's the problem kid they're dealing with. A doctor has a patient to save, or a medical mystery to untangle. A friend has to drive another friend to a certain destination. A father has to find his missing child. A daughter has to get to her dying father's bedside. That's plot.

But the story is more interesting than the plot, because it's not the character's job or their duty or their mission; it's about who they are. Someone else could, if the hero quit, conceivably step in and handle the plot. It's why we don't mind when the cavalry or the police or the soldiers turn up at the end and take the baddies away.

Plots are anybody's. If another character takes over getting the treasure, it won't matter. But stories belong utterly to the characters involved. Story is anything that any character is doing that nobody else in the story can do. Because the story is theirs alone. It tells us about them; what they want, who they are.

Narrative comedy only works because we understand character, and use that knowledge to play its quickfire prediction games. In comedy, making it plain who your characters are, what questions you are asking of them, and then answering clearly, is everything. Comic storytelling is not about mystery and tension, it's about understanding, and comfort. Comic stories represent us and accept us, at both our worst and our best. We love comic storytelling, I suspect, because in its focus on character, it might teach us something useful about ourselves and each other.

... AND THE PUNCHLINE

53

The Secret of Comedy

You could tell round the [writers'] table whether it's been funny or not ... You will have provoked a gurgling noise at the back of the throat from people around the table or you won't.

Michael Palin

And so we near the end, and, as promised, I will reveal to you the Secret of Comedy. Yeah. Really. That was the promise. I'll not cheat.

What's the secret of comedy? Make 'em laugh.

Three words. Make 'em laugh.

Donald O'Connor in *Singin' in the Rain* was right. It's all in there.

I suspect it's really no more complicated than that. It's not like art. 'What's art?' Who knows. It's really up to the artist to decide to declare their work as art, but it may be that something intended as art does not fulfil (and so on and so on). 'What's drama?' It's an attempt to represent the human condition by reflecting realistically, but sometimes it's not... hang on. Yeah. That's hard. 'What's comedy?' Something that makes 'em laugh.

Unlike drama or ballet or sculpture, you know when you've made comedy: it's when people laugh. If people don't laugh then that's not comedy.* And if something is making people laugh, but not you, you don't get to say 'it's not funny' or sneer at it as 'so-called comedy', because it 100 per cent *is* funny, and it 100 per cent *is* comedy, and we know it is, because, hey, it made 'em laugh. Look at them. They laughed. So that's what that thing is over there, doing that. It's comedy.

But because I love slicing up frogs, let's take the three words of the secret of comedy and, with what we have learned so far, break them down, one by one.

Make

Comedy can happen randomly, sometimes, but usually it needs to be made. Comedy, as distinct from 'things that are funny', involves crafting a comic event using a set of established rules; for example, surprise and confirmation. It is a deliberately designed stimulus that will induce a socially contagious action, resulting in a feeling of well-being. We do it on purpose to each other because it's worth doing.

'Em

Comedy is performed for other members of a social group, or to define a subgroup inside it. Its purpose is to share common references and ideas, and solidify tribal bonds. It is an evolution of grooming behaviour designed to allow comfort, play and safety signals to be exchanged without requiring physical contact. Creating comedy makes us valuable within the tribe, and can help establish and

---

* Or at least quietly feel that distinctively joyous, lightened 'laughing' feeling that we all recognise from watching comedy on our own in private. In a world of small personal screens and private earbuds, that essentially human lightness of heart may have to be our New Laughter.

defend hierarchies. The shared assumptions within comedy are a way of asserting communal values.

Laugh

Comedy causes a contagious physical reaction within our equivalent of a primate grooming group that engenders a feeling of safety and kinship. The sense of relief when an error or surprise juxtaposition is resolved to make sense – by applying our past experience, reading verbal, cultural and social cues, and understanding the declared terms of the comedy – causes the group to relax and return to a low-alert state. Sometimes we will feel this relief internally, silently, privately, but we may also make a noise to signal to others that we are united and safe.

That's all this book has been about.

Arguments about what is and isn't funny just come down to one or the other of these key elements failing. The craft was poor, or you disagreed with the values, or you don't feel safe. Get those three things right, and nobody's arguing.

That's comedy.

54

A Joke Amongst Friends

There is an actual difference between male and female comedy writers and I'm going to reveal it now. The men urinate in cups. And sometimes jars.

Tina Fey

In 2002, Amaani Lyle, a recently fired writers' assistant on *Friends*, took out a lawsuit against the hit show's producers, because her job – basically a secretary who keeps notes of all the crazy ideas being thrown around the writing room – meant she had to transcribe conversations between the writing staff that she felt were offensive. The writing team defended their sometimes edgy and confessional banter as a necessary part of the creative process, particularly on a show filled with occasionally risqué jokes about young people's sex lives. The writing team was mainly male and white. Lyle wasn't. Which made her feel very uncomfortable. So she said something.

The writing team's argument was that saying the unsayable was like clearing your throat before speaking. Before getting down to the business of writing broadcastable network comedy, there was a limbering-up period for the group where the only rule had to be *no rules*. *Friends* was a lucrative factory spinning this room's off-colour banter into syndicated comedy gold.

But it was all just a joke, no harm meant. The tribe was safe. What's the problem? It's funny.

And the writers' assistant lost her case. The *Friends* team argued that although the writers' private warm-up conversations, written down cold on paper, could be seen as racist, misogynist and offensive, none of the aggression in the room was directed *at* Lyle personally. It was comedy, not aggression. There is a difference, as we have seen. The writers and producers meant it sincerely. But the feelings of the rejected member of the team tell us loads about comedy's tribal function. What had happened was that the outsider from the writing-room tribe had been told that they had to accept the majority's values or leave the group.

The tribe and its values were secure. Comedy isn't pretty, yeah, and if you can't take a joke. . .

It's unlikely the result would be quite that way today, now we better understand how 'othering' works in social spaces. But in terms of our Golden Rule of Comedy – Make 'em laugh – what had failed was the middle word. While attempting a skilful Make (resulting in lots of killer jokes), the team had experienced a full-scale 'Em failure (by making one member of the supposed tribe feel as if they didn't belong), and, long term, because suddenly everything felt unsafe (to the extent that lawyers were called in), that had led to Laugh levels falling to zero.

Comedy is always used to make a statement of identity. Any one of us might make in-jokes about our hobbies, home towns, families or worldview, and these jokes are designed to only be shared and enjoyed by 'our people'. We do this for entirely positive reasons, to create a feeling of safety, strength and belonging within our tribe. The writers were right to invoke the idea of a 'safe space', because that was exactly the process. The no-holds-barred chat was to create an environment of trust that would enable the writers to relax and start work.

But because the show only had a certain sort of person in that writers' room, and the writers' assistant didn't belong to their tribe, the natural consequence of that was that this outsider was eventually identified and rejected.

HOW WE GOT HERE

The explosive twenty-first-century issue of what we 'can and can't say' is this same question of who is welcomed inside and who is driven outside the room where we make our jokes. And that isn't a side issue with comedy: it's central to what the thing is.

Making jokes requires sophisticated room-reading skills. The room comes first. Before we can even speak the language of comedy, we need to agree on a shared dictionary. And nowadays, whether writing jokes for a living, sharing a gag in the office or posting funny stuff on a social media feed, none of us are in our assumed-safe-space equivalent of a 1990s *Friends* writers' room. We aren't within a sealed and sacred tribe, unless we actively choose to be. Which is fine. But if we do deliberately seal our bubble, shut the doors, make sure nobody outside the gang is listening, we should know what we're doing, and we shouldn't pretend we haven't locked ourselves away.

Being the one person who isn't laughing feels bad, because that's how comedy works. We use the assumed values buried deep inside jokes to tell people who we are, to draw lines around our social group, to create entrance conditions for membership, and make people within that group feel safe. We might then signal that we have stabilised the social group by exchanging a joke that contains a package of our values. And then we'll signal that we now feel safe by laughing.

And if someone doesn't laugh, that's part of the deal. If that person complains that certain jokes make them feel uncomfortable or persecuted, that's not necessarily down to their paranoia, or humourlessness, or censorship. Yes, sure, they *are* a killjoy, but that's just a literal description of what's happening when someone within the assumed shared values of a joke doesn't share those values. Doing that kills the joy.

Unfortunately, 'making someone outside the gang feel shitty' might just be a blunt description of one of the things jokes are meant to do.

IT'S SUPPOSED TO DO THAT

There's a great 1970s Ray Lowry *Private Eye* cartoon of the *Hindenburg* airship disaster. Most of the half-page drawing is a chaotic inkblot of flame. A tail fin pokes limply out of the fireball. Canvas and ribbing rain down. Far below, a tiny crowd on the ground looks up, and one of them is saying:

> *Does anybody know whether they're supposed to do that?*

That's where comedy is now. We're all looking up at the explosion of hurt feelings and fears of censorship and wondering, 'Does anybody know if comedy is supposed to do that?'

And the answer is: yes.

Comedy isn't meant to make everyone laugh at the same things. It's meant to divide us, and delight us, to appeal to niche audiences. It's not meant to bring the world together in harmony to laugh at the ultimate joke that tickles us all equally. It's meant to gather us in small tribes under the flag of whatever joke we, and only we, like best.

Comedy is like our teenage taste in music but turned up

to ten. There are jokes that everyone kind of likes, but usually nobody loves those ones. Those are the ones that fall out of Christmas crackers. And though nobody is going to reject a load of weak but functional puns as 'not jokes', you're not going to feel this one was just for you.

Comedy is tied up with identity and safety and comfort. It's divisive and toxic and, sorry, it *is* meant to do that.

JOY/DIVISION

We have to accept that jokes aren't ever 'just funny'. They're funny because of what's inside the joke, and how it reacts with what's already inside our heads. Every joke defines its own audience: who gets the joke, who feels safe. They're the ones who laugh. And every joke has the potential to reject others, who feel confused, or isolated, and maybe even threatened. They're the ones who don't laugh.

So the important thing for anyone who creates or uses comedy is to acknowledge that comedy is both uniting and divisive. Because that is what it is designed to do. To claim 'no harm meant' about a joke whose main purpose is to gather your gang closer (and push others away as a consequence) is disingenuous. Even if you only know it subconsciously, thanks to the little buzz of communal warmth and belonging that comes with every joke, we all know what we're doing.

We joke for our friends, amongst our friends, to tell them that they are our friends, and to declare that we have this joke in common and that's why we are friends.

We are giggling with a sibling in the back row of a funeral again, and we will not be sharing the joke with the rest of the congregation, because it's not *for* them. They wouldn't get it. And if you really didn't know you were shutting some people out when you cracked your mates up, and those excluded people complain, the least you can do is either own it and say 'that was the whole point' or, alternatively – and this might seem a maverick option – you can say 'sorry'.

MEANWHILE, IN THE EMBASSY ROOMS

In *Comedians*, Trevor Griffiths' seminal 1975 play about the very early birth pangs of the alternative comedy scene, one of the hopeful evening-class clowns offers an unpleasantly misogynist limerick. Veteran stand-up Eddie Walters, leading the class, dismisses it with the classic putdown:

That is a joke that hates women.

Griffiths had written his play after watching an episode of Granada TV's *The Comedians*, the hit showcase for working-men's-club comics that launched provincial stars like Bernard Manning into the mainstream. The acts' jokes were designed to bond their club audiences together with a loud declaration of shared values. The punchlines made clear the rules of admission and exclusion. To Griffiths, a left-wing progressive university-educated dramatist, every joke was 'a lead pellet aimed at somebody in . . . my society'. But though the open sexism, homophobia and racism of the average 1970s Manning routine feels shocking today, the show's jokes were only doing what Griffiths' own jokes do: bonding his tribe together, marking the edges.

Of course, laughing from the gut is more fun than laughing from the head, thinking all the bloody time. Of course, we worry about killing the fun of laughing-without-a-care, but like Griffiths' comedy class, we do need to be students of the jokes we tell.

The most intelligent way to make good comedy, and to demonstrate any love and feeling for the craft, is to understand the nature of the tools we are using. Once you realise that dividing people is something that comedy does – not as an unforeseen side effect, but *as part of its job* – it becomes your responsibility as a user of comedy, amateur or pro, to ensure you're using the equipment correctly.

Just like you would if you were using a hedge trimmer. Read the instructions. Follow the safety advice. Keep an eye on where the cable is trailing. Know which bit is the sharp bit.

Because if you know what this tool is for, and accept full responsibility for being in charge of it, you're less likely to wave it in someone's face and then act surprised when it cuts their nose off.

55

Comedy is Big and Clever

*The meanest jokes rarely make it into the script,
although they often make the room laugh the hardest.*

Nell Scovell

The idea that comedy is tribal and divisive might seem a
bit upsetting. Comedy should be about feeling safe.
That's what this book has been about. We laugh when
we're safe. This doesn't feel safe. This feels very dangerous indeed. Is comedy just providing the tools to make
things more tribal, more exclusionary and spiteful?
And then offering the universal excuse that it was all
'just a joke'?

It would be awful if comedy were the painkilling pill
that masks the symptoms of a harmful disease without
doing anything to arrest its effects.

But there is hope. Because, as we have seen, comedy
has several functions, and tribal bonding is only one of
them. Comedy's other function is to sharpen our minds.
Because it's a game we play with our problem-solving,
our pattern detection and our theory of mind. So we can
use comedy to train our brains to be faster, cleverer,
more effective, more imaginative and, best of all, more
empathetic.

Yes, comedy is a place where we laugh best when we
feel safest. We only laugh when the aggression and danger

is dissipated. The sound of comedy – the laugh – according to any observations in nature, isn't the sound of rage and division and danger. It's the sound of a bunch of us getting together and signalling to one another that there is no outside threat, that we're safe to let our guard down. . . and play. We can get that cosy feeling when we have expelled outsiders, sure, but we also feel like that when we have gathered ourselves together and expressed what we all have in common.

So even though comedy has a tribal function in dividing us into small groups and reinforcing our secret comic handshakes, humour's use of mind-sharpening puzzles gives us the tools that might help to bring us together. By playing comedy games, we can improve our understanding of why people are different, how we interact, why we sometimes do inexplicable things. We can learn to think outside the box, or try seeing the implausible from a crazy angle that tilts it back into sense.

We can learn to guess what even the most inexplicable people within and without our social groups might be about to do, and adjust accordingly.

We can gain confidence in taking wild intuitive leaps to find answers.

We can even learn which words sound like other words, and that sometimes there's no reason for a chicken to cross the road, but that's OK, because some jokes are meta, and even little kids get that.

And that's all aside from comedy's broadest tribal function of uniting us all in happy opposition to the non-comedy-sharing community: the lizards, fungal outgrowths, geological formations and dour Bavarian quantity surveyors with whom we share the planet but who noticeably don't swap jokes. And then we can bond together based on what we, deep down, as members of the social group 'humanity', all agree is funny.

Which, as we all know, is manhole accidents, and farts.

56

Hack Comedy

I used to keep pictures of the Hubble Telescope on the wall of the writing room at Seinfeld. It would calm me when I would start to think that what I was doing was important.

Jerry Seinfeld

I got speaking at a party a while back with a very skilled, successful stand-up who was preparing her new show. Because we were off-guard, and nicely cushioned with wine, she was being disarmingly honest about the grind of coming up with new material.

'What's the point?' she said. 'I've been doing this for so long. I know it might sound boastful, but... I'm quite good at this. I do it every night. I've got the skills. I worked to get them. And...' – she dropped her voice under the surrounding chatter – 'I've started to worry that... I could just deliver anything at all, and it would follow the right rhythm, and rise and fall in the right place, and everyone would laugh, and I'd be doing my job. So... why come up with new material at all? Why kill myself worrying that I need something important to say? Is that bad of me?'

And that was music to my ears, because I think comedy is music, so I asked the inevitable horrible question.

'How much of when you get a laugh is down to craft,

not content? How much is structure, shape and technique, and how much is down to the actual material?'

And she said, without hesitation, 'Ninety per cent. Ninety per cent is the shape. Ten per cent is what I'm saying.'

It was a noisy room. Nobody could overhear us. So we felt safe.

And we both laughed.

MAKE YOUR OWN KIND OF MUSIC

I think that her assessment of the balance of skill and expression that comedy requires was almost certainly a slight exaggeration for comic effect (solid craft, that), but it got me thinking. Because that's what this book is about. I believe that there is an underlying, unbreakable music to comedy that allows the content to sit on top as a separate thing. The tune is the tune, and if you've got a catchy enough tune, the words can be anything you like.

And that means, of course, that you can deliver what you suspect is pretty hack material and still get a decent laugh off the shape and the rhythm and the surprise alone without worrying much about what you're saying. The Construct, the Confirm, the Confound in comedy are sometimes enough. Just as a three-chord song like 'Louie Louie' can have dumb-as-hell lyrics, and still be a catchy, uplifting classic that lasts as long as pop music has been a thing.

But that is wonderful news.

Because it means you can sing anything you like over the top. As long as the chords stay the same, and you play them confidently, they'll go together and sound great. People are going to enjoy your comic tune, and then you can express anything you want. It's like making up new rude words to a Christmas carol at a school concert, which, as we all know, is amongst the funniest things that can happen to human beings. 'One of the Three Kings is on a scooter!'

The strength of the underlying building blocks of comedy means that if you've got a joke that you realise isn't quite sending the message you want, or has upset the wrong people, or is making some other, different wrong people laugh in a way that is slightly uncomfortable, you can change it to say something else without breaking it. You're not wedded to the content, only the container. Because the lyrics can be anything. It's the tune that's funny.

Rewrite. Polish. Change. Improve.

If the original version of the joke is still the one that makes you laugh the most, maybe that's just a way of telling you which audience it is for, or learning something about yourself. There is no joke that is 'just funny'. Except the shape of the joke itself. Which can't be broken. If your bucket is strong, but you realise the content stinks? Just empty it out. And try something else inside instead. It'll hold anything.

Maybe you can put something amazing in there.

57

Her Majesty

Plum [P. G. Wodehouse] woke up. 'What's going on?' he asked, sleepily.
'It's an audience laughing at Jeeves and Bertie,' I said.
Plum said, 'What a lovely way to wake up!'

Frank Muir

When Britain's Queen Elizabeth II died in 2022, she was celebrated for her long reign and her powerful role as a symbol of national continuity, representing a stable bond over time with generations of our own families. Even staunch republicans, who disagreed with the idea of monarchy itself, found themselves able to talk of her dignity and sense of duty.

But I was interested in how she seemed to be remembered by the public. Though commentators fixated on the ancient trappings of her role, the glittery ceremonies, pomp-stuffed rituals and half-inched jewellery that encrusts the monarchy, the public seemed to place her within pop culture. To most of us, we were marking the passing of that woman off *The Crown*. The one our grandparents bought a black-and-white set to watch in 1953, or rushed into a neighbour's house to see on the telly. Elizabeth II was the woman who had that annual show you watched with a paper hat on, between sprouts and Wallace and Gromit.

And most of all, she was the woman who did two great comedy sketches that became as nation-uniting as anything Morecambe and Wise ever did.* We loved her in her two best double acts, with James Bond and Paddington Bear. And even though Bond was played by Daniel Craig in Her Majesty's first big national comedy sketch, she didn't team up with Craig's own gritty take on Bond, the troubled agent with the sad past and lashings of toxic regret. She was paired with Craig playing the funny Roger Moore Bond, with his Union Jack parachute, cocked eyebrow and selection of dad jokes.

In both *Regina vs Bond* and *Regina vs Bear*, it was the ultimate Eric and Ernie unlikely star turn, full of broad, communal in-jokes, which we all got. Both routines were built on solid, shared Construct notes, with a couple of storming Confounds and a load of lovely Confirms to make it work. We knew all the rules, understood all the references, and didn't see any of *that* coming. Lovely.

These vivid, comic moments seemed to be closer to the public's hearts than all Her Majesty's dutiful years of opening things and waving out of things and patiently watching traditional Commonwealth dances. From the evidence of the piles of soft bears and marmalade sandwiches left in tribute after her death, and the published recollections of the creators of the Bond stunt, you might have thought we'd just lost one of the nation's comedy stars, not its queen. We were, it seemed, waving farewell to someone who'd recently cheered us up in a couple of cracking double acts.

---

* As Barry Cryer always used to write on a crumpled fag packet, and hand to the star at the end of any recording before they went to thank the audience and crew, MENTION THE FUCKING WRITERS. So the royal sketch at the 2012 Olympic Games opening ceremony was by Frank Cottrell-Boyce (with Danny Boyle), and the Paddington sketch for the 2022 Platinum Jubilee was written by Frank Cottrell-Boyce, Jon Foster and James Lamont.

In that (now maybe hard-to-recall) post-pandemic daze of fatigue and unaddressed trauma, the country felt about as divided as it was possible to be. But to find comfort and agreement, we had chosen to remember when a major public figure had acted as a genuine tribal unifier. Her real legacy wasn't duty or royalty or monarchy at all. It was a couple of warm, inclusive, culturally resonant routines about three iconic national characters (two fictional, one maybe slightly more real), and we'd all agreed to get the jokes.

A head of state had been turned into a shared token of comic culture that seemed to burst the bounds of our own tribe, and become almost global. The gags travelled. They really did.

Everyone knows Bond, and the bear, and the Queen. Well, almost everyone. The whole tribe could gather round a single fire for a minute and laugh. It was magical, unprecedented and funny. And we remembered that.

'I keep mine in here.'

That was your catchphrase, Ma'am.

And that's how comedy works.

ACKNOWLEDGEMENTS

Thanks to everybody I've talked to about comedy theory in pubs or on long walks. You have all shaped the ideas in this book, and some I've probably adopted wholesale and used so often I forgot where I learned them. There are too many friends, DM-thread fillers and twitmongers to mention, but I've made a note every time I've said something in the text that I'm pretty sure I can trace back to a chat online or in person, and so specific thanks to the helpful and inquisitive likes of Will Maclean, Carrie Quinlan, Jonathan Key, Robin Ince, Jason Hazeley, Paul Putner, John Finnemore, Alasdair Beckett-King, Madeleine Brettingham, Simon Kane, Ed Morrish, Lyndsay Fenner, Sarah Morgan, Rhodri Marsden, Josh Weinstein, Eddie Robson, Toby Davies, Tony Way, John Luke-Roberts, Alex Morris, Robin Halstead, Sarah Kendall, Davey Jones, Matthew Holness, David Tyler, David Quantick, Charlie Brooker, Ben Caudell, Laurence Rickard, Rufus Jones, Cariad Lloyd, Adam Tandy, Stewart Lee, Simon Blackwell, Abigail Burdess, Kay Stonham, Andy Riley, Will Smith, Roger Drew, Alice Lowe, Chris Addison, Danielle Ward, Margaret Cabourn-Smith, Jon Holmes, Kev Cecil, Andy Riley, Jim Field-Smith, Tom Neenan, Paul King, Simon Farnaby, James Cary, Richard Hurst, Andy Miller, Andrew Ellard, David Reed, Izzy Mant, Kevin Eldon, Katy Brand, Henry Trotter, Chris Waitt, Simon McLean, James Kettle, Gareth Edwards, David Mitchell, Robert Webb, Robert Thorogood, Neil Forsyth, Natt Tapley, Justin Edwards, Lucy Porter, Marc Haynes, Matthew Hawn, Leah Earl, Sam Bain, Jesse Armstrong, Tony Roche, Lucy Prebble, Rowland White, Robert Popper, Phil Clarke, Robert Katz,

Chris Morris, Geoffrey Perkins, John Lloyd, Richard Curtis, Rowland White, Daisy Buchanan, John J. Hoare, Robin French, Jonathan Dryden-Taylor, Gráinne Maguire, Christine Rose, Julian Dutton, Aisling Bea, Christopher Thorpe-Tracey, Rufus Gerard-Wright, Annemarie Cancienne, Tom Hemmings and Melanie Gutteridge.

Thanks to everyone who's ever been on one of my podcasts, because those are mainly an excuse to get clever people to sit down and try out some new ideas. Podcasting pays like a paper round, so there has to be another reason to do it, and to me it's like booking a regular session of mind tennis. It's a privilege to play with such amazing partners (and then painstakingly edit out all my foot faults).

Huge thanks to neuroscience wizards Professor Sophie Scott and Professor G. Neil Martin for their help, encouragement and sympathetic 'peer review-lite' reading of the sciencey bits. Huge gratitude for further academic assistance and advice to Dr Greg Jenner, Professor Anil Seth, Dr Sophie Quirk and Dr Bob Nicholson. Any stylistically convenient fudges of the hard science and proper history are entirely my fault, but all their advice and guidance has been invaluable. The philosophy and craft stuff is all mine, but that's less contentious, because that's not a peer-reviewed discipline. Peer review is like homework, and I never liked handing in homework – ask my tutors. Oh, and thanks to my tutors and teachers at school, art college and university, who managed to get me thinking like this in the first place, to understand that there's usually a reason for things being the way they are if you stare at them hard enough and try not to fall asleep in a sunbeam in the college library. Mmm. Sunbeams.

Big thanks to the brilliant Mackenzie Crook for permission to use the extract from his script for *Detectorists*. (I think technically it's under the length for quoting for academic review, but, y'know, manners.)

Modern-style thanks to someone I've never met, Craig Mazin, whose forty-five-minute lecture on story theory is definitely the best single fuss-busting tool for writers that I've ever encountered, and whose various podcasts on writing (solo and with other writers, particularly John August, Neil Druckmann and Damon Lindelof) have sparked endless pondery walks, and discussions with my own fellow writers, all of which helped lead me to a lot of the thoughts I've put in this book. Listening to a podcast is a weirdly intimate way to share hours of your day with the brain of an interesting stranger, and I don't think I'd have gone down a lot of these conceptual alleys without the ideas and advice he's been generous enough to share over the years. So thanks.

Thanks to the writers who first made me think comedy writing could be a job. To Barry Took and Marty Feldman for putting a cartoon of themselves on the cover of the *Round the Horne* LP, showing the pair of them sitting behind a typewriter, and giving away the secret. To Spike Milligan, Eric Sykes and Larry Stephens, whose *Goon Show* scripts were the first time I'd seen comedy written down like that. And to Douglas Adams, who seemed to be so effortlessly in charge of a universe where his own brain was the star, and his own butterfly attention span the only nemesis. I think that's the usual set-up, and it remains an appealing offer as a career option.

Thanks to my original professional mentors, who encouraged me when I was barely out of my teens and said there was a career in writing funny stuff (even if it wasn't actually going to pay properly, and would I please stop asking that): Ian Davidson, Peter Vincent and Barry Cryer.

Thanks to everyone at Unbound, particularly Mathew Clayton, John Mitchinson, Flo Garnett, Suzanne Azzopardi and Rina Gill.

Huge thanks to my agent Ed Wilson, and the much-missed Cat Ledger, who I hope would have enjoyed this book and making a special index card for its tiny hand-written sales figures to live on.

And of course. . . all the love in the world to Julia and Douglas, who put up with only seeing my back at my desk for months, hunched over, with headphones on like the bloke from *The Lives of Others*. You might find out what the front of me looks like now. Hope it's not a shock.

EPIGRAPH SOURCES

Opening epigraph, p. xiii
Line from: Marty Feldman, *eYE Marty: The Newly Discovered Autobiography of a Comic Genius*, Coronet, 2015.

Comedy is Important, p. 3
Line from: E. B. White and Katharine S. White, 'The Preaching Humorist', *Saturday Review of Literature*, 18 October 1941.

Chapter 1, p. 11
Line from: Gurpall Gosall, in Richard Wiseman & British Science Association, LaughLab, 2001, richardwiseman.wordpress.com/psychology-of-humour/

Chapter 2, p. 14
Line from: Mark Twain, 'The Lowest Animal', 1897/1905.

Chapter 3, p. 19
Line from: Brent Forrester, in John Ortved, *Simpsons Confidential: The uncensored, totally unauthorised history of the world's greatest TV show by the people that made it*, Ebury, 2009.

Chapter 4, p. 25
Line from: Ken Dodd, in Ned Sherrin, *Oxford Dictionary of Humorous Quotations*, Oxford University Press, 2008.

Chapter 5, p. 32
Line from: 'The Blood Donor', *Hancock's Half Hour*,
written by Ray Galton and Alan Simpson, reproduced by
kind permission of Galton & Simpson estate.

Chapter 6, p. 39
Line from: Thomas Hobbes, *Human Nature: Or, The
fundamental Elements of Policie*, 1650.

Chapter 7, p. 45
Line from: John-Luke Roberts' stand-up routine,
reproduced by kind permission of John-Luke Roberts.

Chapter 8, p. 49
Line from: Will Hay, 'How I Make You Laugh', *Film
Weekly*, 2 March 1934.

Chapter 9, p. 57
Line from: 'Gas', *Bottom*, written by Adrian Edmondson
and Rik Mayall, Season 2, Episode 1, BBC, 1991,
reproduced by kind permission of Adrian Edmondson.

Chapter 10, p. 61
Line from: David Nobbs, *The Fall and Rise of Reginald
Perrin*, Penguin, 1976.

Chapter 11, p. 66
Line from: Steve Martin, *Comedy Is Not Pretty!*, Warner
Bros. LP, 1979.

Chapter 12, p. 73
Line from: 'Fog', *Dinnerladies*, written by Victoria Wood,
Season 4, Episode 2, reproduced by kind permission of
Good Fun Revisited Limited.

Chapter 13, p. 81
Line from: P. G. Wodehouse, *Author! Author!*, letter to
William Townend, Simon & Schuster, 1962.

Chapter 14, p. 84
Line from: Neil Innes, *Rutland Weekend Television*,
BBC2, 1976, reproduced by kind permission of Yvonne
Innes.

Chapter 15, p. 89
Line from: Geoffrey Willans and Ronald Searle,
'Back in the Jug Agane: Molesworth's Guide to the
Skool Piano', *The Compleet Molesworth*, Penguin,
1987.

Chapter 16, p. 95
Line from: David Gross, Twitter, 18 October 2022,
twitter.com/davidgrossTV/status/1547426159951982592

Chapter 17, p. 102
Line from: Lewis Carroll, *Alice's Adventures in
Wonderland*, 1865.

Chapter 18, p. 108
Line from: Steve Martin, *Born Standing Up: A Comic's
Life*, Simon & Schuster, 2007.

Chapter 19, p. 115
Line from: 'The Aristocrats', Trad.

Chapter 20, p. 120
Line from: *The Goon Show*, written by Spike Milligan,
BBC Radio, reproduced by kind permission of the
Milligan estate.

Chapter 21, p. 126
Line from: Lewis Carroll, *Through the Looking-Glass* (first published in 1871), *The Annotated Alice: The Definitive Edition*, 1985.

Chapter 22, p. 132
Line from: Jim Abrahams, in Will Harris, 'Surely you can't be serious: An oral history of *Airplane!*', *AV Club*, 17 April 2015.

Chapter 23, p. 141
Line from: *Cheers*, NBC sitcom, 1982–1993.

Chapter 24, p. 147
Line from: Peter Cook and Dudley Moore, *Dud & Pete: The Dagenham Dialogues*, Methuen, 1988.

Chapter 25, p. 151
Line from: Denis Norden, in David Bradbury and Joe McGrath, *Now That's Funny!: Writers on Writing Comedy*, Methuen, 1998.

Chapter 26, p. 157
Line from: Konrad Lorenz, *On Aggression*, Methuen, 1966.

Chapter 27, p. 162
Line from: Victoria Wood, in David Bradbury and Joe McGrath, *Now That's Funny!: Writers on Writing Comedy*, Methuen, 1998.

Chapter 28, p. 169
Line from: Neil Gibbons, Rob Gibbons, Armando Iannucci and Steve Coogan, *I, Partridge: We Need to Talk About Alan*, HarperCollins, 2011.

Chapter 29, p. 174
Line from: Douglas Adams, *The Hitchhiker's Guide to the Galaxy*, Pan Books, 1979.

Chapter 30, p. 178
Line from: Gilda Radner, *It's Always Something*, Simon & Schuster, 1989.

Chapter 31, p. 183
Line from: George Carlin, *3x Carlin: An Orgy of George*, Hyperion, 2006.

Chapter 32, p. 189
Line from: Stewart Lee, *Snowflake*, BBC, 2022, reproduced by kind permission of Stewart Lee.

Chapter 33, p. 197
Line from: Jack Handey, *Deep Thoughts: Inspiration for the Uninspired*, Berkeley Books, 1992.

Chapter 34, p. 202
Line from: Tina Fey, *Bossypants*, Sphere, 2011.

Chapter 35, p. 207
Line from: Joel Morris, Trad.

Chapter 36, p. 211
Line from: *Derry Girls*, written by Lisa McGee, Channel 4, Season 1, Episode 1, reproduced by kind permission of United Agents/Lisa McGee.

Chapter 37, p. 221
Line from: Spike Milligan, *Milligan Preserved*, EMI, 1961, reproduced by kind permission of the Milligan estate.

Chapter 38, p. 230
Line from: Eddie Braben, *The Book What I Wrote: Eric, Ernie and Me*, Hodder & Stoughton, 2004.

Chapter 39, p. 234
Line from: 'Chains', *Blackadder II*, written by Ben Elton and Richard Curtis, Season 1, Episode 6, BBC, 1986, reproduced by kind permission of Ben Elton/Richard Curtis.

Chapter 40, p. 239
Line from: Unknown.

Chapter 41, p. 243
Line from: Iona and Peter Opie, *The Lore and Language of Schoolchildren*, Oxford University Press, 1959.

Chapter 42, p. 247
Line from: Chuck Jones, *Chuck Amuck: The Life and Times of the Animated Cartoonist*, Avon Books, 1990.

Chapter 43, p. 252
Line from: Bill Watterson, *The Calvin and Hobbes Tenth Anniversary Book*, Warner, 1995.

Chapter 44, p. 256
Line from: Bob Mortimer, *And Away. . .*, Simon & Schuster, 2021.

Chapter 45, p. 259
Line from: 'Bambi', *The Young Ones*, written by Ben Elton, Rik Mayall and Lise Mayer, Season 2, Episode 1, BBC, reproduced by kind permission of Ben Elton.

Chapter 46, p. 271
Line from: John Cleese, *The Pythons Autobiography*, The Pythons, Orion, 2003.

Chapter 47, p. 278
Line from: John Sullivan, in David Bradbury and Joe McGrath, *Now That's Funny!: Writers on Writing Comedy*, Methuen, 1998.

Chapter 48, p. 285
Line from: James Acaster, reproduced by kind permission of James Acaster/PBJ Management.

Chapter 49, p. 291
Line from: Aaron Sorkin, *This Cultural Life*, BBC Radio 4, 2 April 2022.

Chapter 50, p. 296
Line from: Pete Docter, in Ed Catmull, *Creativity Inc.: Overcoming the Forces that Stand in the Way of True Inspiration*, Bantam, 2014.

Chapter 51, p. 303
Line from: Nell Scovell, *Just the Funny Parts: . . . And a Few Hard Truths About Sneaking into the Hollywood Boys' Club*, Dey Street Books, 2018.

Chapter 52, p. 311
Line from: Douglas Adams, *The Hitchhiker's Guide to the Galaxy: The Original Radio Scripts*, Pan Macmillan, 1985.

Chapter 53, p. 319
Line from: Michael Palin, in *The Pythons Autobiography*, The Pythons, Orion, 2003.

Chapter 54, p. 322
Line from: Tina Fey, *Bossypants*, Sphere, 2011.

Chapter 55, p. 329
Line from: Nell Scovell, *Just the Funny Parts: . . .And a Few Hard Truths About Sneaking into the Hollywood Boys' Club*, Dey Street Books, 2018.

Chapter 56, p. 331
Line from: Jerry Seinfeld, in Judd Apatow, *Sick in the Head: Conversations about Life and Comedy*, Random House, 2016.

Chapter 57, p. 334
Line from: Frank Muir, *A Kentish Lad*, Bantam, 1997.

RESOURCES

In the introduction I defined comedy as:

an art form whose peaks of expression for me personally would include a 1950s greaser in a transport café singing 'Mr Boombastic' on a Kirby wire, a drag Viking miming extremely tight raspberries, and an American newsreader playing jazz flute to strangers under the door of a toilet stall. It's the art form in which the magic words 'for you, Lord Delfont...' can act as a bonding signal to old friends, and where the happiest moment of your childhood might be you and a sibling crying with laughter as you pass each other a spoof advert featuring a smiling man furiously pedalling a bicycle wheel that goes up his arse. Its craft is contained in the book title Doctor Who and the Shreddies of Nabisco, *the name of the American football star 'Quiznatodd Bidness' and the little village of Wabznasm. It's a man in a bowler hat eating wax fruit, a huge Gaulish warrior eating most of a cake, and a schoolgirl eating a colossal Wagon Wheel so marshmallow goes all over her face. It's a cat chasing a mouse that is suddenly two more enormous mice who turn out to be circus elephants in disguise. It's a man who starts to tell you a story but can't because he farts continuously for three minutes straight. It's hiding a cow creamer from a fascist lingerie entrepreneur in ridiculous shorts.*

These are references to a handful of things I remember laughing at really, really hard. I could have chosen hundreds more. For the quizzers amongst you, here are the answers.

1. *Shooting Stars* Christmas Special by Reeves and Mortimer.
2. Spike Milligan in *Q*.
3. Will Ferrell in *Anchorman*.
4. Julie Walters in *Victoria Wood: As Seen On TV*: Behind the Scenes of *Acorn Antiques*.
5. *Viz* comic: 'Clag Gone' advert.
6. *Not 1983*, Science Fiction Book Club catalogue (by Douglas Adams and John Lloyd).
7. *Key & Peele*: College Bowl Football.
8. *The Day Today*: Emergency Broadcast.
9. Laurel and Hardy, *Sons of the Desert*.
10. *Asterix and Cleopatra* by Goscinny and Uderzo.
11. French and Saunders.
12. *Tom & Jerry*: Jerry and Jumbo.
13. *Absolutely*: Frank Hovis on the Lavatory.
14. *The Code of the Woosters* by P. G. Wodehouse.

The Incredibles: Full Breakdown

As promised, here's the whole of *The Incredibles*, broken into Yes-No beats.

PRELIMINARY SCENES
How we got here. The story so far. . .
THE QUESTION: *Can we balance our need for success and self-expression with our responsibilities to our family?*

1. Superheroes are interviewed about their tricky split identities. NO.
2. We see Mr Incredible at work. He is brilliant at it. YES.

3. Mr Incredible meets Elastigirl. She tells him he needs to be more flexible. NO.
4. A big superhero adventure breaks out. Mr Incredible saves the day. YES.
5. Mr Incredible arrives late to his own wedding to Elastigirl. She cautions him. NO.

THE QUIET QUESTION (See later)

Elastigirl whispers the film's central quandary to her new husband...

ELASTIGIRL: *To make this marriage work, you have to be more than Mr Incredible.*

ACT ONE

We set up the world: basically 'Marvel's Fantastic Four are a sitcom family'.

THE QUESTION AGAIN: Can we balance our need for success and self-expression with our responsibilities to our family?

6. The superheroes' colourful antics have seen them banned. Mr Incredible has a dull job. The family are settled, but frustrated. Nobody is themselves. NO.
7. Mr Incredible and old super-friend Frozone do some secret hero work. YES.
8. Elastigirl tells her husband he is ignoring family life. 'You are missing this.' NO.
9. Mr Incredible's superheroic side explodes at work, doing what he is good at. YES.
10. The incident is covered up for him but he loses his job. He can't keep doing this. NO.
11. Mirage, a mysterious woman, asks for his help. 'You can still do great things.' YES.
12. Mirage's exciting superhero-mission-briefing message explodes, wrecking the family home (and nailing the central theme of the film). NO.

13. Mr Incredible lies that work is sending him to a conference. Maybe he can have both lives, career and domestic, after all! YES.

ACT TWO

Mr Incredible is leading a double life again.

THE QUESTION AGAIN: Can we balance our need for success and self-expression with our responsibilities to our family?

14. Mr Incredible on a heroic mission on a secret island. He defeats a giant robot. YES.
15. The mysterious woman, Mirage, flirts with him over dinner. Home is forgotten. NO.
16. Back home, Mr Incredible is a new man, reinvigorated. YES.
17. Elastigirl thinks he's still at his old job. He is lying to her. A betrayal of the woman he loves. NO.
18. Mr Incredible secretly goes to get a new superhero suit from Edna. YES.
19. Elastigirl suspects he is having an affair. She says she loves him, but he barely responds. NO.
20. Mr Incredible reinvigorated on the glamorous secret island. YES.
21. Elastigirl finds clues and suspects her husband has been lying to her. NO.
22. Elastigirl readopts her old superhero identity to speak to Edna. YES.
23. Mr Incredible meets supervillain Syndrome, who outwits him. NO.
24. Mr Incredible survives but is forced into hiding. YES.
25. Syndrome thinks he has killed Mr Incredible, and is depicted as triumphant. NO.
26. Edna designs outfits that will allow the family to all be heroes. YES.

27. Edna sows doubt in Elastigirl's mind: is Mr Incredible having an affair? NO.
28. Mr Incredible infiltrates the villain's lair in classic style, discovers his plans. YES.
29. Elastigirl uncovers all of Mr Incredible's deceptions, and accidentally triggers his capture. NO.
30. Edna tells Elastigirl to be her superhero self. YES.
31. Elastigirl struggles to leave the kids, to stop them joining her. NO.

ACT THREE

Thanks to Mr Incredible's selfishness, the family are now fractured and in danger.

THE QUESTION AGAIN: Can we balance our need for success and self-expression with our responsibilities to our family?

32. Elastigirl approaches the secret island, heroic, capable and maternal. YES.
33. Mr Incredible is tortured by Syndrome, who threatens the family. NO.
34. Elastigirl finds the kids have stowed away on the plane. All are in superhero costume. YES.
35. Syndrome destroys the family's plane. NO.
36. The family's superpowers mean they survive the crash. YES.
37. Mr Incredible thinks the family are dead. Syndrome mocks his weakness. NO.
38. Elastigirl and the kids infiltrate the villain's lair, working together. She trusts them. YES.
39. A dark scene between Mirage and Syndrome; superheroics and reality don't mix. NO.
40. Elastigirl breaks into Syndrome's facility using cool superpowers. YES.
41. Syndrome's rockets are launched; the vulnerable kids are in danger. NO.

42. Elastigirl in superhero mode locates Mr Incredible. YES.

43. The kids, left alone, are in more and more danger. NO.

44. Mirage rebels, releases Mr Incredible and tells him the family are alive. YES.

45. Elastigirl spots the pair embracing. Thinks it's an affair. NO.

46. Mr Incredible declares his love for Elastigirl. They are on the heroic mission together. YES.

47. The kids are chased by henchmen, really in trouble now. NO.

48. The kids and their parents unite, use their powers and defeat the henchmen. YES.

49. Syndrome captures the whole family. Explains his plan. They are helpless. NO.

50. Mr Incredible apologises. 'You are my greatest adventure.' Using powers, they escape. YES.

51. The city is under attack from Syndrome's killer robot. NO.

52. The Incredibles arrive in a motorhome, a sitcom family and superheroes at once. YES.

53. Mr Incredible won't let the family fight alongside him. 'I can't lose you again. I'm not strong enough.' NO. Not just NO. But NOOOOOOOOOO!*

54. Elastigirl says everyone should be their authentic selves, but openly, not secretly, integrated with their other selves, and they should exist as heroes and a family. 'We're superheroes.' YES.

55. But the family are outclassed by Syndrome's killer robot. NO.

56. Together, using their powers, and their family bonds, they work out how to defeat it. YES.

---

* This is the big killer NO! The All Is Lost moment in the story. How do I know this is the big NO? Because I cry at this bit every time I watch it. The answer to the question from the top of the beat sheet is NO. The answer has been reached: that the hero will never be happy. Bang. A punch in the tear ducts. Also, notice that this scene is as quiet as the question scene at the start. The audience get a breather to hear it clear as a bell. It has its own space. The answer has come. And it's a big NO.

EPILOGUE

Well, that appears to have answered that! Drink, anyone? Oh. Hang on. Can we see the conclusion in action? Maybe test it. A mirror act to the opening, where we see the characters doing their thing again, but with the new knowledge they have gained by answering the question. Let's see how they've changed.

THE QUESTION AGAIN: Can we balance our need for success and self-expression with our responsibilities to our family?

57. Everything seems good now. The government say they can be themselves. YES.
58. Syndrome kidnaps the Incredibles' baby. NO.
59. The family uses their powers together to save their baby and defeat Syndrome. YES.
60. A new villain appears. NO.
61. But the family are united, and heroic, and ready for anything. YES!

CONCLUSION

Yes.

THE QUESTION AGAIN: Can we balance our need for success and self-expression with our responsibilities to our family?

By being open about their needs and integrating their secret identities with their super identities (balancing their work life and home life) the family are strong enough not only to work together, but to work within society. THEY HAVE FOUND A CLEAR ANSWER TO THE STATED QUESTION. And it is YES. What a clever bunch of storytellers.

TITLES

Books

Judd Apatow, *Sick in the Head: Conversations About Life and Comedy*

Philip Ball, *The Music Instinct: How Music Works and Why We Can't Do Without It*

Richard Boston, *An Anatomy of Laughter*

David Bradbury and Joe McGrath, *Now That's Funny!: Writers on Writing Comedy*

Joseph Campbell, *The Hero with a Thousand Faces*

Jimmy Carr and Lucy Greeves, *The Naked Jape: Uncovering the Hidden World of Jokes*

Lewis Carroll, edited by Martin Gardner, *The Annotated Alice: The Definitive Edition*

Lewis Carroll, *Symbolic Logic*

Ed Catmull, *Creativity, Inc.: Overcoming the Unseen Forces That Stand in the Way of True Inspiration*

Charles Darwin, *The Expression of the Emotions in Man and Animals*

William Goldman, *Adventures in the Screen Trade: A Personal View of Hollywood*

Susan Greenfield, *The Human Brain: A Guided Tour*

Trevor Griffiths, *Comedians* (play)

Andrew Hankinson, *Don't Applaud. Either Laugh Or Don't.*

John Higgs, *The Future Starts Here: An Optimistic Guide to What Comes Next*

Matthew M. Hurley, Daniel C. Dennett and Reginald B. Adams Jr., *Inside Jokes: Using Humor to Reverse-Engineer the Mind*

Robin Ince, *I'm a Joke and So Are You: Reflections on Humour and Humanity*

Steve Kaplan, *The Hidden Tools of Comedy: The Serious Business of Being Funny*

Gary Larson, *The Prehistory of the Far Side*

Stewart Lee, *How I Escaped My Certain Fate: The Life and Deaths of a Stand-Up Comedian*

Sharon Lockyer and Michael Pickering (eds), *Beyond a Joke: The Limits of Humour*

Rob Long, *Set Up, Joke, Set Up, Joke*

G. Neil Martin, *The Psychology of Comedy*

Iona and Peter Opie, *The Lore and Language of Schoolchildren*

Dan O'Shannon, *What Are You Laughing At?: A Comprehensive Guide to the Comedic Event*

Steven Pinker, *The Language Instinct: How the Mind Creates Language*

Sophie Quirk, *Why Stand-Up Matters: How Comedians Manipulate and Influence*

Jem Roberts, *Fab Fools: The Last Untold Beatles Story*

Jude Rodgers, *The Sound of Being Human: How Music Shapes Our Lives*

Nell Scovell, *Just the Funny Parts: ... And a Few Hard Truths About Sneaking into the Hollywood Boys' Club*

Anil Seth, *Being You: A New Science of Consciousness*

Jonathan Silvertown, *The Comedy of Error: Why Evolution Made Us Laugh*

Blake Snyder, *Save the Cat!: The Last Book on Screenwriting You'll Ever Need*

Will Storr, *The Science of Storytelling: Why Stories Make Us Human, and How to Tell Them Better*

Christopher Vogler, *The Writer's Journey: Mythic Structure for Writers*

John Vorhaus, *The Comic Toolbox: How to Be Funny Even If You're Not*

Bill Watterson, *The Calvin and Hobbes Tenth Anniversary Book*

John Yorke, *Into the Woods: A Five-Act Journey Into Story*

Articles and Webpages

www.psychologytoday.com/gb/blog/beastly-behavior/
201705/why-play-is-important

www.wired.com/2011/04/ff-humorcode/

www.strangehistory.net/2018/04/03/the-history-of-why-
did-the-chicken/

Ted Chiang, 'CHATGTP is a blurry JPEG of the web',
The New Yorker, 9 February 2023

John Lahr, 'Puzzled Puss' (on Buster Keaton), *London
Review of Books*, 19 January 2023

Justine T. Kao et al., 'A Computational Model of Linguistic Humor in Puns', *Cognitive Science*, Volume 4, Issue
5, July 2016, doi.org/10.1111/cogs.12269

Sophie Scott, Ceci Qing Cai and Addison Billing, 'Robert
Provine: the critical human importance of laughter, con-
nections and contagion', Philosophical Transactions of
the Royal Society of Biological Sciences 377:20210178,
25 February 2022

Chris Westbury et al., 'Telling the world's least funny
jokes: On the quantification of humor as entropy', *Jour-
nal of Memory and Language*, Volume 86, January
2016, doi.org/10.1016/j.jml.2015.09.001

A NOTE ON THE AUTHOR

Joel Morris is a BAFTA-winning comedy writer. A long-time collaborator with Charlie Brooker and the co-creator of dimwit pundit Philomena Cunk, he has written for countless TV and radio shows, including *Mitchell and Webb*, *Miranda* and *Murder in Successville*, as well as the *Paddington* films. He co-created cult spoof newspaper *The Framley Examiner*, the hit *Bollocks to Alton Towers* tourist guides and the chartbusting *Ladybird Books for Grown-Ups*. He is also an award-winning podcast producer and presenter (for *Comfort Blanket* and *Rule of Three*), a member of the band Candidate and a regular contributor to *Viz*.

Unbound is the world's first crowdfunding publisher, established in 2011.

We believe that wonderful things can happen when you clear a path for people who share a passion. That's why we've built a platform that brings together readers and authors to crowdfund books they believe in – and give fresh ideas that don't fit the traditional mould the chance they deserve.

This book is in your hands because readers made it possible. Everyone who pledged their support is listed below. Join them by visiting unbound.com and supporting a book today.

Lee Bates
Paul Bayne
Richard Beach
Rick Bean
Dan Bean -
    @alatereviewer
Sean Beattie
James Beck
Richard Beckett
Alasdair
    Beckett-King
Dan Beeston
Colin Bell
Daniel Bennett
Ross Bennett
Simon Bennett
Philip Benson
Steve Berry
David Bertenshaw
Gabby Best
Dave Bevan
Colin Beveridge
Claudia Biedert
Big Day Out
David Billcliffe
Emily Bird
Joel Bishton
Ashley Blaker
Tom Blakeson
Karl Blanks
Dave Blundell
Nicky Bond
Tom Bond
Paul Boswell
Martin Boulton
Jon Bounds
Alec
    Bowman_Clarke
Richard Bowyer
Thomas Bowyer

Matt Box
Ben Boyer
Carolyn Braby
Jesse
    Bradley-Amore
Toby Braithwaite
Juliet Brando
Hal Branson
Brant
Lucy Brennan
David Breslin
Barry
    Brett-McStay
James Brew
Matt Brew
Emma Bridge
Matt Brito
David Brocklebank
Holly Brockwell
Kristian Brodie
Tim Bromfield
Brad Brooks
Stephen Brooks
Ed Broom
Jack Brough
Nicola Brown
Rick Brown
Brian Browne
Paul Brunger
Hannah Bryan
Guy Buckland
Nick Bull
Chris Burgess
Douglas Burgess
Gareth Burgess
Tom Burgess
Ross Burman
Jonathan Burton
Richard Busby
Matt Butler

Iain Cairns
Ian Calcutt
Howard Calvert
Ian Calvert
Al Campbell
Douglas Campbell
Neil Campbell
Andrew
    Campbell-Howes
Annemarie
    Cancienne and
    Tom Hemmings
Glyn Cannon
Peter Capel
Heckity Carbide
Victoria
    Cargill-James
Jon Cartwright
Daragh Carville
Ande Case
Dermot Casey
AH Cassells
Steven Cassidy
Kevin
    Caswell-Jones
David Catley
Ali Catterall
Chrissie Caulfield
Chris Cawte
Michael Channell
Suw
    Charman-
    Anderson
Norman Chella
Robert Chilton
Matt Chorley
Toby Clark
Graham Clarke
Phil Clarke
Rosie Clarke

Shannon Clarke
Paula Clarke Bain
Gillian Claus
Mathew Clayton
Tom Cleaver
Matt Clifton
Steven Cockcroft
Ilya Colak-Antic
GMark Cole
Jo Coleman
Peter Coleman
Jenny Colgan
Stevyn Colgan
Alex Collier
Mark Collyer
Brendon Connelly
Blake Connolly
Paul Conroy
Benjamin Cook
James Elliot Cook
Michael Cook
Benedict Cooke
Helena Cooke
Peter Coombe
Joseph Cooper
Stu Cooper
Darren Corcoran
David Corney
Kerin Cosford
David Cottis
Philip Cotton
Helen Coutts
Martin Coyle
Andrew Craggs
Fiona Craig
Simon Craven
John Crawford
David
    Creasey-Benjamin
Peter Crocker

Emma Crossland
John Crowther
Brendadirk
    Crumplesnatch
Kristofer
    Cullum-Fernandez
Graham Cumming
Jules Curran
Peter Curran
Steve Curran
Stuart Curran
Bruce Daisley
Patrick Dalton
Tom Darby
Tim Darlington
Glenn Davidson
Jo Davidson
Aden Davies
Russell Davies
Stephen Davies
Jonathan Day
Kat Day
Elizabeth Daykin
Chloe de
    Lullington
Michael Deacon
Jo Dear
Jo deBank
Ian Delaney
Dr Alison Diaper
Steven Dick
Ian Dickson
Sammy Dobson
James Docherty
Steve Doherty
Kevin Dolby
Adam
    Donald-George
Iain Donaldson
Justin Doran

Rory Dormer
Kevin Dowling
Sam Downes
Lawrence T Doyle
Kathryn Drumm
Neil Dube
Alexis Dubus
Melanie J Duck
Abe Duenas
Leah Duncan
William Dunlop
Chris Dunn
David Durose
Leah Earl
Dan Early
Jamie East
Hilary Edgcombe
Brian Edwards
Daryl Edwards
Hywel Edwards
Andrew Ellard
Håvar Ellingsen
Samantha Ellis
James Ellison
Andy Elms
Joel Emery
Neil Emery
Louis Emmett
Daniel K. Eng
ES
David Evans
Jamie Evans
Stephen Evans
Zack Evans
Pauline Eyre
Daniel Fahey
Paul Fairie
Lee Farley
Colin Farrell
Simon Fathers

Joe Fattorini
Lyndsay Fenner
Mike Fensom
Tom Fern
Mark Ferres
Cornish Darren
   Fewins
Lottie Field
Andrew Fielder
Hector Figueroa
Paul Fillery
John Finnemore
Steve Fiori
David Firth
Gwyn Fisher
Paul Fitzsimmons
Dermot Fitzsimons
Richard Flagg
Michelle Flower
Chris Floyd
Grant Flynn
Scott Foale
Nic Ford
Mark Forsyth
Neil Forsyth
Chris Fosten
Andrew Fothergill
Deborah
   Frances-White
Eliza Fraser
Pete Fraser
Rob Fraser
Peter Frederick
Thomas Alexander
   Frederiksen
Dean Freeman
Joseph Freeman
Rossfrom Frends
Ashley Frieze
Thomas Futter

Suzi Gage
Justin Gamblin
Paco B. Garcia
Paul Gardiner
Alan Gardner
Mark Gardner
Martin Gardner
Steve Gardner
Chris Garland
Hugh Garry
Louis Gawin
Mark Gelder
Dan Gent
Rory Geoghegan
Rufus
   Gerrard-Wright
T Ghelani
Jonathan Gibbs
Sara Gibbs
Julie Giles
Chris Gillies
Richard Gillis
Rob Gilroy
Paul Ginn
Robin Gissing
Matt Goddard
Jake Godfrey
Scott Goodacre
G.P. Goodall
George Goodfellow
David Goodsell
Marc Goodson
Pravin Gorajala
Al Gordon
Boštjan Gorenc
Dave Gorman
Ben Gosling Fuller
Will Goulden
Tom Gowans
Jon Gowshall

Christian Gradl
Jonny Grady
Keith Grady
Andrew Graham
Wren Graham
Mark Granger
Lee Grant
Richard Grant
Barry Gray
Simon Gray
Dickie Graylin
Nathan Green
Nige Green
Simon and Catherine
   Greenwood
Louise Gregory
Steph Grey
Gavin Griffiths
Mark Griffiths
Laura Grimshaw
Stuart Grimshaw
Lorien Gruchalla
Mei Gwilym
Gareth Gwynn
Joanna Hagan
Peter Haindl
Greg Haiste
Phil Halford
Phil Hallam
Chris Hallas
Francis Halsall
Tom Halsey
Damian Hammond
Andrew Hankinson
John Harding
Mark Harland
Simon Harper
Benny Harris
Mark Harris
Sophie Harris

Ali Hart
Ned Hartley
Kathryn Hartopp
Dylan Harvey
Pete Hathway
Gary Hayton
Rob Hayward
Tim Hayward
Chris Hazell
Andy Healing
David Healy
Dave Hearn
Peter Hearn
David Hearsey
Stuart Hedges
Peter Hegarty
Scott A M
  Henderson
Paul Hennell
Christopher
  Hennessey
Andrew Henry
Ian Herbert
Stuart Heritage
Richard Herring
Thomas Hewett
Andrew Hickey
Lucian Hicks
Stu, Katherine &
  Izzy Higgins
John Higgs
Daniel Hill
Thomas Hill
Ed Hind
James Hingley
Robert Hinton
Kai Hirdt
Tony Hirst
Duncan Hiscock
Alan Hitchin

John J. Hoare
John Hodgkinson
Lucy Holbrook
Stephen Holbrook
Matt Holdcroft
Bob Honey
Harry Hong
John William
  Hopkins
Hilman Hor
Sean Horgan
Nik Horne
Dudley Horque
Stuart Houghton
Mike Houldsworth
Rufus Hound
Rhys Howell
Bernard Hughes
Jim Hughes
Jonathan Hughes
Rob Hughes
Simon Hugo
Graham Hull
Fiona Hulme
Andy Hume
Derek Hummerston
Oliver Humpage
Philip Hunt
Sebastian Hunt
Graeme Hunter
David Hurst
Richard Hurst
Aaron Husain
Robert Hutton
Simon Hynd
Jason Hynes
Robin Ince
Sean Ingham
Oliver Ings
Hazel Ireland

Nick Ireson
Darren Izzard
Alexander Jackson
Andrew N. Jackson
Liam Jackson
Adam Jacobs
Katherine Jakeways
Alex James
Fiona James
Pete James
Simon James
Simon J. James
Steven James
Josh Jeffery
Tom Jellett
Chris Jenkins
Chris Johnson
David Johnson
Liam Johnson
Michael B. Johnson
Tim Johnson
Zack Johnson
Paul Johnstone
Dave Jones
Davey Jones
Gareth Jones
M Jones
Mitchell Jones
Oliver Jones
Peter Jones
Ralph Jones
Rufus Jones
Sarah Jones
Steve Jones
Neil Jones
  (@neiltaffy)
Toby Jones Toby
  Jones
JRWI
Hari Kanth

Alex Keal
The Kearns Family
John-Paul Keates
Steven Keevil
Yvette Keller
Karen Kellock
Katharine Kelly
Justin Kemp
Norm Kemp
Jo Kendall
Fergus Kennedy
Fiona Kennedy
Steven Kennedy
Stephen
    Kent-Taylor
Hilja Kepponen
Youssef Kerkour
David Kerr
Ben Kersley
Jonathan Key
Elyas Khan
Dan Kieran
Patrick Kincaid
Al King
Matthew King
Stuart King
Tom Kingsley
Dave Kinsella
Nick Kirk
Jim Kleefeld
Hilary Knight
Donna Knight-Olds
Sanjeev Kohli
Allison Koster
Kit Kriewaldt
Martin Kudlac
Chris Kydd
Pierre L'Allier
Duncan Ladkin
Yvonne Lam

Tom Lancaster
Chris Lane
Roger Langridge
Ali Larkin
David Lars
    Chamberlain
Christopher Law
Shaun Lawrence
Stafford Lawrence
Elaine Lawrie
Adam Le Boutillier
Elisabeth Le
    Maistre
Darren Leathley
John Leavey
Andrew Lee
Lee
Jon Leigh
Fiona Lensvelt
Fraser Levey
Emma Levin
Justin Lewis
Owain Lewis
Magnus
    Lewis-Smith
Adrian Lightly
Michael Linwood
Andy Lloyd
Paul Lockyer
D Lodge
Log
Chad Long
Stephen Longstaffe
Dougal Lott
Mark Lougheed
Shanti Love
Nicholas Lovell
Anna Lowman
Peter Lunnon
Stuart Lutes

Alex Lynch
Helen Lynch
Vincent Lynch
Martin Lyons
Jack Lyttle
Carleo M
Laura MacDonald
Euan MacInnes
Tommy Mackay
Euan Mackenzie
Seonaid Mackenzie
Adrian Mackinder
Darrell Maclaine
Will Maclean
Sue Macmillan
Adam Macqueen
Tim Madden
Jamie Madge
Diviya Magaro
Dirk Maggs
Shauneen
    Magorrian
Dara Maguire
Gráinne Maguire
Angus Main
Andrew Male
David Malki!
Bob Mallett
Ciaran Mallon
Iain Maloney
Andy Malt
James Maltby
Rowan Manahan
Kenneth Mann
Ginni Manning
Matthew
    Mannion
Ian Mansfield
Izzy Mant
Rob 'follow

@fesshole now'
Manuel
Anthony
  Maplesden
Katie Marsden
Ian Martin
Lenny Martin
Prof GN Martin
Sean Mason
Jamie Mathieson
Claire Maw
Gary Mawby
Charlie Mawer
Andy Mawn
Adam Maxwell
Simon Mayo
Ian Mayor
Fraser McAlpine
David McCalmont
James McCann
Trevor McCarthy
Gaynor McClarey
Mark McConville
Sanchia
  McCormack
Peter McDonald
Kevin McGee
Jane McGrath
Andy McGregor
Rob McGregor
David McGuinness
Mark McIntosh
Sean McKenna
Colin M. McKeown
Gareth McKibbin
Steven McKiernan
Adam McLean
Simon Mclean
Joe McNally
Ian McQue

Gavin McWhirter
Neil McWilliam
Joanne Mead
James Medd
Joel Mellinger
Chris Mellors
Peter Merre
  @topicalcomedian
Andy Merrills
Justin Merritt
Carl Mesner Lyons
Joseph Midgley
Scott Millar
Katie Miller
Jonnie Milne
Fil Milton
Mark Minto
Alastair Mitchell
Barry Mitcheson
John Mitchinson
Mixima
Dave Moore
Davey Moore
John Moore
Kerry Moore
Peter Moore
Thomas Moore
Simon Moorfield
Claire Mora
Caitlin Moran
James Moran
Steve Morey
David Morgan
Roger Morgan
Rosemary Morgan
Alex Morris
John & Marion
  Morris
Ed Morrish
Oliver Morrish

Jim Mortleman
Paul Mosley
Tim Mouncer
Kerry Moyles
Kenneth Mullins
Rob Mullins
Dec Munro
Joe Murphy
Owen
  Murphy-Evans
@mutablejoe
John Myhill
Rick N
Knut Nærum
Fly Wrangler: Craig
  Naples
Al Napp
Carlo Navato
Joanna Neary
Nebolland
Rich Neville
Sian Neville
Christopher J
  Newman
Doug Newton
Tim Nicholls
Al Nicholson
Simon Nicholson
Gary Nicol
Aija Nieminen
Stewart Noble
Kevin Nolan
Ken Norman
Vaun Earl Norman
Caroline Norris
Clare Norris
Kirk Northrop
Andrew Nugent
Tom O'Brien
Emm O'Connell

Geri O'Donohoe
Fionnuala
 O'Driscoll
Simon O'Hare
Conor O'Loughlin
Mark O'Neill
Shannon O'Neill
Sophie O'Neill
Seamas O'Reilly
Rick O'Shay
Phil O'Brien
Phil Oakes
Alex Oates
Oblivity Podcast
 Team
Mugren Ohaly
Himanshu Ojha
Chris Ollis
Wanda Opalinska
Stuart Orchard
Peter Orr
Connal Orton
David Oswald
Mark Oswin
A.N. Other
Christopher Owens
Mathew Owens
Martin Oxnard
Erica Packington
James Pain
Jon Palin
Jim Pallett
Jessica Pan
Lev Parikian
Matthew Parker
Russell Parker
Claire Parsons
Andy Paterson
Jenny Pearce
Chris Pembury

Ed Percival
Leonie Percival
Matt Perdeaux
Greg Perkin
John Perks
Matthew Perret
Claire Perry
Henrik Persson
Benjamin Pert
James Petts
Marianne Philipson
Jason Phillips
Matthew Phillips
Trevor Phillips
Grant Philpott
Samuel Pickard
Alessandra Pino
David Pipe
Dan Platts
Tom Pleasant
Ian Pointer
George Poles
Justin Pollard
Andrew Pope
Richard Porter
Daniel Postgate
Gareth Potter
Arran Potts
Steve Potz-Rayner
John Poveromo
Tom Powell
Tracy Powell
Gordon Prenter
Stuart Presnell
Geraint Preston
Pete Prodge
Owen Pullar
Caroline Pulver
Ian Purser
Paul Putner

David Quantick
Carrie Quinlan
Tony Quinlan
Sam Raby
Julia Raeside
Duncan Raggett
Mark Rainey
Nic Ransome
Chris Ratcliff
Jon Rayment
Dan Rebellato
Victoria Redfern
David Reed
Howard Reed
Rob Reed
Tom Rees-Williams
Billy Reeves
Nanette Regan
Bryan B. Rhodes
Dan Rhodes
Gwen Helen Louisa
 Rhodes
Paul Rhodes
David Richardson
Rachel Riley
Gareth Rimmer
Teme Ring
Stephen Risness
John Rivett
Jonathan Roberts
Andy Robertson
James Robilliard
Carolyn Robinson
Ian Robinson
Eddie Robson
Keith Roche
Jane Roe
Geraint Rogers
Matt Rooke
Jesse Ross

Mathew Ross
Matthew
Rowbotham
Su Rowbotham
Jonathan Royle
Hypnotist
Simon Rueben
Iain Rushworth
Benjamin L Russell
Robert Russell
Tanya Sabrina
Tom Salinsky
Tia Salisbury
John Sanders
Ben Sansum
Kevin Sargent
Alasdair Satchel
Paul Saunders
Shrikant Sawant
Katie Sayer
Lesley Scarles
Dave Schofield
Torn Scone
Ben Scott
River Scott
James Seabright
Henry Seal
Jack Seale
Jason Searle
Joe Shafer
Marsha Shandur
Johnnie Shannon
Helen Sharpe
Dale Shaw
Paul Sheehan
Mike Sheldon
Daniel Sherlock
Myra
Shikimachi-
Stickney

Dan Shires
Katy Sidwell
Bartosz Siepracki
Silky
David Simpkin
Rex Singlehurst
Ed Singleton
Rickard Sisters
Charles Skinner
Chris Skinner
Peter Smailes
Andrew Smith
Chris Smith
Dan Smith
David Smith
Mat Smith
Matt Smith
Oscar Smith
Patrick Smith
Phillip Smith
Stacy Smith
Stuart Smith
Matthew Solly
Rich Sommer
Charlotte Sones
Ian Sorensen
Ross Spalding
Chris Spear
Nick Speed
David Standen
Maureen Standen
Jason B. Standing
Mark Stay
Zoë Steel
Allan Stephens
Darren Stephens
Edward Stern
Toby Stevens
David Stevenson
David Stewart

James Stewart
Andy Stilp
Graham Stock
David Stokes
Jon Stones
Mark Stringer
Tobias Sturt
Rachel Sumner
Louise Sutton
Graham Swann
Nathaniel Tapley
Dylan Taylor
James Taylor
Mark Taylor
Neil Taylor
Patrick Taylor
Vicky Tazzyman
Erika Tebbens
Howard Teece
Dan Tetsell
The Cambridge
Geek
Andy Theyers
Ben Thomas
Chris Thomas
Gregg Thomas
Tracey Thompson
Jim Thornton
Simon Thorp
C J Thorpe-Tracey
Tiffany the Wonder
Horse
Stephen Tilbury
Nick Timms
Richard Tingley
Katrina Tipton
Mike Tobyn
Zoe Tomalin
Kara Tompsett
Samuel Toogood

Mike Tope
David Toyne
John Tracey
Joe Tracini
Ross Tregaskis
S Troeth
Henry Trotter
Rachel Turner
Callum Tyler
Ben Van der Velde
Will Vandyck
Joel Veitch
Mark Vent
E. K. Victor
Timothy Victor
Gabriel Vogt
Felix von Stumm
Richard Vranch
Ian Wacogne
Christopher Wade
Stephen Wademan
Simon Wagstaff
Richard Wainman
Julia Wainwright
Jack Waley-Cohen
Eliot Walker
Ian Walker
James Wallin
Eleanor Walsh
Nina Wanat
Antonia Ward
Duncan Ward
Greg Ward

Lee Ward
Roy Ward
Simon Ward
Rebecca Warren
Fraser Waterfield
Alex Watts
Will Watts
Andrew Waugh
Tony Way
Gemma Webb
Tom Webb
Robin Webber
Carrie Weekes
George Weeks
Josh Weinstein
John Welch
Glen West
Rob Western
Levin Wheller
Mark Whitby
Jonathan White
Paul 'Silky' White
Rob White
Stephen Whitener
David Whittle
Gregor Whyte
Jason Whyte
Mark Wilden
Rhys Wilkins
Dr Bill Wilkinson
Sam Wilkinson
Colin Williams
Dave Williams

Katie Williams
Marc Williams
Reuben Williams
Tim Willis
Alex Wilson
James Wilson
Jamie Wilson
Peter Wilson
Richard A J Wilson
Stew Wilson
Adam Windmill
Nigel Wolfin
Pete Wonnacott
Jo Wood
James Woodman
Dan Woods
Tim Woollias
John Worsey
David Wragg
Lyndsey S H Wray
Paul Wray
Joe Wright
Lewis Wright
Simon Wright
Tony Writer
Alaric Wyatt
Phil Wyatt
Adam Yates
Ben Yates
Emerson Young
Helen Young
Peter Young
Ricky Young